The League
That Didn't Exist

ALSO BY GARY WEBSTER
AND FROM MCFARLAND

*Just Too Good:
The Undefeated 1948 Cleveland Browns* (2015)

*When in Doubt, Fire the Skipper:
Midseason Managerial Changes
in Major League Baseball* (2014)

.721: A History of the 1954 Cleveland Indians (2013)

*Tris Speaker and the 1920 Indians:
Tragedy to Glory* (2012)

The League That Didn't Exist
A History of the All-American Football Conference, 1946–1949

GARY WEBSTER

McFarland & Company, Inc., Publishers
Jefferson, North Carolina

LIBRARY OF CONGRESS CATALOGUING-IN-PUBLICATION DATA

Names: Webster, Gary, 1956– author.
Title: The league that didn't exist : a history of the All-American Football Conference, 1946–1949 / Gary Webster.
Description: Jefferson, North Carolina : McFarland & Company, Inc., Publishers, 2019 | Includes bibliographical references and index.
Identifiers: LCCN 2018048494 | ISBN 9781476665344 (softcover : acid free paper) ∞
Subjects: LCSH: All-America Football Conference—History. | Football—United States—History—20th century.
Classification: LCC GV955.5.A43 W43 2019 | DDC 796.332/6409044—dc23
LC record available at https://lccn.loc.gov/2018048494

BRITISH LIBRARY CATALOGUING DATA ARE AVAILABLE

ISBN (print) 978-1-4766-6534-4
ISBN (ebook) 978-1-4766-3420-3

© 2019 Gary Webster. All rights reserved

No part of this book may be reproduced or transmitted in any form or by any means, electronic or mechanical, including photocopying or recording, or by any information storage and retrieval system, without permission in writing from the publisher.

Front cover illustration © 2019 PicturesNow

Printed in the United States of America

McFarland & Company, Inc., Publishers
  Box 611, Jefferson, North Carolina 28640
    www.mcfarlandpub.com

Table of Contents

Preface   1

1. Challenging the NFL   5
2. Ward's Dream   15
3. Battle Stations   34
4. 1946   59
5. Exit Crowley, Enter Ingram   83
6. 1947   103
7. For the Good of the League   126
8. 1948   143
9. Wounded, but Still Alive   166
10. 1949   186
11. The Final Gun   204

Epilogue   213

Chapter Notes   221

Bibliography   225

Index   227

Preface

If at first you don't succeed, try, try again.

Sports-minded entrepreneurs had been trying to form a second football league to compete with the NFL for 20 years before the All-America Football Conference came along. The first American Football League was partially backed by and featured as its star attraction football's most famous player, Red (The Galloping Ghost) Grange. It flopped in 1926, lasting only one season. Grange's star power alone, which was all the first AFL had going for it, wasn't enough to sustain an entire league. Eleven years later, the second American Football League came along and folded its tent after the 1936 and 1937 seasons. One of its teams, the Rams, still survives. The Rams started in Cleveland in 1936 and moved from the AFL to the NFL in 1937. Nine years later, the Rams moved from Cleveland to Los Angeles. In 1995, they moved from Los Angeles to St. Louis. In 2016, they moved back to southern California.

The third AFL was born in 1940 with six teams. It was reduced to five teams for the 1941 season, and to zero teams thereafter, forced to "suspend" operations due to World War II. The league's owners never bothered to revive the third AFL after the war ended. But there were plenty of other businessmen with money to invest in football ready to satisfy the country's craving for sports entertainment after the conflict.

While the NFL's owners were wondering where they'd find enough relatively healthy bodies to field ten teams in 1944, and again, although to a lesser extent, in 1945, three upstart leagues announced their intention to compete with the establishment as soon as the war ended. The United States and Trans-America football leagues soon fell by the wayside, without ever playing a game. The All-America Football Conference, founded by Chicago sportswriter Arch Ward, was made of sterner stuff. Ward recruited men of significant financial means, and his eight-team league kicked off its first season in September of 1946, in front of a crowd of better than 60,000 enthusiastic (and curious) fans in Cleveland. The AAFC lasted twice as long as any challenger the NFL had ever faced and boasted of some historic accomplishments,

Harold (Red) Grange, college football's legendary Galloping Ghost. Grange would serve briefly in 1944 and 1945 as president of the United States Football League, a challenger to the NFL which gave up without so much as even signing a single player (Library of Congress).

such as tearing down professional football's color barrier when Marion Motley and Bill Willis took the field for the Cleveland Browns on that September Friday night in Municipal Stadium. The AAFC lured some of college football's brightest stars and drew more fans to its games than the NFL in 1946, 1947 and 1948. Its owners, according to the league's first commissioner, were worth in the neighborhood of $200 million cumulatively. Why did an enterprise with seemingly so much going for it fail, as those that came before it had failed?

The AAFC suffered the growing pains all fledgling sports leagues suffer. Two franchises changed ownerships, and one changed both ownership and location, after the 1946 season. The Chicago franchise, counted on to be the flagship of the AAFC, had four changes of ownership in its four-season existence. Baltimore's team needed a public sale of stock to raise the funds to keep it afloat after the 1947 season. The Browns, with solid ownership and the sport's best coach, emerged as the league's strongest franchise, burying their competition, losing just four games in four seasons. By 1949, it was a foregone conclusion that the AAFC's other six teams (Brooklyn dropped out after three futile years) were fighting for the right to be runner-up to Paul Brown's juggernaut in Cleveland. That led to declining attendance figures, even in northeastern Ohio, where Browns fans hungered for someone, anyone, to give their team some competition. Only the San Francisco 49ers were up to the challenge. Judging by the decreasing number of people who paid their way into massive Municipal Stadium on game days, even Browns fans got tired of watching their team win every week.

The bottom line may have been, however, that the millionaires who bought into Ward's vision (and his league) never wanted to compete with the NFL. From the time NFL commissioner Elmer Layden responded to questions about the AAFC by suggesting the new league "get a football," a comment that, taken in the proper context, wasn't nearly as inflammatory as historians have made it sound, the AAFC wanted to form a partnership with the established league. The AAFC's owners repeatedly explained that they envisioned a set-up identical to that of major league baseball: two separate but equal leagues, living in peaceful co-existence, tied together by a common draft of college players, with each league's champion meeting in a one-game, winner-take-all playoff at the end of each season. They couldn't understand why the NFL rejected the idea from day one. The NFL continued to reject the idea until one-sided negotiations resulted in the partial merger of the two leagues in December of 1949. Another challenger to the NFL had bitten the dust. It had simply taken longer than usual.

The AAFC did get a football, as Layden suggested. Its eight teams did some interesting things with it during four action-packed seasons. While ultimately failing to achieve its objective, the AAFC had an impact on professional football that is still felt today.

1

Challenging the NFL

Imitation is the sincerest form of flattery. Unless you own a major league sports team.

The American Professional Football Association was formed in an automobile dealership in Canton, Ohio, in September of 1920 and changed its name to the National Football League in 1922. Organized professional football struggled mightily through its first six seasons, but made enough of an impact that it faced the first of several competitors in the fall of 1926. All because Chicago Bears owner George Halas was too tight with a buck.

At least, C.C. Pyle thought so. And so did his client. Known as "Cash and Carry" to his friends, Pyle was among the first sports agents. He represented the greatest and most famous player in the history of college football, Harold (Red) Grange. Grange's exploits for the University of Illinois earned him nationwide acclaim, and he wasted no time turning professional after playing his final game for the Fighting Illini. The day after finishing his college eligibility, Grange signed a contract with Halas' Bears. He then led his new teammates on a 19-game barnstorming tour covering 67 days. Only five of the games counted in the National Football League standings, the rest were exhibitions designed to fatten Halas' bank account. One of the NFL games was played in New York's Polo Grounds on December 6, 1925, against the Giants. It drew better than 68,000 spectators, easily the largest crowd ever to watch a professional football game. The Bears won, 19–7, as Grange secured the victory with a fourth quarter interception return for a touchdown. It was, of course, Grange that the fans had paid to see. Not the Bears. Not the Giants. Halas knew it. So did Pyle and Grange.

When the tour ended, and the profits were distributed, Grange and Pyle decided they hadn't received enough for their labors—particularly Grange. He and his agent wanted a bigger slice of the financial pie for the 1926 season. When Halas wouldn't meet their terms, Pyle decided to start a league of his own. He had, after all, football's greatest player as his client. All he had to do was build an entire league around Grange. It proved to be far easier said than done.

Pyle called his new enterprise the American Football League and awarded franchises to Boston, Chicago, Cleveland, Philadelphia, Brooklyn, Newark, and New York. Grange would play for the club in the media capital of the nation, and would share ownership along with Pyle. The AFL also had a pair of road teams: Rock Island, Illinois, and Los Angeles. Rock Island defected from the NFL to join Pyle's league. The Los Angeles team, known alternately as the Pacific Coast All-Stars and as George Wilson's Wildcats after its star player, would have its business office in southern California, but not its home field. Neither Rock Island nor Los Angeles would have a home field. They'd play all of their games on the home field of their opponent.

Aside from Grange, the AFL had little going for it. And few thought one star player, even a player as great as Grange, could single-handedly sustain an entire league. "Red Grange is the goods the new American League has to offer," wrote sports columnist Sam Otis. "How he is going to be delivered in several cities at one time we cannot figure out. While he is performing in one town, what are the other clubs going to do to attract audiences? Pyle must have more goods if his league is to prosper."

Otis didn't think the AFL could lure enough stars away from the NFL (or from colleges) to entice fans to attend its games. Boston and Philadelphia didn't allow sporting events on Sundays, so their clubs would have to play their home games on Saturdays, in direct competition with college football, which was far more popular (and respected) in 1926. Otis also noted that the NFL had failed in Cleveland, despite that city's team winning the 1924 league championship. He held out scant hope for the AFL's success.

"It doesn't look as if Mr. Pyle is going to get very far bucking the National League," Otis wrote. "And if Red Grange should happen to be injured...."[1] Otis didn't finish the thought. He didn't have to.

The AFL's Cleveland Panthers were typical of many of its clubs, with the exception of New York and Los Angeles, both of which were owned and operated by Pyle and Grange. The Panthers were coached by Ray Watts and played their home games in a 40,000-seat stadium hastily built on the grounds of Luna Park, an amusement park on the city's southeast side. The club's president was Charles Zimmerman, who also happened to operate Luna Park. Zimmerman appeared to have joined the AFL in the hopes it would draw fans to its games who'd then spend more money touring the amusement park, ignoring the fact that football games were played in October, November and December, when the park would be closed. Cleveland's roster included Doc Elliott, Dave Noble and Dick Wolf, who had played on the city's NFL champions two years earlier. However, coach Watts was reported to be searching for players just three days before the Panthers' opener against Grange's New York club in Cleveland.

Cleveland won its opener, 10–0, before a reportedly raucous crowd of better than 22,000. The Panthers held the mighty Grange in check and kept the powerful visitors off the scoreboard. Things then deteriorated rapidly for the Panthers and the AFL.

Cleveland's third game of the season, scheduled for Newark on October 10, was canceled when the owners of the Newark team said they wouldn't be able to pay either the league-required visitor's guarantee to the Panthers, or their travel expenses. Newark had failed to meet both obligations for its October 3 game too. Attendance at Philadelphia's home game against Chicago, played on Saturday, October 2 against competition from local colleges, was a pathetic 891. Philadelphia's owner said he was "sorry [we] ever entered the organization."[2]

On Halloween, the Panthers lost to Los Angeles, 6–0, in a game that, in the words of the *Cleveland Plain Dealer*'s correspondent, nearly put him and the few spectators in the Luna Park stadium to sleep. No mention was made of the attendance, just as no mention had been made of the attendance at the Panthers' previous home game, a 23–7 victory over Rock Island on October 17. There was a good reason for the Cleveland players' lethargic performance against Los Angeles, and it was revealed the next day.

On November 1, the Panthers met to discuss disbanding the club over the small matter of not being paid for their services. The game against Los Angeles the previous day had been delayed by 45 minutes because the players refused to take the field in protest over not having received their salaries for the previous week's game in Chicago. To forestall a strike, someone in club management distributed the receipts that had been received at the Luna Park ticket windows that afternoon. Each player got 67 percent of his salary for the previous week's game, with the understanding that there was nothing in the till to pay them for the game against Los Angeles, undoubtedly explaining their listless performance. The visiting Wildcats wanted their money, too, and were told to take the $2,500 visitors share they were guaranteed under league rules out of a $3,000 "franchise forfeit."

Charles Zimmerman was nowhere to be found, having, according to newspaper accounts, "withdrawn some time ago."[3] The players said they'd be willing to re-negotiate their contracts and accept less money if a new owner would come forward, but none did. Max Rosenblum, owner of Cleveland's professional basketball team, and Sam Deutsch, former owner of Cleveland's 1924 NFL champions, both said they wanted nothing to do with Pyle's AFL. The Panthers' debt was reported to be $5,000. The club's assets consisted of "33 muddy uniforms."[4]

In spite of the confusion, Boston's club arrived in Cleveland mid-week for its game scheduled for Luna Park on November 7. The Panthers were placed in receivership on November 5, and were declared to be "dis-franchised," along with the bankrupt Newark club, on November 6. That was a typical development in Pyle and Grange's new league.

Pyle had signed a five-year lease for his New York team to play in Yankee Stadium. That proved to be two years longer than necessary. New York, Los Angeles, Chicago and Philadelphia (despite its owner being sorry he'd signed up with Pyle's league) made it through the season. Cleveland, Boston, Rock Island, Brooklyn and Newark were "dis-franchised" at various points of the year. Grange's Yankees finished second in the AFL at 10–5, joined the NFL for 1927, and stayed through 1928. Chicago, Philadelphia and Los Angeles disbanded. That was the end of the first American Football League.

As a measuring stick of how close the first American Football League was to "major" status, the Yankees, after winning ten games in the AFL in 1926, were 7–8–1 in the NFL in 1927, as Grange missed much of the season due to a knee injury. Grange sat out all of 1928, and the Yankees were 4–8–1. The Yankees folded after the season and Grange (minus Pyle, with whom he'd parted company) returned to the Bears.

The second American Football League arose in 1936. With the United States still in the grip of the Great Depression, the country was barely able to support one major football league, let alone two. And to consider the second American Football League a "major" league would be giving it the benefit of the doubt. As a case in point, Cleveland's entry was to be guided by a fellow named Buzz Wetzel, who was a cartoonist by trade. Wetzel had played football at Ohio State and declared in early September of 1936 that Cleveland had pulled out of the AFL due to ownership problems. Wetzel was determined not to put a weak club on the field and said he'd seek strong ownership and try again in 1937. Two weeks later, Wetzel announced that he'd found strong ownership in the person of Homer Marshman, and Cleveland was back in the AFL. It would field a team to be known as the Indians and would participate in the league's 1936 season. Cleveland's playmates would be Pittsburgh, Boston, New York, Brooklyn and Syracuse. Only Cleveland and Syracuse didn't share their cities with an NFL team.

Boston won the 1936 championship with a record of 8–3. Cleveland's team, thrown together at the 11th hour by Wetzel and Marshman, changed its name from Indians to Rams and finished second at 5–2–2. The Rams then defected to the NFL for the 1937 season. Defecting has been a trademark of the Rams. They left the AFL for the NFL in 1937, then left Cleveland for Los Angeles in 1946, Los Angeles for St. Louis in 1995, and St. Louis for Los Angeles in 2016. They are the lone link to the second American Football League that exists to this day.

The second American Football League was plagued by the kind of problems most infant sports leagues face. Boston's Shamrocks were the only team to play a full 11-game schedule. New York played ten games. Cleveland played nine. Pittsburgh played only six games and averaged just 2,500 fans per home game. Syracuse attracted only 5,000 customers to its home games and moved east to Rochester after six contests. After one game representing Rochester, the club disbanded, leaving behind an unsightly 1–6 record. The Brooklyn club then re-located to Rochester for the rest of the year, completing its abbreviated seven-game season with a record of 0–6–1. It's little wonder Wetzel and Marshman wanted to get their Rams out of such a disorganized mess.

In spite of the carnage left behind by the loss of the Cleveland, Syracuse and Brooklyn teams, the second AFL plowed ahead in 1937. The re-organized league had franchises in New York, Boston, Pittsburgh, Cincinnati, Rochester and Los Angeles. The second AFL thus became the first "major" league (and again, the term is used loosely) to place a team on the west coast. The first AFL had a team headquartered in Los Angeles, but it played all of its games on the road. The champion Shamrocks had Boston all to themselves after Redskins owner George Preston Marshall moved his team south to Washington, D.C. Marshall was disgusted that his Redskins had barely out-drawn the upstart Shamrocks at the gate and decided to seek greener pastures.

The second season of the second AFL was every bit as chaotic as the first. Pittsburgh quit after losing its first three games by a combined 69–7. New York, Boston, Rochester and Cincinnati played only seven games. Los Angeles played eight and won them all, thus technically laying claim to being the first undefeated, untied team in modern major league football history. The Bulldogs, whose application for NFL membership had been denied, overwhelmed their opponents, out-scoring them 219–69. None of those opponents posted a winning record, however, and only Cincinnati out-scored its opponents (102–89). In spite of that, Cincinnati won just two of its seven games. The Bulldogs were undefeated, but their claim to rank alongside the 1948 Cleveland Browns of the All-America Conference (15–0) and the 1972 Super Bowl champion Miami Dolphins (17–0) is tenuous at best. The second American Football League was a "major" league in name only. As proof, the Rams team that finished second in the AFL in 1936 won only one of its ten games in the NFL in 1937 and was out-scored 207–75.

The second AFL folded after the 1937 season. The third American Football League was born in 1940, with teams in Milwaukee, Buffalo, New York, Boston, Cincinnati and Columbus, which won the championship with an 8–1–1 record. Boston dropped out before the 1941 season began, leaving the third AFL to struggle through the campaign with just five clubs. The schedule was reduced to only eight games, with each team playing four at home and four on the road. Columbus' 5–1–2 record was good for its second league championship.

The third AFL was backed by men of significant financial means and appeared to have a chance to compete with the NFL. Detroit was granted an AFL franchise for 1942, replacing Boston. Philadelphia and Baltimore applied for admittance but were rejected because the owners didn't want to expand

Washington Redskins owner George Preston Marshall presents President Franklin D. Roosevelt with a gold season pass in September of 1938. Marshall would be the AAFC's main antagonist (Library of Congress).

too quickly and had decided to keep the league's membership at six for the 1942 season. The Second World War put an end to any thoughts of the third American Football League seriously challenging the NFL. Operations were suspended in September of 1942, and the league wasn't revived after the war.

The NFL struggled through the years of the Second World War. Manpower shortages forced some teams to suspend operations (the Rams sat out the 1943 season) and others to merge in order to survive. The Eagles and Steelers played as the Phil-Pitt Steagles in 1943. When the Eagles decided to go it alone in 1944, the Steelers combined with the Chicago Cardinals to form Card-Pitt. In 1945, the Brooklyn Tigers and Boston Yanks joined forces. But entrepreneurs were thinking ahead to the end of the conflict, when Americans with money to spend would be looking for ways to relax and have fun after the stress and sacrifice of the war years. No less than three new professional football leagues announced their formations between March of 1944 and January of 1945, even as the NFL was fearful of having to suspend operations for the duration due to a lack of players.

The March 6, 1944, edition of the *Pittsburgh Post-Gazette* reported that a meeting scheduled in that city the previous day to form a new football league had been postponed until April 2 due to bad weather. The newspaper said ten potential club owners were to have attended the meeting, and that the proposed league would have franchises on the east and west coasts. The re-scheduled meeting took place on the appointed day, and Pittsburgh was selected as the headquarters of the un-named league. Local industrialist Roland Paynes was elected acting president. Certificates of operation were awarded to groups representing Pittsburgh, New York, Washington, Baltimore, Philadelphia, St. Louis, Cincinnati and Seattle. The certificates meant that, if negotiations regarding financial backing, playing sites, and, in the words of the United Press, "other details pertinent to organization"[5] were successfully completed, those cities would have franchises. Akron, Ohio, was represented at the meeting but wasn't given a certificate. Detroit, San Francisco, Los Angeles, Boston and Chicago were said to be in negotiations for certificates. Paynes said the new league would start playing games in 1945, providing the war had ended and conditions were feasible.

By mid-summer, Paynes' new league had a name. The United States Football League, according to the United Press, had issued nine certificates of operation, the ninth having been granted to a group representing Honolulu. Airplane travel would not only make franchises on the west coast feasible, but also a team on an island in the middle of the Pacific Ocean. Paynes said the growth of professional football would probably require the formation of a government commission to regulate the sport. He said the USFL's owners would have the money needed to compete with the NFL for college players as well as to lure established professionals to switch leagues. He also said he didn't think it would take long for the owners to get tired of trying to out-bid each other for talent and put their heads together to find a better way to run the sport. That was where the government commission would be needed. Paynes said the commission would give the USFL and NFL owners a forum to discuss their differences and arrive at solutions without driving any teams bankrupt.

The USFL scheduled its first draft of eligible college players for December of 1944. There's no record of that draft ever taking place.

On November 26, the USFL made a splash by electing football's biggest name as its president. Red Grange was lured out of retirement to serve as the leader of the fledgling league. Grange played his last professional game for the Bears in 1934 and was earning a living selling insurance, and writing about and broadcasting football, when the USFL came calling. Grange said the USFL would be incorporated in Illinois, and its headquarters would be moved from Pittsburgh to Chicago. His affiliation with the USFL gave the league, which still consisted of nothing more than a bunch of certificates of organization, immediate credibility.

As of the day Grange accepted the league presidency, the USFL had granted franchises to Akron, Baltimore, Boston, Chicago, Honolulu, New York, Philadelphia, and Washington. Akron had replaced Pittsburgh. Seattle, Cincinnati and St. Louis were out. Each city posted a $10,000 guarantee. Grange said he'd thoroughly investigated the prospects of professional football and was convinced the United States could support a second major league. Grange had been co-owner of the New York and Los Angeles clubs of the first American Football League in 1926.

Grange said the men who'd invested $10,000 in USFL franchises were "good businessmen, not millionaires, and they're not entering this thing just on a gamble." He said the USFL wouldn't sign any players currently under contract to the NFL, but as for eligible collegians drafted by the NFL who hadn't signed, "that's another story. The final choice should be up to the player himself."[6] When Grange became eligible to turn professional in the fall of 1925, he had his pick of teams to choose from and signed with the Bears. Since 1936, college players had been subject to the NFL's draft and played with the team that selected them or didn't play professionally at all. At least not in the NFL.

The fact that none of the USFL owners were millionaires may have doomed the league to failure before it even got started. It took a lot of money to create a professional sports league, especially one aspiring to major status, and the USFL's owners, good businessman though they may have been, didn't have it.

In January of 1945, John (Chick) Meehan, the former football coach at Syracuse University, New York University and Manhattan University, introduced the Trans-America Football League, of which he would be president. Meehan said franchises had been granted to Dallas, Brooklyn, Philadelphia, Baltimore, New York and Los Angeles. Other cities were also under consideration. Meehan had a message for those who scoffed at the TAFL's chances of taking on the NFL, and the USFL.

"There is nothing tentative about our set-up," he said after meeting with the ownership group of the Dallas club. "These six cities have already been granted franchises, leased stadia on which to play, and are eager to start. Two other cities—Denver and Houston—may be added before the league begins operations."[7] Meehan made the remarks before leaving Dallas to head for Houston to check out that city's bid for a major league football franchise. He gave no indication when the TAFL planned to start playing games.

Among the buildings Meehan claimed to have been leased by the TAFL was Yankee Stadium, the most famous sports venue in the United States. Meehan said the New York franchise of the TAFL had the rights to Yankee Stadium even though the ballpark, and the baseball team that played there, had recently been sold to Del Webb and Dan Topping. Topping also owned the Brooklyn Tigers of the NFL and wanted to move them into Yankee Stadium. Webb and Topping had purchased the Yankees (and the stadium) from the estate of the late Colonel Jacob Ruppert. However, Meehan said J. Basil McGuire, the owner of the TAFL's New York franchise, had an agreement with Ruppert, allowing him to lease the stadium. McGuire was identified in wire service stories as the husband of one of Ruppert's heirs. Meehan insisted the agreement was binding despite Ruppert's death and the subsequent sale of the stadium to Topping. Meehan counted on a New York team playing in Yankee Stadium to serve as the foundation of the Trans-America Football League.

Neither the United States Football League nor the Trans-America Football League ever so much as signed a player to a contract, let alone played a game. Both expired the same week in June of 1945. On June 1, Red Grange stepped down as the USFL's president. Grange had actually resigned in May, but didn't make a public announcement until June. When he was hired in November of 1944, Grange said he was certain a second major football league could achieve financial success. Six months later, he'd changed his mind.

"I would not advise anyone to start in pro football right now," he said. "Pro football is on shaky footing and anything can happen." Grange had decided that professional football faced two problems. "Players are holding out for $400 and $600 a game when they used to get $150. The various leagues are bidding against each other for players, and the salaries are getting too high. The competition for players is becoming too stiff." Grange had apparently forgotten that he'd been able to sell his services to the highest bidder when he left the University of Illinois 20 years earlier. He also conveniently forgot how he and C.C. Pyle started their own league when they didn't get what they felt was their fair share of the profit from George Halas and the Bears. Now that Grange was management rather than labor, he felt the hired hands wanted too much money. It would be expensive to compete with the NFL, and the USFL's "non-millionaire" owners couldn't, or wouldn't, pay the price. Grange reached the conclusion that professional football teams would "have to draw a hell of a lot of people just to break even" in 1945 and beyond.

The other problem Grange foresaw was a lack of playing facilities. "Professional football can never be on a sound basis until it owns its own parks, or until baseball club owners organize their own [football] league and use their own parks." He said of NFL owners "all they really have are contracts and uniforms, and if baseball ever decides to forbid football teams to play in its parks, the National League—or any league—is ruined." Of the NFL's ten clubs in 1945, only the Green Bay Packers didn't lease their stadium from a major league baseball team. Losing access to those stadiums was unlikely since baseball owners didn't see professional football as a threat, and they enjoyed the rent money paid by football teams to use baseball stadiums.

Grange said of the job he'd resigned from that "the office requires a big promotional job, and my insurance business prevents me from giving it the necessary time." He said he quit because professional football "does not know where it is going."[8] He said he'd earned no salary during his half-year as president of the USFL, but that he hadn't accepted the job to make money. He said he didn't anticipate returning to professional football in any future capacity.

The USFL refunded the $10,000 franchise fees it had collected from owners in Akron, Boston, Baltimore, Philadelphia, Washington, New York and Chicago. Some of those owners wanted to replace Grange and forge ahead. Instead, the USFL, which had suspended operations in December of 1944 for the duration of the war, officially went out of business on June 4.

Chick Meehan's Trans-America Football League folded the same day. On June 2, NFL commissioner Elmer Layden announced that the New York Giants would drop their claim to territorial rights and allow Dan Topping's Brooklyn Tigers to move from Ebbets Field to Yankee Stadium. Yankee Stadium was about a mile from the Polo Grounds, where the Giants played, and the Mara family, which owned the Giants, asserted their territorial rights to the Bronx to keep the Tigers in Brooklyn. With a rival league trying to get a lease at Yankee Stadium, the Giants relented. The Maras didn't want anyone playing in Yankee Stadium, but they'd rather have an NFL team across the Harlem River from the Polo Grounds than an interloper from an upstart league. And that was the end of Meehan's TAFL.

"Now that the National League has obtained the New York Yankee stadium, we are bowing out," he said. "With Yankee Stadium, I had plenty of ammunition. Without it, I just had conversation. The Brooklyn Tigers have the stadium. We are through."[9] All the brave talk from the USFL and TAFL about their ability to compete against the NFL amounted to just so much bluff and bluster.

That left one challenger to the NFL still standing. The All-America Football Conference would prove to be made of much sterner stuff than the USFL, the TAFL, or any of the American Football Leagues that came before it.

2

Ward's Dream

Arch Ward had an idea.
Make that *another* idea.
As of the late summer of 1944, two of Ward's ideas were firmly entrenched parts of America's sports scene. Ward's day job was columnist for one of the country's largest newspapers, the *Chicago Tribune*. As the city prepared to host the 1933 World's Fair, Ward thought it would be a good idea for the festivities to include a baseball game between the best players in the American League and the best in the National League. Ward recruited the Comiskey family, owners of the White Sox, to make Comiskey Park available for the exhibition. The owners, players and fans responded enthusiastically. Connie Mack, then in his 33rd year as manager of the Philadelphia Athletics, piloted the American League All-Stars. John McGraw, who'd retired in 1932 after three decades managing the New York Giants, was in charge of the National Leaguers. Babe Ruth's two-run homer was the difference as the Americans defeated the Nationals, 4–2, in front of a sell-out crowd. Ward meant for the game to have been a one-shot deal as part of the World's Fair. It proved to be so well-received that no thought was given to dropping the event.

In 1934, Ward conceived the college all-star football game. In an era when the college game was more popular, and more highly regarded, than the professional version, Ward came up with the idea of putting together a team of the previous season's best college seniors and matching them against the NFL champions in an exhibition to kick off the football season. The game was played in Chicago's mammoth Soldier Field, and the proceeds were given to charity. Early on, the collegians held their own against the NFL's champions and even managed to win occasionally. The college all-star game started every football season through 1976, with the exception of 1974, when it was canceled by a players' strike. By the mid–1970s, the pros had won 12 straight games, most of them non-competitive, and the public had lost interest. The *Tribune* dropped its sponsorship. For the record, the collegians defeated the pros nine times and tied them twice.

By the late summer of 1944, baseball's All-Star game was a mid-season fixture, and the football game had drawn more than 98,000 fans to Soldier Field on August 30. So when Ward held a press conference on September 2 to introduce a new professional football league, fans took notice. There were skeptics and scoffers, but Ward's involvement gave the enterprise a credibility all the other challengers to the NFL had lacked.

At a meeting in Chicago on September 1 and 2, a plan to create the All-America Football Conference (often incorrectly called the All-*American* Football Conference) was finalized. Ward said the groundwork had been laid several months earlier, and seven cities had been awarded franchises. Ultimately, eight to ten "key cities" would be represented in the AAFC, and the teams would be owned by "men of millionaire incomes."[1] Ward introduced the franchise owners:

Trucking company owner John L. Keeshin in Chicago.

Oil company president Ray Ryan and Mrs. Eleanor Gehrig, widow of New York Yankees legend Lou Gehrig, in New York.

Former world heavyweight boxing champion Gene Tunney in Baltimore.

Oil company executives James Breuil and William Bennett, and construction magnate Sam Cordovano in Buffalo.

Radio and film star Don Ameche and former newspaper syndicate editor Christy Walsh in Los Angeles.

Tony and Vic Morabito, Allen Sorrell and Ernest Turre in San Francisco. The Morabito brothers and Sorrell had earned their money in the lumber business. Turre made his fortune in construction.

Arthur (Mickey) McBride, the founder of the Yellow Zone Cab Company, was the principal owner of the team in Cleveland.

Ameche and Walsh may have been the new league's most interesting ownership tandem, Ameche with his Hollywood background and Walsh by virtue of his association with America's most famous sports figure, Babe Ruth. The immature and impulsive Ruth was smart enough to know he needed someone to handle the money he'd earn playing baseball lest he squander every penny of it. He hired Walsh as his business manager, and Walsh not only saved Ruth from going broke, he added to Ruth's fortune by securing outside income from sources such as product endorsements, movie contracts, recording deals, and a newspaper column bearing Ruth's name but ghost-written by Walsh.

Ward's new league needed at least one, and possibly three, more members. Negotiations were underway with potential investors in Detroit, Philadelphia and Boston. The plan was to begin play in 1945.

At the meeting that solidified the AAFC, Ward said the owners agreed on a pair of resolutions that "are certain to shape the success of the confer-

2. Ward's Dream

Notre Dame's legendary 1924 backfield, christened the "Four Horsemen" by sportswriter Grantland Rice. Jim Crowley (far left) would become the commissioner of the AAFC. Elmer Layden (next to Crowley) would become the commissioner of the NFL. They spent the 1946 season at odds with each other in those capacities (Library of Congress).

ence."[2] The first resolution prohibited the employment by the AAFC of any player or coach under contract to an NFL team. The second barred the AAFC from signing any player who had collegiate eligibility remaining. Neither resolution lasted long.

The AAFC's ban on signing anyone under contract to the NFL was abandoned in late November. The NFL's commissioner in 1944 was Elmer Layden, one of the legendary "Four Horsemen" of University of Notre Dame fame. Layden and his teammates had been immortalized by sportswriter Grantland Rice after the Fighting Irish's stirring victory over Army at New York's Polo Grounds in 1924. One of Layden's backfield mates on that Saturday afternoon had been "Sleepy Jim" Crowley, the left halfback. With Layden running the NFL, it was likely no coincidence that the owners of the AAFC teams chose Crowley as their league's first commissioner.

Crowley had been a successful head coach at Michigan State College from 1929 to 1932, and Fordham University in New York from 1933 to 1941. Fordham's 1936–37 teams featured a defensive line which has gone down in football lore as "the seven blocks of granite." One of those blocks was a young man named Vince Lombardi, who would go on to become arguably the NFL's greatest coach. Another block was future Pro Football Hall of Famer Alex Wojciechowicz. Crowley's teams at Michigan State, Fordham and the North Carolina Pre-Flight School, which he coached in 1942, compiled a record of 86–23–11.

Crowley was a lieutenant commander in the Navy and had just returned to the United States after 16 months in the south Pacific. He was serving as athletic director and head football coach at the Sampson Naval Training Center in Sampson, New York, when he accepted the AAFC's offer to become its commissioner. The AAFC conveniently ignored the fact that Crowley was under contract to coach the Boston Yanks of the NFL after the war ended. So much for resolution number one. Crowley secured his release from his obligation to the NFL and signed a five-year, $125,000 contract with the AAFC.

On the same day the AAFC announced Crowley's hiring, it also announced that applications for franchises from Boston, Atlanta, Miami and Detroit would be considered at a league meeting in December.

With a commissioner and seven franchises in place, the AAFC started signing players. According to sports editor Sam Otis of the *Cleveland Plain Dealer*, AAFC teams which he didn't identify had signed college stalwarts Glenn Dobbs, Bill Daley and Paul Governali, whom Otis anointed "real topnotchers." Otis used the signings, which he publicized in his column of December 5, to show his readers that Ward's new league meant business.

The owners of AAFC teams met in New York on December 8 and 9 and selected a committee to write the circuit's constitution and by-laws. Former Cleveland mayor Ray T. Miller was hired as the AAFC's legal counsel. A franchise was awarded to Miami, with Harvey Hester serving as its president. Gene Tunney's Baltimore group was out. No explanation was given for Baltimore's withdrawal. It would prove to be temporary. As for Hester and Miami, their acceptance would be one of the biggest mistakes the All-America Football Conference would make.

The NFL announced its regular season attendance figures for 1944 on December 12. The league drew 1,234,750 fans to its games, or 57,681 more fans than had come through the turnstiles in 1943, for an increase of just under 5 percent.

The AAFC's search for head coaches had begun. Columnist Gordon Cobbledick of the *Plain Dealer* wrote on December 18 that he had it on good authority Notre Dame head coach Frank Leahy, who was then serving in the Navy, would coach a professional team after the war. Leahy had compiled a sparkling record with Boston College and Notre Dame (46–5–3), and guided the Fighting Irish to the 1943 national championship. What Cobbledick didn't tell his readers was that the team pursuing Leahy was McBride's Cleveland entry.

2. Ward's Dream

On Christmas Eve, Hester's Miami AAFC team announced the hiring of former Rice and Auburn University head coach "Whispering" Jack Meagher as the team's coach. Meagher was a lieutenant commander in the Navy and had coached the Iowa Pre-Flight team to a 10–1 record in 1944. His overall collegiate coaching record was 84–64–10. He signed a two-year contract.

On the day after Christmas, the question was raised as to whether there would be any professional football in 1945. Baseball and football had survived 1944, but an announcement from War Manpower Commissioner James F. Byrnes caused concern that there simply wouldn't be enough able-bodied men to field professional sports teams in 1945. Byrnes said that the status of all 4-F athletes (who dotted the rosters of major league baseball and football teams) would be re-examined, and those deemed unfit for military duty would be required to find work in a war-related industry. Although baseball had been given a green light by President Franklin D. Roosevelt in 1942 to keep playing and provide recreation for the folks on the home front, it didn't qualify as a "war-related industry." Neither did professional football, which lacked Roosevelt's blessing to continue for the sake of the country's morale. Doomsayers feared Byrnes' decision would require professional sports to shut down for the duration of the war.

NFL commissioner Layden didn't feel a suspension of professional sports was necessary, however. He explained his league's position regarding the Byrnes declaration. "We have been taking the situation as we found it since the beginning of the war," he said. "I believe we have contributed to the war effort in this respect. We have provided some relaxation to the home front. We have not sought deferments for our players and don't intend to do so. Their military status is up to the Selective Service boards. We don't have the same kind of football—or the same kind of meat—we had, but we have operated within wartime regulations. If we felt we were interfering with, or retarding, the war effort, we would have quit long ago."

Layden said about 500 NFL players were serving in the military. The league had employed 280 players in 1944, all of whom were of draft age. About 20, according to Layden, had been classified as 4-F. "Many of these worked in war plants during the week, and most of them would gladly enter the armed services if necessary,"[3] he pointed out.

There was no comment from Jim Crowley or any AAFC club owner about the Byrnes decision. But it eliminated any possibility that the new league would start playing games in the autumn of 1945.

The Byrnes decision didn't stop the NFL owners from holding their winter meeting in January of 1945. Washington Redskins owner George Preston Marshall dismissed the claims of some that the meeting was a waste of time since the 1945 season was likely to be canceled. "That's silly," said Marshall, possibly the most influential owner in the NFL, "because right now there is really nothing to prevent us from playing since our games are held on a non-working day."[4] Marshall conveniently forgot the possibility that there wouldn't be enough men available to play those games.

The owners would also discuss applications for franchises from three men who were supposedly committed to the AAFC. Before casting their lot with Ward, Christy Walsh had applied for an NFL franchise in Los Angeles, Tony Morabito had applied on behalf of San Francisco, and Sam Cordovano had filed an application for Buffalo. The NFL had 11 teams following the dissolution of the one-season merger of the Steelers and Cardinals, and publicity director George Strickler acknowledged that a 12th team might be added for 1945. "We tabled all applications at last year's meeting," said Strickler, "but now it looks like one could be accepted."[5] If for no other reason than to deal a blow to the AAFC by stealing one of its owners. Most NFL owners were against adding another team, and the idea went nowhere.

The scheduled four-day confab adjourned early on its second day, much to Marshall's dismay. When the motion to adjourn was made, Marshall protested, then walked out of the meeting. In his absence, the other owners voted 10–0 to go home until the NFL's spring meeting, scheduled for April. Marshall declared the vote to adjourn null and void since he hadn't voted, and the NFL's constitution required a unanimous vote on all such matters, even adjournment. Commissioner Layden ruled that since all the owners present had voted in favor, the motion had carried legally. It wasn't the fault of the rest of the owners that Marshall had pouted and left the room.

According to Marshall, the abbreviated meeting was "a direct violation of the league's constitution and by-laws. As far as I'm concerned, the meeting was never held. I was not present [at the vote to adjourn] and it takes a unanimous vote of the owners to adjourn such a meeting."

Marshall, who was accustomed to getting his own way, suggested that he may boycott the spring meeting and, with three other leagues looking to challenge the NFL, joked, "I guess I'll have to look for a new league."[6] He didn't, but he wasn't about to let Layden overrule him without getting some revenge.

Less than a week after the abbreviated league meeting, Marshall floated a rumor that Layden was going to leave his post with the NFL and accept the job as head coach of the Chicago franchise of the AAFC. "Persons who put Layden in as our commissioner have organized the All-American [sic] Conference, and it's entirely plausible he will become coach of the Chicago entry in the circuit, which doesn't plan to operate until 1946."[7] Marshall was the first to mention that the AAFC had decided not to field teams in 1945. No such announcement had been made by commissioner Crowley or any other league official.

Layden, who was accustomed to Marshall's shenanigans, fired back. "The suggestion is silly and without fact and should not be dignified by comment."[8] Layden's $25,000 yearly contract as NFL commissioner would expire in March of 1946.

On January 27, millionaire sportsman Dan Topping, whose family owned the prosperous Anaconda Copper company, purchased the New York Yankees along with his partner, millionaire real estate tycoon Del Webb. The most famous, and successful, major league baseball team in history was purchased from the estate of Colonel Jacob Ruppert, and the deal included Yankee Stadium. That had potential repercussions not only for the NFL, but the AAFC.

Possibly the most fateful moment in the history of the All-America Football Conference occurred about a year-and-a-half before it played its first game. On February 8, 1945, the AAFC's Cleveland franchise signed Paul Brown as its head coach and general manager. Brown was synonymous with Ohio football. He'd played at Massillon Washington high school, one of the strongest prep programs in the country. Massillon is about ten miles west of Canton, the birthplace of the NFL. Brown quarterbacked the football team at Miami University in Oxford, Ohio. At the age of 23, Brown accepted the head football coaching position at Severn Prep in Maryland, then returned to Ohio in 1933 to coach at Massillon. Many questioned whether a 24-year-old with one year of head coaching experience, even at an exclusive prep school such as Severn, was ready to take command of one of the highest profile high school football programs in the United States. Those fears seemed to be justified when Massillon lost four games in Brown's first season and three in his second. The board of education ignored calls for Brown's firing, and Massillon suffered just one more defeat over the final six years of Brown's tenure, which concluded in 1940.

Brown's record of 80 victories and only eight defeats at Massillon got the attention of Ohio State University athletic director Lyn St. John, who was in the market for a new football coach after dismissing Francis Schmidt following a mediocre 1940 season. Brown's fellow high school coaches endorsed him highly, first because they knew he had the right stuff to lead the Buckeyes, and second because they were tired of losing to his Tigers and wanted to be rid of him. St. John hired the youthful Brown, and again questions were asked as to whether a mere high school coach was prepared to take on the challenge presented by a powerhouse like Ohio State. Brown answered those who criticized St. John by leading Ohio State to a 7–1–1 record in 1941 and winning the 1942 national championship. Brown's 1942 Buckeyes achieved the school's first number one ranking during the season and held it, finishing 9–1. The Buckeyes lost most of their 1943 squad to military service and won just three of nine games, Brown's only losing season as a head coach. They then lost Brown to military service. He enlisted in the Navy, achieved the rank of lieutenant junior grade, and was placed in charge of the football team at the Great Lakes Naval Training Station in Chicago in 1944.

It was assumed that Brown would return to Columbus and pick up where he left off when World War II ended, but the 1944 Buckeyes threw a monkey wrench into that assumption. Under the guidance of coach Carroll Widdoes, who'd been an assistant under Brown, Ohio State didn't lose a game in 1944 and was ranked number two in the nation at season's end. Suddenly, Brown's return to Columbus wasn't quite so cut-and-dried. Widdoes wasn't to be cast aside so easily after such an outstanding accomplishment, and when Brown asked St. John for assurance that the job would be waiting for him when he was discharged from the Navy, he didn't like what he heard. So he accepted Mickey McBride's offer to coach the Cleveland team in the AAFC.

Brown wasn't McBride's first choice to coach his team. McBride had reached a handshake agreement with Notre Dame head coach Frank Leahy, who was then, like Brown, also in the Navy. Leahy's Fighting Irish had succeeded Brown's Buckeyes as national champions in 1943. Notre Dame officials asked McBride to re-consider and appealed to his loyalty as the father of a Notre Dame alum. McBride's son had graduated from Notre Dame, and both were rabid fans of the Fighting Irish. McBride relented and hired Brown on the recommendation of sportswriter John Dietrich of the *Cleveland Plain Dealer*. It turned out to be a fateful decision for both the Cleveland team and the AAFC's future.

"I leave Ohio State reluctantly," said Brown on the day he signed a five-year contract worth $125,000 to coach McBride's team. He'd also receive a monthly stipend of $1,500 for the duration of the war. "I appreciate the wholehearted support I enjoyed during my three years there, from the fans of Ohio and members of the athletic board. The time arrived for me to decide whether I was to continue as a professor or a businessman. In addition to a generous salary, I have been offered a share in the profits of the Cleveland club. I simply couldn't turn down the deal in fairness to my family. I have every confidence in professional football and especially the future of the All-American [sic] Conference. It has been thoroughly organized. It embraces the key cities of the country. I am convinced professional football will continue to prosper."[9]

Although college football was far more popular than professional football in 1945, Ohio State couldn't possibly have exceeded, or even come close to matching, McBride's offer to Brown. Brown's first contract with Ohio State, in 1941, called for a season's salary of six thousand dollars. His Cleveland contract would pay him $25,000 per year with, as he mentioned, a share of the team's profits, assuming there was a profit to be shared. And that was highly questionable at the time, despite Brown's expressed confidence in the new venture.

McBride said Brown would have "complete charge of operations, both on and off the field." Brown wouldn't have accepted anything less than total control of the football team. Like many successful businessmen, McBride was smart enough to know what he didn't know. And he readily admitted that he knew nothing about football, his passion for Notre Dame notwithstanding. He was more than willing to turn his team over to a man who knew everything about football and get out of the way.

"Everything will be in Brown's hands," McBride said. "I believe in getting the man you want for the job and letting him handle it." Brown was the third coach to cast his lot with the AAFC. San Francisco had signed Lawrence (Buck) Shaw of Santa Clara, and Jack Meagher had been hired by Miami.

McBride had tried unsuccessfully to buy the Rams from Dan Reeves in 1941. He wasn't aware Reeves had a plan for the Rams that didn't involve keeping the team in Cleveland. He explained why he hooked up with the AAFC. "Because people said it was impossible," he said simply. McBride enjoyed a challenge, and going head-to-head with the NFL in Cleveland represented one.

After his bid for the Rams was rejected by Reeves, McBride said "I forgot about [owning a football team] until I heard that Arch Ward, the sports editor of the *Chicago Tribune*, was organizing a new league. I had never met Ward but walked into his office and asked if I could get the Cleveland franchise. He wanted to know whether or not I had the financial backing, and I convinced him that I had. About a week later, I received word that I was in."[10]

McBride wasn't fazed by the prospect of winning the battle for the loyalty (and ticket dollars) of Cleveland's football fans, who had shown little interest in the professional game. The Rams had been in business in the NFL since 1937 (with a one-year hiatus in 1943) and never turned a profit.

"We have all the vast population of northern Ohio to draw from, and a stadium with 80,000 seats," said McBride, who had secured a lease on cavernous Municipal Stadium on Cleveland's lakefront. "I believe the public will go for new faces and new teams, particularly if we show them headline players. Our schedule will be much different from that of the National League. Each team will play every opponent two games a season, on a home-and-home basis, giving each club 14 games. Since we have clubs in Miami, Florida; Los Angeles and San Francisco, we plan that long hops will be by air."[11]

Although McBride would have no input into the team's player personnel, that department being Brown's responsibility, he understood the value of star power. And one of college football's biggest stars was Les Horvath, a native of the Cleveland suburb of Parma who won the 1944 Heisman Trophy playing for Ohio State. Cleveland's AAFC team (which didn't yet have a nickname) had its eye on Horvath, and Horvath expressed a desire to play for his college coach, Brown, if he chose to play professional football.

"I doubt very much if I will play pro football," Horvath said the day after

Brown's hiring was announced. "But if I do, I'd like to play for Paul." Then, sounding very much like someone who intended to give the professional game a whirl, Horvath added, "Of course, if another club comes along with a better offer ... well, I graduate from dental school in June and I will make up my mind then whether or not I will play pro ball." Horvath had been drafted by the Rams and was on the team's "reserve" list. He was considered the property of the NFL (at least by the NFL) even though he hadn't signed a contract, and any NFL player signing with another professional league would be banished from the NFL for five years. That didn't discourage Horvath.

"That won't bother me," said the Ohio State star. "If I go into the new league, I don't intend to play longer than one season, if that."[12] Signing a player of Horvath's stature away from the NFL would have been a coup for the AAFC.

Said McBride of his adopted hometown, "I've always figured this was a good sports city, if you aimed your sights high, right from the start. But you have to be big time. You have to give the fans the best of everything, and I've started by signing the best coach in the business."[13] By signing Brown, McBride may have simultaneously assured the success of his team and the failure of the All-America Football Conference.

The best coach in the business wouldn't be able to start building his team until the war ended, but he was looking ahead to that moment. "You know me.... I'm going to try to build a football dynasty in Cleveland," Brown said. "I will have complete freedom to pick my own coaching staff, as well as the business staff and, of course, our players. Yes, I have a pretty good idea of some of the players I'm going after."

"It will be a tough go, but that's the way I like it," Brown continued. "I realize that it will take more than a year or two to build, but we're not going to waste any time. Cleveland is basically a good sports city. They want the best and they come out for the best. But the possibilities have never been scratched below the surface. I can see the day when we have two powerful, professional leagues, the All-America and the National. It will make the game healthier."[14] Throughout the four-year professional football skirmish, Brown held fast to the hope that the AAFC and the NFL could peacefully co-exist as the National and American leagues did in major league baseball. He never realized that dream.

McBride, Brown and the team they built in Cleveland will be mentioned often in this book, possibly too often. Part of the reason is the fact is the author is a life-long Browns fan with an admitted bias toward his favorite team. The main reason, however, is the story of the AAFC is the story of the Browns. It wouldn't be inaccurate to call this book "The Cleveland Browns and Seven Other Teams," since that's essentially what the AAFC amounted to. Arch

2. Ward's Dream

Ward envisioned the league's Chicago franchise being its crown jewel, but it didn't work out that way, and that was partly because of the determination of McBride and Brown to put together "the greatest show in football." And that determination may have led to the eventual demise of the AAFC.

On February 13, John Keeshin, the owner of the AAFC's Chicago team, announced the signing of a ten-year lease for it to play its home games in massive Soldier Field, the home of the annual college all-star football game, another Ward creation. Soldier Field hadn't had a regular football tenant since 1930, when Notre Dame played there while its football stadium was being constructed on the South Bend campus. The NFL's Bears played in Wrigley Field, home of the Cubs, and the Cardinals used Comiskey Park, the home of the White Sox. Each facility had more than enough seats to accommodate the crowds the teams drew. Keeshin said he'd ask the AAFC to schedule as many night home games as possible for his team in September and October in order to avoid conflicting home dates with Chicago's established NFL teams. Leases had been signed with Soldier Field and Cleveland's Municipal Stadium, and another would soon be signed with the Los Angeles Memorial Coliseum, giving the AAFC three of the largest venues in the country. But could the league fill those seats?

According to published reports, Keeshin's agreement with the Chicago Park District board called for the team to pay 10 percent of the gross gate per game up to $100,000; 9 percent of the gross gate on the next $50,000; and decreased to 6 percent of the gross gate over $250,000. The Chicago franchise would never experience a single-game gate of $250,000.

With a stadium secured, Keeshin went looking for a coach. Talks between Keeshin and Ed McKeever, the acting football coach and athletic director at Notre Dame (substituting for Frank Leahy) began in late February. McKeever told the United Press on February 25 that he and Keeshin were still talking. "We didn't come to any agreement, and at present negotiations are still pending."[15] Those talks proved fruitless, although McKeever would eventually find his way to the sideline at Soldier Field.

By the end of February, Keeshin's team not only had a place to play, but someone to coach it. Chicago announced the hiring of Marine Lt. Col. Richard (Dick) Hanley as head coach and general manager on February 28. Hanley was well-known in Chicago, having coached Northwestern University from 1927 to 1934 and posting a record of 36–26–4. He said his salary in the AAFC would be substantially higher than he'd been paid while coaching the Wildcats. Hanley had been head coach of the El Toro, California, Marine base's football team in 1944 and would be assisted in Chicago by Marine Capt. Ernie Nevers, the former Stanford University and NFL star. Nevers was the athletic officer at the San Diego Marine base. The 48-year-old Hanley signed a three-year contract.

The March 1945 issue of Ohio State's alumni magazine reported that Lyn St. John had offered Paul Brown an annual salary of $15,000 if he'd return to coach the Buckeyes after the war—$10,000 less than McBride had offered. St. John readily admitted that Ohio State couldn't match the financial package McBride gave Brown. Instead, he tried to convince his former coach that he was better off in Columbus than in Cleveland. St. John noted that Brown's long-term security as a tenured professor and coach at Ohio State were assured, while the prospects for professional football were murky at best. St. John also tried (and failed) to convince Brown that he'd be happier coaching college students than professional athletes. Brown denied that any such offer was made.

According to sports columnist Jack Clowser of the *Cleveland Press*, Brown had a master plan for building the dynasty in Cleveland that he'd spoken of when he was hired. Clowser revealed that plan to his readers on February 27. He said that Brown planned to turn Cleveland's AAFC franchise into Ohio State north. The team would adopt scarlet and gray as its colors, and Brown would hire as many of his former Ohio State assistant coaches and players as possible. He'd "depend on his magnetic personality, plus very attractive financial terms" to construct a team that would be loyal to him. Loyalty was extremely important to Brown. Clowser said Brown planned to make Cleveland's team "the scarlet scourge" of the AAFC. One Ohio State assistant had already declined an offer to join Brown's coaching staff. Paul Bixler would remain with the Buckeyes in 1945, and replace Carroll Widdoes as head coach in 1946.

As the United States and its allies marched relentlessly toward victory in Europe in the late winter of 1944–45, questions continued to swirl as to whether there would be a professional football season come the autumn. Charles (Chile) Walsh, general manager of the Rams, saw no reason not to move forward. "As it stands now, I see no reason why we should not be hopeful of operating this year. We play only on Sundays, and it is possible for our players to work a full schedule in war plants. The only thing that could stop football, as I see it, would be a definite change for the worse in the war situation. And from the way things are going now, there is reason to believe it will be much better instead of worse."

Walsh was asked about the specter of competition from the AAFC once the war ended. "It's one of those if-and-when things for after the war,"[16] he said. He also denied a report by the Associated Press that the Rams planned to move to Los Angeles, possibly prior to the 1945 season. Walsh noted that the Rams had a five-year lease at League Park, Cleveland's tiny and antiquated ballpark on the city's near east side. Despite its seating capacity of just 22,000, League Park had proven more than large enough to accommodate the small crowds the Rams had drawn since their inception eight years earlier. Walsh had no comment about McBride's lease at Municipal Stadium, with its nearly 80,000 seats. The Rams hadn't yet drawn 80,000 fans for a full season, let alone for a single game.

Despite George Preston Marshall's claim that the AAFC would not start playing games until the autumn of 1946, no official decision had been made. McBride, however, said on March 25 that he believed the lack of available quality players would necessitate holding off for another year. "My experience in Cleveland is that the fans will support anything that has quality and quantity. We do not want to start with a weak team, disappoint the fans, then have to win them back. When we open, we want to have something real to offer, so that our fans will stick."[17]

McBride's coach met with reporters in Cleveland in late March to detail his plans for his team. Brown quickly let his boss know what he'd gotten himself into by signing on with the AAFC.

"I want to win if it costs every cent he's got," said Brown with a grin, looking directly at McBride. "I have small hope that we will be able to operate this year, but I certainly am hopeful of getting started in 1946,"[18] Brown said. McBride reportedly swallowed hard but forced a smile.

McBride revealed his co-owners to the writers after Brown addressed them. Former Cleveland mayor Ray T. Miller; Dan Sherby, McBride's partner in his cab company; finance expert Smith Davis; and Bob Gries, a former executive with Cleveland's May Company department stores, had invested in the AAFC. "We are not in this just to make money," McBride insisted. "We are interested in all sports, and in the city of Cleveland, where all of us have lived a long time."[19] That comment may have been a direct slap at the Rams, who had been owned since 1941 by Dan Reeves, a New Yorker who was rarely seen in Cleveland and had little interest in the city. Cleveland's AAFC team would be owned and operated by Clevelanders.

The spring NFL owners meeting, which Marshall had threatened to boycott but didn't, got underway on April 6. As a result of the manpower shortage, Dan Topping's Brooklyn Tigers merged with Ted Collins' second-year Boston Yanks. The team would play its home games in Boston. The Associated Press reported that the owners were considering expanding to 12 clubs for the 1946 season, as a response to the AAFC and what they anticipated (hoped?) would be a growing demand for professional football after the war.

Ten days after the NFL owners met, their counterparts in the AAFC got together to discuss the status of the league. It was expected that a decision would be announced as to whether the AAFC would begin playing games in the autumn of 1945, but that expectation wasn't met. The owners did appoint a two-man committee, consisting of Cleveland coach Paul Brown and Chicago owner John Keeshin, to meet with NFL commissioner Elmer Layden. The purpose of the committee was to assure Layden and the NFL that the

AAFC was ready to play ball, and to find out what suggestions Layden may have to guarantee a peaceful co-existence between the two leagues. The AAFC wanted to avoid a costly bidding war for playing talent.

"We want to tell Mr. Layden that we believe that two major leagues should be formed, such as in baseball," said the AAFC's vice president, Christy Walsh. "In that way we want to make arrangements not to tamper with each other's players or territorial rights—to be friends."[20] The idea that the NFL would welcome competition from the AAFC proved to be wishful thinking, as did the hope Layden would meet with the new league's representatives.

In response to the AAFC's overture, Layden issued a statement to the press. "All I know of new leagues is what I read in newspapers. There is nothing for the National Football League to talk about as far as new leagues are concerned until someone gets a football and plays a game."[21] The statement has been shortened into the famous "let them get a football!" retort quoted in numerous football history books. Regardless of whether Layden intended the statement to be inflammatory or not, the message was clear: the NFL had no intention of meeting with anyone connected with the AAFC. As of late April of 1945, the AAFC had seven franchises, some of which had yet to secure leases at venues in which to play their games. Only 30 players were under contract to AAFC teams. Layden can hardly be blamed if he, and the owners who employed him, saw no reason to negotiate with an entity that was still little more than a gleam in Arch Ward's eye.

Another anticipated development at the AAFC meeting was a get-together between the new league's owners and general manager Tom Gallery of the NFL's Brooklyn Tigers, who'd been officially merged with the Boston Yanks earlier in the month. Gallery was to explore the possibility of moving Dan Topping's Tigers into the AAFC whenever it began play, so the team could play its home games in Yankee Stadium. The Tigers were blocked from playing in Yankee Stadium as long as they remained in the NFL unless John Mara was willing to surrender his New York Giants territorial rights to the Bronx, which Mara showed no inclination to do. Gallery denied he'd attend the meeting, which was held in Chicago.

"Chicago is my home, and I am here with my wife and daughter to meet a relative who has been overseas,"[22] Gallery said. "I will not attend the All-America meetings and I have no intention of joining the league as long as Brooklyn is treated fairly in the National League."[23] True to his word, he didn't meet with the AAFC owners. But that didn't mean Topping wasn't interested in the AAFC.

Other business attended to by the AAFC owners included adopting a $15,000 per game minimum guarantee for visiting teams once the league started playing games. Visiting teams in the NFL were guaranteed $10,000 per game. The AAFC owners deferred a decision on an application from a group represented by Dr. D.M. Nigro and former Notre Dame star Marchy Schwartz, seeking a franchise for Kansas City. Nigro admitted his group hadn't secured a home field for a team and wasn't certain it could.

The Los Angeles franchise was the only AAFC team without a head coach, and rumor had it one of the team's owners, Don Ameche, had approached University of Southern California coach Jeff Cravath about the position. Cravath had coached the Trojans to Rose Bowl berths in 1943 and '44 and was said to be reluctant to commit to the AAFC until after the 1945 college season, which was still more than four months away. With all of its rivals having head coaches in place, it was doubtful that Los Angeles could afford to wait until early in January of 1946 for Cravath to make a decision.

One other piece of business the AAFC owners dealt with at the meeting involved an unusual scheduling request from Harvey Hester of the Miami franchise. Hester had some interesting ideas about how a football team should be run, and one of them pertained to his club's home schedule. Hester asked that all of his team's home games be scheduled for the second half of the AAFC's 14-game season. Hester believed snowbirds escaping the oncoming winter would have flocked to south Florida by late in October, and they in turn would flock to his team's home games in the Orange Bowl. He apparently wasn't concerned about the effect opening the season with seven straight road games would have on his players.

Cleveland's Rams left no stone unturned in their search for players. General manager Chile Walsh told the *Plain Dealer* on May 5 that he'd contacted the coaches of more than 200 college teams, asking for recommendations regarding players with professional potential. Any coach suggesting a player who earned a spot on the Rams' 1945 roster and played at least three games would receive a $100 war bond as a reward. "If the player makes good and stays with the team, the reward will be increased in proportion to his performance," said Walsh.

While the Rams were reaching out to college coaches, their AAFC competitors were reaching out to college players. Lou Groza, a native of Martins Ferry, Ohio, who'd played on Ohio State's freshman team in 1942 before joining the military, wrote a letter to OSU assistant coach Ernie Godfrey in May of 1945 from his post in Okinawa. The letter informed Godfrey that Groza would forego his college eligibility and turn professional when he returned home after the conflict. "As you know by now, I have changed my mind about collegiate football," Groza told Godfrey. "I am still going to complete my collegiate education, however."[24] Groza was a private in the Army medical corps in the spring of 1945, and had been a tackle and placekicker for the Buckeyes in 1942. He'd be eligible to play professional football because his college class would have graduated by the time he was discharged from the Army.

Groza's correspondence with Godfrey led to an investigation by the

Western Conference (now the Big Ten) into whether the Buckeyes' former coach, Paul Brown, was actively recruiting his former players to join his Cleveland team in the AAFC. Brown denied the charge, on a technicality.

"I haven't talked to any men," he said. "Our league cannot hope to operate until the 1946 season, and the availability of those 1942 freshmen now in service is contingent upon how long it takes to whip the Japanese."[25] The Germans had already been whipped. Brown made the comments three days before Germany surrendered on May 8. Brown also noted (this is the technicality) that all contract negotiations were being handled by John Brickels, who was running Cleveland's front office in Brown's absence. Brown said nothing about Brickels contacting the men who'd played for him at Ohio State.

Shortly after it was revealed that Groza planned to turn professional rather than return to Ohio State, Godfrey leveled another accusation at Brown, the Cleveland team, and the AAFC. Godfrey, along with head coach Carroll Widdoes and assistant Paul Bixler, who'd declined an offer from Brown to join his staff in Cleveland, visited the Willard, Ohio, home of running back Joe Whisler in early May. Whisler had been a star on the Buckeyes' 1942 freshman team and was then serving in the military.

"We have just been shown by Mrs. Whisler a contract under the terms of which the Cleveland club would pay Joe Whisler $3,000 for the season, plus $100 a month bonus for every month he remains in the service," said Godfrey. "The bonus would be for signing, of course. Joe is one who definitely wants to come back to college and complete his college education and his period of college football after the war. When Paul Brown starts going after boys like that, boys whose college classes will not finish school until June of 1946, he's in for it. We're all determined that if that's the way Brown wants to play the game, then we're in for the biggest knock-down, drag-out fight to protect our interests that you ever saw. We definitely are not going to stand by and see these boys go into pro football while they still have seasons of college eligibility left and want to play them."[26] According to Jack Clowser, the author of the story, the AAFC, unlike the NFL, had no rule against signing college players whose class hadn't yet graduated, as Whisler's class hadn't. Clowser had either forgotten, or was unaware of, the resolution passed by the AAFC owners in September of 1944 prohibiting the signing of college players with eligibility remaining. The league's Cleveland team had adopted a broad interpretation of that resolution. Paul Brown saw no reason not to sign players with eligibility remaining if they had decided not to use that eligibility.

Widdoes also said Brown had offered contracts to Groza and offensive guard Hal Dean. Widdoes was depending on Groza, Whisler and Dean returning to Columbus after their discharge from the service. Groza and Whisler had three years of eligibility remaining, and Dean had one.

Brown didn't deny offering Whisler a contract. "If it's to be a war with Ohio State, it'll be a one-sided war as far as I'm concerned," he said. "We're not doing anything that should cause a fight with the university. In a case like Joe Whisler's, all that boy has to do is tell us that he's not interested in playing professional football, and we would contact him no further. What Ohio State didn't tell you is that, along with the contract that went to Whisler, he received a letter declaring that our thoughts hadn't changed a bit about his completing his education."

"In any case, we're not trying to sign up boys for this year," he went on. "Our league doesn't plan to operate until the 1946 season, and by that time, the class with which Whisler entered college will have graduated. That would make him eligible for pro football under the regulations of any league. We're not trying to snatch athletes who want to return to college. However, we're going to run our business aggressively—that means to win—and if a boy, or his parents, comes to us and says he would rather play pro football, that's another thing."[27]

Asked about whether or not his team was enticing collegians, particularly Ohio State players, with eligibility remaining to turn professional, Mickey McBride professed ignorance as to how many players his club had signed and who they were. "That is Brown's concern, and since he is in the Navy he cannot negotiate with players in any way. Whoever we have signed, Brickels would know."[28]

Brickels vehemently denied offering contracts to college players with eligibility remaining. "You men who know Brown know he is only interested in wholesome young men. His record proves it. No tramp athletes." He then added a significant caveat.

"But in some cases, where we find young players who have part of their college work to complete, and do not care to return to their old school, we will point out to them the advantages of Cleveland. We have four fine colleges around Cleveland.... Case [Institute of Technology], Western Reserve, John Carroll and Baldwin-Wallace ... where they can finish their work and still play pro football."[29] Brickels didn't say whether he, or Brown, or anyone else in the organization tried to influence certain "wholesome young men" like Groza, Whisler and Dean into deciding not to return to Ohio State.

While denying that the Cleveland team was targeting Ohio State's players, Brickels said the team had signed a big-name player: All-American halfback Eddie Prokop of Georgia Tech, a native of Cleveland who was anxious to perform for his hometown team. He'd never get that chance, due to a highly unusual circumstance.

The NFL owners met in a "secret" session at the Hotel New Yorker, on June 1 and 2, which both the Associated Press and United Press managed to find out about and report on. The purpose of the gathering was to formulate a strategy to deal with the AAFC. The NFL's first priority was to dissuade major college players from signing with the upstarts. Several college stars already had. The NFL's second priority was to keep the AAFC from gaining a foothold in New York City by persuading John Mara to waive his territorial rights to the borough of the Bronx and allow Dan Topping's Brooklyn Tigers to play their home games in Yankee Stadium, which Topping owned, beginning with the 1946 season. Topping's Tigers had merged with the Boston Yanks for 1945.

"The New York football Giants," announced commissioner Layden on June 2, "acting for what they believe to be the best interests of the National Football League and the fans of New York City, have granted the Brooklyn Tigers the privilege of playing their home games in the Yankee Stadium."[30] That announcement came as a surprise to Tigers general manager Gallery, who represented Topping at the "secret" meeting.

"I understand that George Strickler, the National League publicity director, is saying that we are 'completely satisfied' with the agreement drawn up at the league meeting here last weekend," Gallery said. "That is 100 percent wrong, and he definitely is out of line for saying so. He has no right to speak for us." According to Gallery, "We have never officially heard what their proposition is." Gallery added that the NFL was demanding 13 different concessions from the Tigers in order to waive the Giants' territorial rights to Yankee Stadium, and several of those concessions were "unbelievable demands." He said he'd walked out of the negotiations under the assumption the Tigers and the league had reached an impasse.

"That's why I was amazed to hear that everybody is happy, including me. I talked to commissioner Layden at Chicago by telephone yesterday and told him that we couldn't agree to anything we hadn't even seen. He said the agreement would reach me by mail in a day or so." Gallery called the NFL's tactics "high-handed"[31] and said in the absence of a suitable agreement to allow the Tigers to play their home games in Yankee Stadium (which, it can't be too strongly emphasized, Topping owned) the team would explore the option of joining the AAFC in 1946.

The summer of 1945 passed quietly for professional football. The end of the war in Europe in May, followed by the end of hostilities in the Pacific in mid–August, meant troops would be discharged by the tens of thousands in the coming months, alleviating any concerns that the NFL might not be able to field ten teams of relatively able-bodied and at least marginally competent players. The title hopes of many of those teams would be determined by how soon their stars were released from their military obligations.

While the NFL prepared for the 1945 season, the AAFC prepared for the fall of 1946. Paul Brown angered the residents of Columbus yet again on July 10 when the Cleveland team (then called the Panthers, a nickname that wouldn't last long) announced they'd signed Gene Fekete, a star running back on Ohio State's 1942 national champions. Fekete decided to turn professional after injuring a knee while preparing for the college all-star game in the summer of 1943. He was inducted into the Army shortly afterward, and the injured knee was a factor in his early discharge. Fekete didn't know how long the knee would stand up under the strain of playing football and jumped at the opportunity to play for pay with Cleveland rather than return to Columbus, where he had two seasons of college eligibility remaining. He felt the risk of sustaining a career-ending injury while playing for the Buckeyes was too great.

With the NFL about to begin its exhibition season (and even in 1945, commissioner Layden instructed the teams to refer to the games as "pre-season" contests), the AAFC owners met in Chicago to start planning for the fall of 1946, when they'd be putting teams on the field and competing with the established league. Commissioner Jim Crowley made the official announcement that the AAFC would begin play in September of 1946. It would be split into two divisions. To distance itself from the NFL, which had an eastern division and a western division, Crowley said the AAFC would have four teams in its "northern section" and four teams in its "southern section." The north would consist of Cleveland, Chicago, New York and Buffalo. The south would consist of Los Angeles, San Francisco, Miami, and an eighth team to be named later. It was anticipated that Baltimore would be the AAFC's eighth franchise, and that the announcement would be made during the meeting being held in Chicago during the first few days of September. Baltimore had been one of the AAFC's original cities, then quietly bumped for reasons never explained. But no such announcement was forthcoming.

The AAFC would play a 14-game schedule, with each team facing every other team home-and-away. Crowley said that each of the league's seven franchises had secured stadiums in which to perform. The winner of the north section would clash with the winner of the south section for the AAFC championship, and the south winner was awarded home field advantage for 1946. With the war over, following Japan's surrender on September 2, Crowley declared open season for the procurement of players. He said the new league had more than 150 players under contract.

"We originally resolved not to tamper with the National League players. But since the NFL snubbed us, I see no reason why we can't hire their players." Responding to Layden's challenge that the AAFC "go get a football," Crowley had a message for his former Notre Dame teammate. "The All-America league has a football, and it's blown up!"[32]

3

Battle Stations

As of September 1945, the National Football League had one challenger still standing. The United States Football League and Trans-America Football League had abandoned their dreams of taking on the establishment three months earlier. The third incarnation of the American Football League, which had been backed by men of substantial financial means and had shown some promise, despite fielding just five teams in the fall of 1941, had chosen not to pick up where it left off after "suspending" operations in September of 1942.

That left Arch Ward's All-America Football Conference, which had finally announced what everyone already knew. In order to give itself a fighting chance against the NFL, the AAFC would allow a year for its seven (eventually to be eight) teams to get themselves organized and wouldn't compete until autumn of 1946. The peaceful co-existence with the NFL Ward and the men he'd recruited to back the teams in his league had hoped for was shattered when commissioner Elmer Layden refused to meet with an AAFC delegation to discuss conditions under which that co-existence might flourish. Layden and the NFL chose to stick their heads in the sand, refuse to acknowledge that the AAFC even existed, and hope it would quietly fade away, as all three American Football Leagues, the USFL and the TAFL had.

The 12 months between September of 1945 and September of 1946 were filled with growing pains for the AAFC. Without even having played a game, the AAFC experienced its first franchise transfer in October. Bill Cox, the former owner of baseball's Philadelphia Phillies, announced that he had assumed control of the AAFC's New York club and was moving it (but not very far) to Brooklyn. Cox introduced Gerald Smith, Charles Grimes, and Dr. Mal Stevens as his business partners. Stevens had been the "holder" of the AAFC's New York franchise, and would own stock in the Brooklyn team. He'd also coach it, when he wasn't in the operating room. In addition to being a football coach, Stevens was also a practicing surgeon. Stevens compiled a record of 54–45–10 coaching Yale from 1928 to 1932, and New York University from 1933 to 1941. He hadn't coached in five years when he was given the reins of the club that would be named the Dodgers. Cox, Smith and Grimes were the other shareholders in the team, which would play its home games in Ebbets Field. Cox announced that his group had signed a 12-year lease with the owners of the Brooklyn Dodgers baseball team, which used Ebbets Field from April to September, and occasionally into October.

Cox had hired former Dodgers pitcher "Fat" Freddie Fitzsimmons to manage his Phillies midway through the 1943 season. Fitzsimmons resigned in June of 1945 and was hired by Cox to serve as his football team's business manager. Fitzsimmons owned no stock in the club.

That Cox had been forced out of baseball by commissioner Kenesaw Mountain Landis at the end of the 1943 season didn't bother commissioner Jim Crowley or the AAFC owners. Landis, who despised gambling, demanded that Cox sell the Phillies after it was revealed that he'd placed bets on them, to win.

The wire service stories about Cox's acquisition of the New York franchise noted that the AAFC still hadn't awarded its eighth franchise. No timetable was given for that decision, which had been expected a month and a half earlier.

Six weeks after Crowley announced that NFL players whose contracts were expiring or had expired were fair game for the AAFC, three such players agreed to switch leagues. Quarterback Parker Hall, who'd played for the Rams from 1939 to 1942, and halfbacks Len Eshmont and George Franck of the New York Giants signed AAFC contracts. So did Bob Dove, an All-American end for Notre Dame in 1943. But it was the signing of another All-American end that caused the biggest commotion.

Wisconsin's Elroy (Crazylegs) Hirsch had been the Rams' top draft choice in 1944. Hirsch declined a contract offer from the Rams and accepted one from Chicago's AAFC club. At least, that was what the club announced on October 16.

Two days later, Hirsch denied the story. He acknowledged that owner John Keeshin had made an "interesting offer, but I haven't accepted it."[1] Hirsch said he planned to return to Wisconsin and finish his college playing career before turning professional. Like so many players not yet discharged from the armed forces, Hirsch's class would graduate before the AAFC's first kick-off in September of 1946. Hirsch's college coach, Harry Stuhldreher (like Layden and Crowley, another of Notre Dame's famous Four Horsemen) denied Keeshin's claim that Hirsch had signed a professional contract. Stuhldreher said the story was "absolutely untrue."[2]

Keeshin wasted no time responding to both Hirsch and Stuhldreher. "I am not in the habit of making false statements. The original story as reported in today's Chicago *Tribune* was 100 percent correct. I might add, however, that it omitted one significant detail. We already have paid Hirsch $900 on his contract. If Hirsch wants to return to Wisconsin and complete his collegiate career before reporting to the Chicago All-America eleven, we will raise no objections. He is legally bound to us, and his professional career will be with the Chicago All-America team."³

When Stuhldreher again denied Keeshin's claim to have signed his star player, Keeshin unloaded. He went easy on Hirsch, saying "the kid is in a tough spot." If Hirsch had accepted $900 from Keeshin's team, his college eligibility had been forfeit. As for Hirsch's coach, Keeshin said "Mr. Stuhldreher, however, better be careful what kind of statements he makes. You tell him that Mr. Keeshin does not tell falsehoods. Hirsch has signed to play professional football with us, and that is final!"⁴

On October 21, the Rams defeated the Bears, 41–21, in Wrigley Field. The usually powerful Bears sustained their fourth straight loss (against no victories) despite the presence in their backfield for the first time of halfback Edgar (Special Delivery) Jones. The former All-American from the University of Pittsburgh ran eight times for 41 yards, and caught one pass for no gain. Jones signed with the Bears minutes before the noon Saturday deadline for submitting their active roster to the NFL for Sunday's game. The Rams had no idea Jones was a Bear until they noticed a player they didn't recognize warming up before the kick-off. Rams general manager Charles Walsh wasn't happy about the deception, but didn't file a protest since his team won the game.

It proved to be Jones' only appearance in the NFL. He'd been playing with the San Francisco Clippers of the Pacific Coast Football League before he signed with the Bears, who broke an NFL regulation by signing him. That's because Jones was already under contract to the Cleveland Browns for 1946, and Layden had decreed that any player signed to an AAFC contract was ineligible to play in the NFL in 1945.

"Our management signed Jones four months ago when he was still in the Navy," said Paul Brown. "When he recently got his discharge, he asked the club for permission to play professionally this year, but he did not reveal what team he planned to join. His request was granted."⁵ Jones signed with the minor-league team in San Francisco, then with the Bears. Brown apparently had no problem with Jones toiling for the Bears for the rest of the 1945 season, but the other NFL clubs did, and asked Layden to rule on the question of Jones' eligibility. Layden had little recourse but to nullify Jones' contract with Chicago.

"The policy of the National Football League, previously practiced, recently announced, is not to permit *alleged* player contracts with an *unrecognized league* to play football in the National Football League, when it is such a player's intention to play in the National Football League for but one year."⁶ It was a painful ruling for Layden to make, because by making it he was admitting the existence of the AAFC, which the NFL had chosen to not only ignore, but to deny altogether. Layden said the Bears' signing of Jones had been proper because Jones indicated to Bears general manager Ralph Brizzolara that he intended to play in the NFL beyond 1945.

The Bears accepted Layden's decision grudgingly. "We knew Jones was signed for the All-America when we signed him," Brizzolara admitted. "We will abide by the ruling so that law and order will prevail."[7]

Jones would contribute to four AAFC championship teams in Cleveland. "Mr. Layden knows now that if we haven't got a football, at least we have a player the National League would like very much to have,"[8] chortled Jones' boss, Browns owner Mickey McBride.

The AAFC's eighth franchise was awarded to Baltimore on November 7. Commissioner Crowley informed the city's park board of commissioners of the league's decision in a letter. The document identified Baltimore resident R. Bruce Livie as the "holder" of the franchise, along with associates who weren't named.

The first coach of the Baltimore team would be Edgar (Rip) Miller, who was the line coach at the U.S. Naval Academy. Crowley conducted the negotiations with Miller, on behalf of Livie. "I have not talked to the franchise owner," Miller said when asked about his new job. "Until I do, I have no statement to make."[9]

The awarding of a team to Baltimore was contingent on Livie's group reaching a lease agreement on the stadium that would become known as Babe Ruth Stadium and later Memorial Stadium. The park board of commissioners controlled the stadium, explaining why Crowley's letter was sent to them. Negotiations with Livie and his associates were to begin immediately.

On November 13, the *Cleveland Plain Dealer* reported that Paul Brown had been offered the head football coaching job at the University of Kentucky. Brown didn't deny the story but said it was only a rumor. Kentucky's president, H.L. Donovan, said Brown hadn't been officially offered the job. It was speculated that Wildcat alumni had approached Brown and planned to submit his name for consideration to the university's athletic department at the appropriate time. Browns owner McBride said he wouldn't release his coach from his contract.

"No, we just couldn't release Mr. Brown from his contract," said McBride. "By the end of the year, we will have at least $100,000 invested in the Browns in players, coaches, and other expenses, and Paul is the key man in our setup. We just couldn't let him go. I doubt if Paul is very much interested in the Kentucky offer anyway."[10]

Kentucky's head football coaching job paid $5,000 annually. McBride was paying Brown $25,000 a year to coach the Browns, in addition to a monthly stipend estimated at $1,000 to $1,500 for the duration of his time in the Navy. Brown was still fulfilling that obligation in November of 1945. The overture from Kentucky wasn't the first Brown would receive, or, at least, be rumored to receive. He'd spend his four years in the AAFC denying stories that colleges were trying to lure him away from Cleveland. The denials weren't always true.

In its formative stage, John Keeshin established himself as the AAFC's most high-profile owner. Keeshin announced on November 25 that the entire El Toro, California Marine base's powerful football team had chosen to stick together after their discharges by playing for his Chicago franchise. El Toro's head coach, Lieutenant Dick Hanley, agreed to a three-year contract with Keeshin, and he brought along his top assistant, legendary former Stanford University and NFL running back Ernie Nevers.

"I predict the Chicago All-America Conference team will battle the National League winner in 1947," Keeshin declared. "For, after two years of play, the National loop will have to recognize us, and the public will demand a truly championship play-off."[11] El Toro's team featured quarterback Paul Governali of Columbia University; 300-pound tackle "Wee Willie" Wilkin of the Washington Redskins; All-America tackle Bob Dove of Notre Dame; and Crazylegs Hirsch, who'd already signed a contract with Keeshin. Keeshin brushed aside questions about Hirsch's alleged distaste for playing in Chicago.

Keeshin made another splash when he announced on November 28 that his team would be part of the first AAFC game to be played in the summer of 1946. Keeshin signed a contract, and posted a $1,000 guarantee, for an exhibition game between his club and either the Los Angeles or San Francisco team, to be played in Denver. The game date wasn't specified. The purpose of the game was to help raise money for a municipal stadium in which Denver area high school teams could play football.

Keeshin's promotion of his team undoubtedly brought a smile to Arch Ward's face. As a columnist for the *Tribune*, Ward envisioned Chicago's team being the crown jewel of the AAFC. It would need to be, in order to grab the attention of Chicago's football fans away from the entrenched Bears and Cardinals. As much as the AAFC needed a successful team in New York, as all sports leagues do, Ward believed that in order for his new league to excite the nation's football fans, it had to have a strong franchise in Chicago.

The AAFC's chances of having a team capable of competing with the Giants in New York increased on December 5. Dan Topping, owner of the Brooklyn Tigers, who'd merged with the Boston Yanks for 1945, announced that he was moving the team into the new league in 1946. Topping owned Yankee Stadium and wanted his Tigers to play there, only to be thwarted by his fellow owners, particularly Giants co-owner John Mara. Mara claimed his Giants, who played in the Polo Grounds, across the Harlem River no more than a mile from Yankee Stadium, owned territorial rights to the Bronx and refused to waive them for Topping. Although Mara had said before the 1945 season that he'd rather have an NFL team in Yankee Stadium than a representative of the AAFC, or one of the other leagues that were still on the drawing board, he eventually stuck to his guns. He wanted no part of any team, even an NFL team, playing in Yankee Stadium. Layden and the other NFL owners agreed, so a frustrated Topping opted for the AAFC.

"We're better off without them in the National Football League," said Mara of the Tigers. "Let them go over to the other league. It won't last long."[12]

Layden declared the Brooklyn franchise vacated on December 17. The owners approved the decision. Topping wouldn't be taking any of the players under contract to his team into the AAFC. Only 13 players under contract to the Tigers played for the combined Brooklyn/Boston team in 1945, and their contracts were assigned to Ted Collins, owner of the Yanks. Like all the other AAFC teams, the New York Yankees would start from scratch. But they'd play their home games in Yankee Stadium, the most prestigious sports venue in the country.

Within weeks after defecting to the AAFC, Topping issued a challenge to his former cohorts in the NFL. He offered to pay $25,000 to any team willing to take on his football Yankees in an exhibition game in the fall of 1946. Bears owner George Halas declined the generous offer.

"We'll be happy to accept Topping's offer," Halas said sarcastically, "providing, that is, that Topping throws in Sonja Hennie and her ice review for entertainment between halves."[13] Topping, in the eyes of Halas and the other NFL owners, was a traitor and a deserter.

Halas was in a particularly surly mood because his Bears had endured a rare poor season on the field in 1945. Chicago won just three games while losing seven, but that didn't stop the AAFC from trying to entice several of his players to jump to the new league. On December 3, Browns owner McBride denied trying to encourage a mass defection of Chicago players to his team. The United Press reported the Browns had offered "fabulous salaries" to center Clyde (Bulldog) Turner, quarterback Sid Luckman, halfback and defensive back George McAfee, tackle Ken Kavanaugh, and tackle Lee Artoe. Turner reportedly told the AAFC he wanted a $30,000 contract, which ended negotiations quickly. Luckman said "I started with the Bears, and I'll finish with the Bears."[14]

Said McBride, "We have no had contact with any of those players, excepting McAfee, whom we contacted when he was in the Navy. We no longer are negotiating with McAfee, either."[15]

Nearly two million fans attended NFL exhibition and regular season games in 1945. The war had ended a few weeks before the regular season started, and war-weary Americans had money and were ready to spend it on recreation. The league's total attendance was 1,918,613, with 1,442,737 of those tickets sold for the league's regular season games. That figure was an increase of 19.8 percent from 1944. Mara's Giants, with the largest population base to draw from, led the way with 282,382 paying customers, an average of 47,063 for their six home games. At the other end of the spectrum, the Chicago Cardinals played just three of their ten games at home and drew 45,291 fans. It's a wonder the Cardinals had any fans, considering they had won a total of 12 games since 1938, including winless seasons in 1943 and 1944. They won once in 1945.

College football was still king in 1945, but it appeared the public was starting to embrace the professional game, and the AAFC was ready to provide it to cities that already had NFL teams, and to cities that didn't (Los Angeles, San Francisco, Miami, Baltimore.) Los Angeles would soon be removed from the list of cities without an NFL team. By the middle of January of 1946, Los Angeles found itself with two professional football clubs.

An un-attributed wire service story claimed on December 20 that the NFL had offered franchises to Los Angeles and San Francisco, which were to have teams in the AAFC in 1946. Layden reportedly offered the owners of the San Francisco Clippers of the Pacific Coast Football League, a minor circuit, a franchise in the NFL for 1946. Although Layden's official position was to deny even the existence of the AAFC, he was obviously aware of it and took its threat to NFL supremacy seriously. The NFL would do whatever it could to knock the legs out from under its challenger.

While Topping searched in vain for an NFL team willing to accept $25,000 of his personal fortune in exchange for playing an exhibition game with his AAFC team, Browns owner McBride floated the idea of a Browns-Rams exhibition match in the fall of 1946. "I think the fans will demand the game next fall, and I don't see how either team can duck it. After all, it's the public we have to please. Paul Brown told me he's in favor of playing the Rams, provided it isn't scheduled until after we get a few games under our belts. We'd need a little time to get organized so that we could make a decent showing. The Rams have a darn good club, but even if they figured to beat us 100–0, I still think the game should be played."

With the addition of Topping's team giving the AAFC nine clubs, McBride said the league would soon add a tenth franchise, most likely either Dallas or New Orleans. "It is tentatively planned to play home-and-home series with each team, but that would mean 18 games. I think we'll probably play about 13."

McBride reiterated his hope that the AAFC and NFL could achieve a peaceful co-existence. "I maintain the two leagues should have a working agreement similar to that of the major baseball leagues. Last summer, Jack Keeshin and I wanted to make a date with Elmer Layden and discuss such an agreement, but he told us to go and get ourselves a football. Well, we've got the football, and we've got some darn good players. We think there's room for two leagues and we're ready to prove we can operate in competition or in co-operation with the National League. It's up to them to decide which it shall be."[16] McBride and his coach spent the four years of the AAFC's existence beating the drum for two professional football leagues co-existing in peace; conducting a common draft of eligible college seniors; and with their champions meeting in a one-game, winner-take-all playoff at the end of the season.

As 1945 ended, Bob Snyder, assistant coach of the newly-crowned NFL champion Cleveland Rams, said he'd been offered the chance to coach the AAFC's Los Angeles team and rejected it. Snyder spoke of his encounter with Los Angeles general manager Ed Madigan. "He told me he'd better any contract the Rams offered me, and that he'd guarantee me an off-season job in the movie industry. I told him that I wasn't interested in the coaching offer, and that I couldn't even double for Donald Duck in the movies. I think I'd be foolish to leave a world championship club to jump to a league which isn't even completely organized as yet. I've been in the National League a long time now, and I'd feel out of place somewhere else."[17]

Snyder played in the NFL from 1937 to 1943, and coached with the Bears in 1944. He'd wind up in Los Angeles in 1946 anyway. Just not with the AAFC.

As the AAFC owners prepared to ring in the new year with an organizational meeting in Chicago, Crowley said five cities were vying for the league's tenth franchise. Groups representing New Orleans, Kansas City, Philadelphia, Dallas and Atlanta had submitted applications. "I can't reveal identities, but I can say those seeking the 10th franchise have a financial parity with the group already accepted for conference membership," he reported. "As to the latter, I'd be conservative in saying their total wealth is approximately two hundred million dollars. Yes, it sure looks like an excessively merry new year starting as of now."

Crowley added that the nine AAFC franchises had about 350 players under contract, and "could take the field tomorrow, if necessary."[18]

The AAFC shrank from a nine-team league to an eight-team league on January 4, 1946. Ed Nielsen, representing Baltimore, told the owners of the other eight franchises that his group had experienced delays in obtaining a lease at the city's stadium, and was far behind its brethren in organizing a team to compete in 1946. He asked that Baltimore's franchise be suspended, and the other owners agreed. "I think this is best for the conference and Baltimore," Nielsen said. "We expect to field a team in Baltimore in 1947."[19]

With the AAFC's membership reduced to the nice round figure of eight teams, the search for an additional franchise was placed on hold indefinitely. Crowley said the applications of New Orleans and Kansas City had been studied, but the league would wait until 1947 before adding a tenth franchise, assuming Baltimore would iron out its problems and re-join the group as its ninth team. Baltimore would have an AAFC team in 1947, but not under the circumstances anticipated.

The terms under which Dan Topping had agreed to move his Brooklyn NFL team into the AAFC were revealed to the public at the meeting, because they first had to be agreed upon by his fellow owners. And while the vote to accept Topping's terms was unanimous, it didn't come without a contentious debate. Topping demanded that he not be required to pay the AAFC's franchise fee of $100,000. He also demanded that each of the other AAFC teams allow him to select one player off their rosters to help him strengthen his team. He was allowed to keep 15 of the players from his Brooklyn NFL squad. The remaining players, and Topping claimed to have had 200 players under contract, were placed in a pool and made available to the other seven AAFC teams.

There was a question as to the ownership of the contracts of the players who'd worked for Topping in 1945. According to Elmer Layden, those contracts reverted to the NFL when Topping's franchise was vacated. Layden assigned them to the Boston club, for which the players had performed in 1945. Topping saw the situation differently.

The players under contract to Topping belonged to him, he insisted, "and there is nothing the National League can do about it."[20] The problem was that, regardless of which team the players were under contract to, they just weren't very good. Topping's Brooklyn teams had always been also-rans, and the combined Brooklyn/Boston team won just three games in 1945, losing six and tying one. Topping, as owner of baseball's New York Yankees, was accustomed to winning. And he wanted to make sure his football Yankees would be competitive in the AAFC. After considerable arm-twisting, he convinced his fellow owners to allow him to select three players from each of their rosters. And those players wouldn't be the dregs, either. This was no "expansion draft." Each AAFC owner was allowed to protect only three players from their rosters, a total of just 21 players. Topping had his pick of the litter of the better than 300 players who remained.

Three owners didn't appreciate waiving the franchise fee as an inducement to Topping to jilt the NFL. And Mickey McBride, John Keeshin and Bill Cox really didn't like the idea of having to surrender three valuable players to Topping and getting nothing (except the presence of his team and Yankee Stadium in their new league) in return. McBride, Keeshin and Cox opposed the agreement, but backed down when Topping warned them that the AAFC would surely fail without a strong team in the nation's media capital. Apparently Cox's Brooklyn team didn't count.

After officially welcoming Topping and his Yankees into the AAFC, the owners conducted a secret draft of over 300 eligible college and service team

3. Battle Stations

players. "Their names will not be announced," Crowley told the press. "The National League has always publicized its draft lists, often embarrassing the players. We hope to stop that practice."[21] The fans wouldn't know which players had been selected by which teams until the player had signed a contract. And not all the players drafted by the AAFC would sign with the new league. Aside from a desire not to embarrass the draftees, maybe the owners wanted to avoid embarrassing themselves by revealing which players had spurned the AAFC to sign with the NFL.

The owners also started working on the schedule for the AAFC's first season. Crowley explained that the plan was for the western and southern teams (Los Angeles, San Francisco and Miami) to visit the northern teams early in the season, when the weather was hospitable. The northern teams would make their road trips to the west and south later in the season, when the climate turned cold in their home cities. Harvey Hester, owner of the Miami team, had already informed the league that he wanted all of his team's home games to be scheduled in November and December.

As the NFL opened its winter meeting in New York on January 9, Rams owner Dan Reeves denied persistent rumors that he planned to move his champions to Los Angeles. "I'm well aware of the rumors," Reeves acknowledged. "I've seen them in the papers here [New York] and I've been asked about them a dozen times. But as far as I'm concerned, they're not true. The Rams definitely will stay in Cleveland."[22]

Three days later, Reeves changed his tune. His team was headed for southern California. "It isn't that I love Cleveland less, but that I love Los Angeles more,"[23] he explained poetically. Reeves had loved Los Angeles for quite a while. He'd been trying to get an NFL franchise for the city since 1937. After purchasing the Rams in 1941 from the Clevelanders who'd started the team in the short-lived American Football League and moved it into the NFL, Reeves asked for permission to move the club to Los Angeles for the 1942 season. War-time travel restrictions made the request impossible, and Reeves' fellow owners denied it. Reeves asked again in 1944 and 1945 and was turned down. He was determined to move the Rams to Los Angeles in 1946, and threatened legal action against the NFL if his request was denied again.

With the Browns ready to open for business in the fall of 1946, the loss of the Rams was taken in stride by Clevelanders who'd never warmed to the team or its absentee owner. Reeves was a New Yorker who was rarely seen in Cleveland. Reeves had lost money each year he'd owned the Rams, including the championship season of 1945. Despite a 9–1 record, the Rams finished ninth in the NFL in attendance, ahead only of the Cardinals. In defense of Cleveland's football fans, the Rams had asked for only four home games in 1945. Just two of the Rams' home opponents, the Bears and Packers, were marquee names. The Cardinals were a perennial doormat, and the Yanks were a second-year amalgamation of the Boston and Brooklyn clubs. Reeves was stuck in ancient League Park, a facility built in 1891 for baseball in a residential section of Cleveland's near-east side. Though the park had been refurbished in 1910, it was inadequate for football. It had just 22,000 seats, and there was no place for fans to park except on the surrounding city streets. The Browns had a lease on Municipal Stadium, with its 80,000 seats and ample parking. Los Angeles, with its much larger population, much better weather, and 100,000-seat stadium, beckoned to Reeves.

Instead of competing with the NFL for fans in Cleveland, the AAFC would be competing for fans against the NFL in Los Angeles. The Browns would have Cleveland all to themselves. But that didn't mean McBride would ease off in his effort to put a championship team on the field in Municipal Stadium.

"While it is regrettable that Cleveland has lost a championship team, I see no reason to go into mourning about it," said McBride's partner in both his taxi cab business and his football team, Dan Sherby. "In the first place, we'll have the highest payroll in either league, which should prove we are willing to spend money for the best talent available. Second, we have in Paul Brown the greatest coach in the country. And, last but not least, we have signed some of the most brilliant college and professional players to be had. We will continue to make every effort to produce a winning ball club. In fact, we are striving to come up with another championship club for Cleveland."[24] Sherby and McBride would succeed in achieving that goal.

The NFL would have a new leader as it battled the AAFC. Washington Redskins owner George Preston Marshall had vowed that Layden would not be re-elected commissioner at the winter meeting. Layden's term expired in March of 1946, and while it appeared he had the seven votes necessary for another three-year term, he announced his resignation, saying simply he wanted to pursue other opportunities. Layden was offered a job as an adviser to the NFL at the same salary he'd earned as commissioner, $20,000 annually. He said he'd think about it.

The moguls turned to one of their own to replace Layden, signing Bert Bell to a three-year deal at $20,000 per season. Bell had been owner and coach of the Philadelphia Eagles from 1936 to 1940, then sold his interest in the Eagles and bought into the Pittsburgh Steelers with Art Rooney. Bell coached the Steelers for two games in 1941 (losing both) before resigning. Bell said he'd assume his new duties and move the NFL office to New York as soon as he divested himself of his stock in the Steelers.

After giving the matter careful consideration for six weeks, Layden decided on February 17 that he wasn't interested in serving Bell as a consultant. He'd concentrate on his duties as president of Shippers Car Line Corporation in New York. On the same day, the Naval Academy welcomed Rip

3. Battle Stations 45

Miller back as its line coach for 1946. Miller was supposed to have been head coach of the AAFC's Baltimore team, but there would be no Baltimore team to coach in 1946.

In late February, Crowley issued the first of many challenges to the NFL, proposing eight exhibition games to be played prior to the opening of each league's regular season. "I am so confident of the potential power of our clubs that I am in favor of arranging a series before the 1946 season, pitting our eight clubs against eight of the 10 selected by the National, with profits going to charity."[25] Crowley may as well have been talking to a wall. Bell, on orders from his employers, continued Layden's policy of refusing to acknowledge the AAFC's existence. There was no possibility of the NFL accepting Crowley's challenge, which he'd issued with the support of Paul Brown and John Keeshin. The established league had nothing to gain and everything to lose. For the AAFC, it was just the opposite.

To prove that the AAFC was growing stronger by the day, Crowley said the Los Angeles Dons had 38 players under contract, and the San Francisco 49ers had secured seven playing dates in Kezar Stadium.

Officially, as far as the NFL was concerned, there was no such thing as an AAFC. Privately, the owners were concerned about the upstarts gaining a foothold on the west coast. The Rams were on their way to Los Angeles, and on February 6, it was reported by the United Press that the NFL was negotiating with the San Francisco Clippers of the Pacific Coast Football League to merge with one of the old league's weakest teams, the Cardinals. The combined Cardinals/Clippers would be headquartered in the Bay Area. The merger never came about.

In Los Angeles, which the AAFC had expected to have all to itself before Dan Reeves intervened, the Dons would battle the Rams not only for fans, but for prime playing dates at the Los Angeles Memorial Coliseum, which would serve as the home field for both teams. As of late in February, the Dons had signed a contract with the Coliseum commission to play on September 15 and 22, October 27, November 3 and either December 14 or 15. The Rams had nailed down four dates of their own, but those weren't revealed.

One of the players most responsible for the Rams' 1945 NFL championship, receiver Jim Benton, made it clear during the winter of 1945–46 that he was ready to switch leagues if the price was right. Benton caught 45 passes for a whopping 1,067 yards in 1945, including an NFL record ten receptions for 303 yards in the Rams' division title-clinching victory over the Detroit Lions on Thanksgiving. He averaged 118 receiving yards per game, and 23.7 yards per catch. Astonishingly, he wasn't named to the all-league team. "Whoever wants me is going to have to pay me $13,000," he said from his home in Arkansas.

Benton said he'd gladly stay in Cleveland, where he had business interests and lots of fans, but "I haven't heard from the Browns. But the All-America Conference team in Los Angeles contacted me. I told [Ed] Madigan that I wanted $13,000 and he said he would have a representative of the team contact me. So far, I haven't heard any more from them. I called [Charles] Walsh last week, and he told me [Rams assistant coach] George Trafton would come down to Pine Bluff to discuss terms with me."

"I don't think I'm asking for too much money," he continued. "After all, the Rams have given [quarterback Bob] Waterfield a $20,000 contract, and I feel that I was some help to him last season."[26] Before Waterfield led the Rams to a 15–14 victory over the Redskins in the championship game, Reeves signed him to a three-year, $60,000 contract. Waterfield, the league's MVP as a rookie, earned $8,000 in his first year in the NFL. Despite the fact his team had already signed Otto Graham, Browns owner McBride said he'd have made Waterfield an offer if Reeves hadn't locked him up for three years.

Benton made it clear he didn't care where he earned his money, whether it was in Los Angeles, Cleveland, or elsewhere. Former Rams player Bill (Red) Conkright, who was the team's chief scout in 1945, chose to stay in Cleveland. Conkright signed with the Browns as a scout and assistant coach on Paul Brown's staff. He wouldn't be the only Ram to choose Cleveland over Los Angeles.

Brown was discharged from the Navy on March 1. He'd been promoted to the rank of lieutenant. He headed for Chicago to represent the Browns at a meeting of AAFC owners. He had purchased a home in Cleveland but said for the time being, he'd commute from Columbus while he built his football team. From that moment on, Brown was in complete charge.

At that meeting in Chicago, Crowley reported that he'd approached Bert Bell about an agreement between the AAFC and the NFL pertaining to the sanctity of player contracts. Although Crowley insisted the AAFC hadn't tried to sign any players under contract to the NFL, the Detroit Lions begged to differ. Halfback Frank Sinkwich, the NFL's MVP for 1944 who entered the armed forces in 1945, had hooked up with Dan Topping's New York Yankees for 1946. Crowley said Sinkwich's contract status with the Lions was "a moot question." Lions owner Fred Mandel didn't think so and was making loud noises about filing a lawsuit against Topping and the AAFC.

Crowley told the owners that "any agreement is still in the offing. I'm going to hear further from Bell, if I'm going to hear."[27] Bell denied that he'd had any discussion with Crowley about the topic of contracts, or about any other topic.

The other significant announcement to come from the gathering in Chicago was that the AAFC would kick off its first season on Sunday, September 8. The season would conclude on December 15, and the championship game was scheduled for December 22. Not all of the league's games would be played on Sundays. The San Francisco 49ers' agreement with Kezar Stadium stipulated that the professionals could only play there on Friday nights. And John Keeshin, owner of the Chicago Rockets, wanted to avoid going head-to-head with the Bears and Cardinals by playing his team's home games on Fridays. Although none of the actual playing dates were announced, it was known that Topping's Yankees would play most of their home games in the middle of the season, competing directly with the New York Giants. That was how Topping wanted it.

In the words of the International News Service, "This represented yet another concession in the endless line of salaams the All-Americans have made to Mr. Topping." Not every AAFC owner was happy about granting Topping's every wish, but the alternative was losing his franchise and Yankee Stadium. An owner of Topping's stature and bank account, plus the prestige of Yankee Stadium, gave the AAFC instant credibility.

Crowley visited Cleveland on March 19 to meet with Mickey McBride and Paul Brown and the city's press corps. He said he foresaw a "World Series of professional football" championship game between the AAFC's champion and the NFL's champion, although he conceded the game probably wouldn't happen after the 1946 season. He called the NFL's policy of ignoring the AAFC "a waiting game."

Said Crowley, "We have the cities, the stadiums, coaches and playing talent. I believe that all the National League is waiting for to declare a truce is to see how we do at the gate." The commissioner said the AAFC had signed over 100 former NFL players, and brushed off the threatened legal action over the Yankees' signing of Sinkwich as "mere ballyhoo." Crowley said he expected all eight teams to be strong contenders, even the two teams most observers were concerned about: Buffalo and Miami.

"Miami has signed a lot of southern players who prefer to play in Dixie," Crowley said. "Don't worry about them. They'll be good."[28] The Seahawks signed a lot of southern players, plus a coach with a southern background, because owner Harvey Hester was convinced the best football in the country was played south of the Mason-Dixon line. The skeptics who doubted Miami would support a professional football team would prove to be correct. The doubters included Redskins owner George Preston Marshall, who was skeptical about everything pertaining to the AAFC.

As March came to a close, "Fat Freddie" Fitzsimmons was hard at work as business manager of the AAFC's Brooklyn Dodgers. Like Topping's Yankees, Bill Cox's football team borrowed the nickname of the baseball team whose stadium it would share. Fitzsimmons had pitched for the Dodgers from 1937 to 1943, and Cox had a good reason for hiring him. "Fitzsimmons is probably the most loved man in Brooklyn today," he said. "And is he selling tickets? Well, every box seat in our upper grandstand is already taken for next year's games."²⁹ Fitzsimmons may not have been so popular after Brooklyn fans got on eyeful of the team Cox foisted on them in 1946.

While Fitzsimmons was selling tickets to Brooklyn fans, Dan Topping was trying to buy the nickname of his former team from his former business partner. Topping wanted the nickname "Yankees" all to himself and his football team. He offered Ted Collins $10,000 if he'd change his Boston NFL team's nickname from "Yanks" to something else. Anything else. Collins called Topping a spoiled rich kid and turned down the money.

The AAFC made a slight schedule adjustment in early April. After announcing that the league's first regular season games would be played on Sunday, September 8, Crowley said the league would debut on Friday, September 6. The AAFC's first game would pit the Cleveland Browns against the Miami Seahawks in Cleveland's mammoth Municipal Stadium. Filling many, or all, of the building's 80,000 seats would undoubtedly get the NFL's attention. Filling all of the seats would require drawing more fans than the Rams had drawn during the entire 1945 season, not including the championship game.

Among the perks of signing with the AAFC would be traveling to all of one's team's road games by air. The league signed a $230,000 contract with United Airlines on April 13. There would be no train travel in the AAFC. Each team would fly in 44-passenger planes provided by one of the country's premier airlines. That would be just enough seating for 35 players plus coaches and trainers.

To make the players easier for fans to identify, the AAFC adopted a standardized uniform numbering system. Centers would wear numbers in the 20s; guards in the 30s; tackles would wear numbers in the 40s; ends in the 50s; quarterbacks would wear numbers in the 60s; fullbacks in the 70s; and halfbacks in the 80s and 90s.

The leaders of minor league football were just as anxious to put the AAFC out of business as the NFL owners. The AAFC was helping itself to their players, too, and Rufus Klawans didn't like it. Klawans was the president of the Pacific Coast Football League, which had lost San Francisco to the AAFC. He spoke to the NFL owners at their spring meeting on April 30 and proposed a plan he was certain would strangle the AAFC before it played its first game. Klawans suggested football's three minor leagues: the PCFL, the American League and the Dixie League, join forces with the NFL to form an amalgamation similar to organized baseball. NFL commissioner Bert Bell would serve as commissioner of all of professional football, with the exception of the AAFC. Under Klawans' plan, the AAFC would be branded an "outlaw" league, and any player signing with an AAFC team would be banned from "organized" professional football for five years. At that time, most of the AAFC's teams had between 60 and 70 players under contract. Those numbers

The AAFC's teams traveled in style. In this photograph, the Browns await their departure for a road game in 1946 (Michael Schwartz Library, Cleveland State University).

would be reduced to 35 when the season began, meaning some 200–280 players would be out of work. Those that weren't picked up by another AAFC team would be out of luck since no NFL or minor league team would sign them. Klawans hoped his scheme would scare most, if not all, of the players under contract to the AAFC into abandoning the new league. Klawans really wasn't offering the NFL anything new since it had already adopted a policy of a five-year ban for any player signing with the AAFC. A five-year ban it was more than willing to ignore if a prodigal son chose to return home.

The owners rejected a letter from Crowley to Bell seeking a meeting to discuss player contracts and a combined draft. It was yet another in a series of communiqués from Crowley to the NFL in a futile effort to avoid an all-out war between the leagues. Lions owner Fred Mandel, Giants co-owner John Mara, Redskins owner Marshall and Yanks owner Collins were opposed to any kind of co-operation with the AAFC. Bell was told to toss Crowley's letter in the trash. The NFL would continue to refuse to recognize the existence of the AAFC.

Crowley said the letter was the AAFC's final attempt at peaceful co-existence with the NFL. All overtures had been ignored. If the NFL wanted a fight with the upstarts, it would get one.

As for the types of offers NFL players were receiving from the AAFC, the United Press reported on April 29 that John Keeshin was trying to lure an unidentified lineman away from Detroit with an apartment, a car, a permanent off-season job, and a diamond ring at half price. And, presumably, a sizable salary, although the story mentioned nothing about money. "All I can do is hope the boy doesn't take it," moaned Mandel. "I can't find a diamond ring." Mandel was already steaming from the AAFC's effort to entice Frank Sinkwich to jump ship, although he hadn't filed his threatened lawsuit. At least not yet.

Sinkwich wasn't the only player the two leagues were fighting over. The United Press reported on April 29 that Boston had offered former Notre Dame All-American quarterback Angelo Bertelli a contract worth between 20,000 and $24,000. In February, Bertelli had signed a contract worth $12,000 with the Los Angeles Dons. Signed contracts didn't seem to mean much to owners in either league.

Crowley visited Cleveland in May to meet with Mickey McBride and the local press. He lauded McBride's dedication to making his team a winner. "The Browns have been the most aggressive team in our league so far. In fact, they have been so aggressive that I've had to rule against them on a couple of matters."[30] Crowley didn't elaborate as to what those matters were.

What would it cost to attend an AAFC game? In Cleveland, the prices at Municipal Stadium were set at $3.60, $2.40, $1.80, $1.20, and 25 cents. The tickets costing just a quarter were for students 18 years old and under.

The Buffalo Bisons, expected by many observers (but not Crowley) to be one of the AAFC's weakest teams, suffered a blow on May 28 when part owner, vice president, general manager and head coach Sam Cordovano resigned. In his letter to majority owner James F. Breuil, Cordovano explained "due to the heavy press of business and recent rapid development of interests outside of Buffalo, it has become necessary to dispose of all of my interests and sever all of my connections with the Buffalo club."[31] Cordovano didn't explain what those outside interests were, but wire service reports in the early days of the AAFC had described him as a "construction magnate." That was just one of several professions for Cordovano, who'd been an All-American football player at Georgetown and spent 14 years as an assistant coach at Columbia University in New York City. He was elevated to interim head coach on a few occasions in 1943 when head coach Lou Little was sidelined by health problems. Cordovano also made a name for himself as a professional wrestler. While he was largely responsible for signing the players on Buffalo's new AAFC team, he didn't want to coach them, and his resignation wasn't altogether unexpected.

3. Battle Stations

Cordovano's resignation didn't faze Breuil in the least. He hired University of Minnesota assistant coach Lowell (Red) Dawson to replace him as head coach the next day. Dawson had previously been head coach at Tulane University in New Orleans, his alma mater. Dawson's record at Tulane was 36–19–4, and his 1939 team was undefeated until losing the Sugar Bowl to Texas A&M. He was signed to a three-year contract.

While the NFL struggled with the AAFC, major league baseball was dealing with a crisis of its own. The wealthy Pasquel brothers, determined to make the renegade Mexican League a major league, had launched an all-out attack on the American big leagues, luring star players (with valid contracts) south of the border with promises of enormous salaries. The New York Yankees and Brooklyn Dodgers had responded by filing a lawsuit in federal court, asking for a restraining order barring the Mexican League from tampering with players who were already signed to legally binding contracts. Bert Bell told reporters on May 8 that the NFL had no need to follow baseball's lead and seek legal redress against the AAFC. Bell said there had been no contract jumpers in the NFL.

"A mere statement in a newspaper that a player has signed a contract with a club in an unaffiliated league means nothing to us," he explained. "Our clubs hold options for the services of players on their reserve lists, and until such time as we have proof that the player in question does not intend to fulfill that obligation we'll do nothing about it. All players will be offered a hearing before a suspension is made."[32] Like major league baseball, NFL contracts contained the dreaded "reserve clause," which, as far as the owners were concerned, bound the player to his team for as long as the team wanted him. The contract's option year rolled over from one season to the next, renewing itself automatically. The AAFC's position was that when an NFL player's contract had expired, that player became a free agent. Bell's position was that, whether or not a player who'd played in the NFL in 1945 had signed an AAFC contract for 1946, that player hadn't jumped leagues until he failed to report to his former employer's training camp. If and when such incidents began, appropriate action would be taken.

Pass receiver extraordinaire Jim Benton signed with the Rams on May 24. The wire service story announcing the signing didn't say whether Benton would be paid the $13,000 he'd demanded.

Quarterbacks have always been football's marquee players, and the AAFC scored a coup when Angelo Bertelli of Notre Dame signed with the Los Angeles Dons on February 21. Bertelli had quarterbacked the Fighting Irish to the 1943 national championship before entering the Marines. The contract was for two years. On May 21, Bertelli signed a four-year contract with Boston Yanks owner Ted Collins. Attorney Daniel Lyne, representing the Dons, asked for and was granted a temporary restraining order by a judge in Suffolk, Massachusetts, Superior Court on June 5, preventing Bertelli from playing for any team other than the Dons in 1946 or 1947. A spokesman for the Yanks said Bertelli had signed a special services contract with Collins, and the team was confident the contract would stand up in court. The spokesman added, "It's a question of whether these pro football contracts are legal or not."[33]

The first court battle over a player's services between the AAFC and the NFL was at hand. The restraining order was sustained by a judge in Springfield, Massachusetts (Bertelli's hometown) on June 10. At that hearing, a trial date of July 2 was set. Collins was ordered to testify as to why he shouldn't be prohibited from employing Bertelli in 1946 and '47, in apparent violation of his contract with the Dons.

Bertelli didn't appear at the trial. His written response to the restraining order was filed by his attorneys, Michael Kane and Thomas Moriarty. Bertelli denied signing a contract with the Dons in February. He claimed that he'd signed on March 31 "a printed form on which were typed statements including that he would be paid $10,000 a season."[34] Bertelli's response claimed that a party purporting to represent the Dons falsely and fraudulently told him they represented an unidentified person with whom Bertelli wanted to sign a contract. Bertelli said he was told by the Dons' representative that he was legally bound to sign the paper because he'd received $1,000 from the unidentified person Bertelli wanted to sign a contract with. The paper said nothing about Bertelli playing for the Dons in either 1946 or 1947. Bertelli claimed the paper he signed violated the laws of both California and Massachusetts and was null and void. Bertelli asked that the Dons' lawsuit against him be dismissed, and that he be paid damages and attorney's fees. That motion was denied. A judge needed time to digest Bertelli's convoluted claims, and the trial was continued until July 30.

While the Dons were busy in court fighting with the man they hoped would be their star player, they weren't too busy to complete their coaching staff. Former Stanford All-American end Ted Shipkey was hired to assist head coach Dudley DeGroot. Johnny Baker was DeGroot's other assistant. The signing of DeGroot had been a feather in the AAFC's cap, as he'd coached the Washington Redskins into the NFL title game in 1945, losing by a point to the Rams. DeGroot resigned over what he perceived to be interference by the Redskins' front office.

Any fears that Cleveland wouldn't embrace the AAFC after losing the Rams were dispelled by the summer of 1946. The Browns announced they'd already sold 3,000 season tickets, seven times more season tickets than the Rams had ever sold in their eight seasons in Cleveland. The season tickets sold to date put $60,000 in the Browns' treasury. Those numbers increased to 4,000 season tickets worth $80,000 by late in August.

3. Battle Stations

The AAFC announced its 56-game schedule for 1946 on the sixth of July. "We have the best schedule professional football has ever seen, since it brings each of our eight clubs into competition with each other twice,"[35] crowed Crowley. The NFL, after cutting its season to ten games during the war years, expanded it to 11 games for 1946.

While Bertelli was passing Notre Dame to the national championship in 1943, down the road in Bloomington, Indiana, 18-year old freshman tailback Bob (Hunchy) Hoernschmeyer was leading all of the nation's collegians in rushing and passing at Indiana University. Due to the war, freshmen were permitted to play varsity sports in 1943. Like all able-bodied men his age, Hoernschmeyer went into military service following his spectacular freshman season. Upon his discharge from the service, he decided to pass up his remaining college eligibility and turn professional, signing with John Keeshin's Chicago Rockets on July 14. Terms of Hoernschmeyer's contract weren't announced. His signing meant three of college football's biggest stars (Crazylegs Hirsch, Hoernschmeyer, and Bertelli) had spurned the NFL for the AAFC. Providing the court ruled in the AAFC's favor in the Bertelli affair.

The Brooklyn Dodgers were the first AAFC team to open their training camp. Coach Mal Stevens led the Dodgers in drills at their camp in Bend, Oregon, on July 15. The Dodgers needed all the training they could get, but the early start didn't help once the regular season began. It would be a long autumn in Brooklyn.

Bert Bell had said the NFL would take no action against contract jumpers until someone actually failed to show up for training camp while under a valid NFL contract. That happened in late July. Chet Adams, a veteran lineman, had signed with the Rams in October of 1945, then with the Browns in 1946. He explained why. "I signed my contract with the Rams when they were a Cleveland organization, and did so because I wanted to play in my hometown. In fact, that was one of the points played up by Red Conkright. It was about the time the new teams in the All-America Conference were beginning to sign players, and I had several offers. I passed up all of them because I wanted to finish my football career in Cleveland, right where it started. I still do, and I have no intention of reporting to Los Angeles." Adams then succinctly explained why he believed he was no longer under contract to the Rams. "My contract stated I signed with a Cleveland team."[36]

The Rams saw the matter differently and sued Adams and the Browns on July 20. They asked for a restraining order to forbid Adams from playing for the Browns, and to forbid the Browns from trading or selling his contract. News of the court action was the first mention of Adams signing with Cleveland. While AAFC teams were generally overjoyed to announce the defection of an NFL player to the new league, the Browns, for some reason, didn't publicly announce Adams' signing.

Four days later, the Rams were back in court, suing the Browns over the signing of running back Gaylon Smith, who'd been a member of the 1945 Rams and was still under contract to them in their opinion. "Both [Adams and Smith] signed contracts with our club and accepted money when they did so," said Rams general manager Charles Walsh. "Under the contracts, they agreed to abide by the league's constitution and by-laws that give clubs the right to sell or transfer contracts."[37]

In all, four Rams would decide they wanted to stay in Cleveland and signed with the Browns. In addition to Adams and Smith, running back Don Greenwood and defensive back Tom Colella would jump their contracts. The players' argument was, as Adams noted, that their contracts were with the CLEVELAND Rams. When the team moved to Los Angeles, those contracts were automatically voided. In the Rams' opinion, as Walsh pointed out, when the team transferred to Los Angeles, the players' contracts transferred to Los Angeles, just as if they had been traded, in accordance with NFL by-laws. A court would have to sort out the matter.

The New York Yankees departed for their training camp on July 27. Under the direction of Ray Flaherty, the Yankees would train in Spokane, Washington. Flaherty's signing by the Yankees was an even bigger coup than DeGroot's was by the Dons. Flaherty had coached the Redskins to three NFL title games, winning two of them, between 1937–1943.

Angelo Bertelli's trial continued in Boston on July 30. This time, Bertelli was in the courtroom and testified that while he'd signed a deal with the Dons calling for a $1,000 bonus and a $10,000 salary, he'd returned the bonus money before signing with the Yanks. Bertelli said he'd signed with Boston only after his lawyer had assured him the contract with Los Angeles wasn't valid. Among those testifying on Bertelli's behalf were Steve Owen, head coach of the Giants, and Earle (Greasy) Neale, head coach of the Eagles. Both were asked by the judge to describe how the NFL selected players, and both essentially said "we sign the best players we can." The trial was continued.

Brooklyn's Dodgers needed all the talent they could assemble. The Dodgers would win only three games in 1946, and only eight in their three seasons in the AAFC. On August 2, the Dodgers lost the services of Wilfred (Bill) Bangert, who chose to hang up his cleats to pursue a career as an opera singer. Bangert played football at Purdue and Missouri and was the national Amateur Athletic Union's shot-put and discus throwing champion in 1944 and 1945. The article announcing his retirement didn't mention which position he played. Bangert was a baritone, and had an audition with the Metropolitan Opera Company scheduled upon his return to New York. He was hired.

Tragedy struck the Chicago Rockets during their intra-squad scrimmage at their training camp in Santa Rosa, California, on August 3. As a curious crowd estimated at 4,000 looked on, left halfback and placekicker Bill McArthur was forced from the scrimmage after suffering a compound fracture above the left ankle in the second quarter. Coach Dick Hanley said the injury would end McArthur's season before it had started. It wound up ending McArthur's career. The fractured bones in his leg severed arteries and resulted in the leg being amputated on August 10. McArthur's misfortune proved to be a portent of what the Rockets had in store for them during their four-year existence.

Professional football's color barrier was broken when guard Bill Willis reported to the Browns' training camp on the 31st of July. Willis had played for Paul Brown at Ohio State and reportedly "wowed 'em" in the words of the *Cleveland Press*' correspondent, John Dietrich. A week later, bruising fullback Marion Motley became the second African American player in Cleveland's camp. Motley caught Brown's eye when he played for Canton McKinley high school in the late 1930s. McKinley was the bitter rival of Brown's Massillon team. Motley enrolled at the University of Nevada, and wound up playing for Brown at the Great Lakes Naval Training Station in 1945.

"He could play a game tomorrow," said Brown of Motley. "We have the same plays, same formations, same signals we used at Great Lakes."[38] Neither Willis nor Motley had yet signed a contract. Although the Browns and the AAFC like to take credit for shattering professional football's color barrier, just which league and which team deserves the recognition for ending the repugnant practice of excluding players based on their race depends on the measuring stick one uses. Technically, the Rams were the first to sign African American players. They signed halfback Kenny Washington and offensive end Woody Strode, both from UCLA, shortly after moving to Los Angeles. Because the AAFC began its season a few weeks before the NFL, Willis and Motley took the field in a game that counted in the standings before Washington and Strode. Wherever the credit belongs, the color barrier had fallen in professional football in 1946. But that didn't mean Willis, Motley, Washington and Strode would be accepted with open arms by their opponents, and even many of their teammates.

When Cleveland's players reported to training camp at Bowling Green State University, just south of Toledo and about 125 miles west of Cleveland, two NFL players who'd defected to the AAFC, or were supposed to have, were AWOL. Running back Ted Fritsch, who deserted the Packers to sign with the Browns, and linebacker Vince Banonis of the Cardinals, were nowhere to be found when Paul Brown assembled his squad on August 1. Rumor had it that Fritsch, who was born, raised, and lived in northern Wisconsin, was under intense pressure from both Packer management and Packer fans to return to Green Bay in spite of his contract with Cleveland. Banonis' absence was a mystery. With teams in both leagues having opened their training camps,

Among the many innovations Paul Brown brought to professional football was classroom instruction. Here, the Browns listen intently to a lecture from Brown at Bowling Green State University in the summer of 1946 (Michael Schwartz Library, Cleveland State University).

push had come to shove. Would Bert Bell enforce the five-year ban he'd threatened to impose on players who'd jumped to the AAFC, then decided to jump back? Fritsch would prove to be a test case.

Fritsch arrived in Bowling Green on August 2, and the *Press* quoted him as saying he was happy to be there and liked what he saw. But Paul Brown apparently didn't like what he saw. On August 10, the Browns were reportedly close to a ground-breaking deal that would allow Fritsch to return to Green Bay, in exchange for the Rams dropping their lawsuits against Chet Adams and Gaylon Smith for jumping their contracts. The deal would have been ground-breaking because it would have represented the first contact of any substance between teams in the warring leagues. And the teams allegedly involved quickly denied the *Cleveland Plain Dealer*'s story.

"We, or no other member of the National Football League, are making any deal with the All-America Conference or any of its members,"[39] said Charles Walsh on behalf of the Rams.

"I have no right to make deals with players of another conference," said Packers general manager and head coach, Curly Lambeau. "The only one who would be able to do that would be the commissioner of the National League."[40]

Said the commissioner of the NFL, "We're not making any deals with the All-America boys at all."[41]

Fritsch, meanwhile, had returned to Green Bay and signed a contract with the Packers. "I just made a mistake, that's all," he said of his misadventure with the AAFC. "But this makes everything all right."[42] According to the *Plain Dealer*, Brown was willing to release Fritsch because the running back didn't fit the coach's offensive system. Brown also didn't want any players who didn't want to be in Cleveland, and Fritsch clearly regretted his impulsive decision to leave Green Bay.

Vince Banonis reported to training camp on August 7. The training camp of the Chicago Cardinals, that is, the team he'd played for before the war. The Cardinals didn't know Banonis had signed with the Browns and traded him to Detroit. It didn't take the Lions long to learn about Banonis' contract status. Not wanting a protracted legal battle with Cleveland, Detroit voided the deal. Banonis had accepted a $2,000 signing bonus from the Browns, and had been paid a $200 stipend for each of the 13-months he'd been under contract. Nonetheless, his father, Pete, said his son had no intention of honoring his contract with Cleveland. And he didn't. Banonis stayed in the NFL. The Browns didn't put up a fight to force him to play for them.

Rather than agreeing to drop their legal action against Adams and the Browns in exchange for Fritsch's release from his Cleveland contract, the Rams went back to federal court in Cleveland on August 13 and asked that the temporary restraining order they'd obtained in July be replaced by a temporary injunction. The request was taken under advisement, and a hearing on the matter wasn't expected until December, a development that was totally unsatisfactory for all parties involved in the squabble.

The first All-America Football Conference game was played on August 18 in Portland, Oregon, and not Denver as had been originally announced. A crowd estimated at 20,000 watched the Dodgers and Rockets battle to a 14-14 tie in an exhibition game. Brooklyn scored on 78- and 11-yard touchdown passes from Mickey Mayne to Bob Paffrath. Chicago's touchdowns came on short runs by Walter Clay and Bill Boedeker.

On August 22, the AAFC owners announced that Eleanor Gehrig, the widow of the late baseball legend Lou Gehrig of the New York Yankees, had been named a league vice-president. The position had been created especially for her. Her duties weren't specified.

The 1946 football season officially began on August 23, when the College All-Stars stunned the defending NFL champion Los Angeles Rams, 16–0, in

Soldier Field. A gathering of 97,380 watched a pair of AAFC-bound collegians lead their team to an upset victory. Crazylegs Hirsch of the Rockets, performing before his home fans, ran 68 yards from scrimmage for a touchdown, and caught a 62-yard pass from Otto Graham of the Browns for another.

At the request of both the Browns and Rams, neither of whom wanted to wait until the end of the season for a decision in the Chet Adams affair, judge Emerich Freed opened a hearing into the matter on August 27. Attorney Robert Trenkamp represented the Browns and asked Freed to dismiss the Rams' lawsuit. Trenkamp argued that Adams' contract had been signed with the CLEVELAND Rams and was rendered null and void when Dan Reeves moved the team to Los Angeles. Representing the Rams, attorney Thomas Lipscomb, who'd served as the team's president during the 1937 season, admitted he'd warned Reeves about potential contract problems before he uprooted the Rams and headed for Los Angeles.

After a three-day hearing, Judge Freed issued his ruling on August 30. Freed found in favor of the Browns, saying that Adams had signed a contract not with Reeves, but with the Cleveland Rams. In the eyes of the law, when the team moved to Los Angeles, the Cleveland Rams ceased to exist, and Adams couldn't be contractually bound to an entity that didn't exist. A legal precedent was thus set for the cases of Tom Colella, Don Greenwood and Gaylon Smith, who each intended to make the same argument if the Rams chose to take them to court.

Freed's ruling enabled Adams to play in the Browns' first game, an exhibition against the Dodgers in the Akron Rubber Bowl on the night of Friday, August 30. A crowd of 35,964 fans, a larger gathering than had ever watched a Rams game in Cleveland, saw the Browns rally from a 13–0 deficit to defeat Brooklyn, 35–20. The same evening in Baltimore, Buffalo edged Miami, 23–21. The attendance for that exhibition was estimated at 15,000.

The All-America Football Conference was ready to take on the NFL. Whether it would succeed where three previous challengers had failed remained to be seen.

4

1946

Almost two years to the day after it had been introduced by Arch Ward, the All-America Football Conference played its first game on September 6, 1946.

"All I ask is a chance to show what we've got," said Paul Brown, who'd been working to create a professional football dynasty from the day in early February of 1945 that he'd been hired to guide the fortunes of the Cleveland AAFC franchise. The result of his handiwork would be put on display in Municipal Stadium on the first Friday night of September. "I wish we could persuade 50,000 or 60,000 people to come to the stadium for our league opener with Miami. I am certain we could prove to them we have the kind of football and entertainment they have been looking for. We'll give them a good, fast, wide open, hard-hitting game. Arthur McBride has invested more than $250,000 in this enterprise already. We haven't cut any corners in attempting to organize the best football show in the country."[1] Brown had joked that he'd spend McBride's last penny to produce a winner in Cleveland. It didn't come to that, but Brown spent a lot of McBride's money, and he'd spent it wisely.

Before the Browns and Seahawks officially kicked off the AAFC's first season, the 49ers and Rockets concluded the exhibition season on September 1 in Kezar Stadium. A crowd estimated at 35,000 watched the 49ers pound the visitors, 34–14. Three fourth quarter touchdowns erased a 14–13 deficit. That finished the preliminaries.

Brown got his wish on the AAFC's opening night. While a crowd of 60,135 filed into Municipal Stadium, Cleveland's head coach and Miami's owner exchanged pleasantries on the stadium's turf. Harvey Hester had a word of warning for Brown, telling him his team was in for a long night because it hadn't signed enough players from the south. Hester was convinced the best football was played in Dixie, and loaded his team with players from that region. The Seahawks featured a pair of college All-Americans, Roy (Monk) Gafford of Auburn, and Jimmy Nelson of Auburn's arch-rival, Alabama.

Miami's head coach, "Whispering" Jack Meagher, had been head coach at Auburn, so Hester couldn't be accused of failing to practice what he preached. And Hester was right about a long night awaiting one of the teams participating in the AAFC's first game. But it wouldn't be the Browns.

With AAFC commissioner Jim Crowley and league vice president Eleanor Gehrig watching from the press box, and undoubtedly pleased by the size of the crowd, the Browns pulverized the Seahawks, 44–0. Cleveland needed just three minutes and 45 seconds to score the first touchdown in AAFC history, on a pass from quarterback Cliff Lewis to end Mac Speedie. The Browns rolled up 345 yards of total offense and limited the Seahawks to 27, none of them in the first half, when Miami gained 16 yards passing but lost 16 yards rushing. The Seahawks managed just five first downs against Cleveland's smothering defense, led by end Bill Willis. Willis and fullback/linebacker Marion Motley became the first African Americans to play in a professional football game since 1933. Unlike major league baseball's color barrier, which stretched back to 1884, the barrier in major league football was just 12 years old. A handful of black players, most notably Fritz Pollard, saw action in the NFL in the 1920's. Ray Kemp and Joe Lillard were the last African Americans to play professional football prior to Willis and Motley. Kemp played five games for the Pittsburgh Steelers in 1933. Lillard played in 18 games for the Cardinals in 1932 and '33, rushing for 494 yards on 171 carries. Football historian Richard Crepeau has written that the NFL formally banned African Americans at its meeting following the 1933 season. That claim was denied repeatedly and vehemently after the NFL's re-integration by such old-guard owners as Art Rooney and George Halas. According to Crepeau, it was Redskins owner George Preston Marshall's idea to bar African Americans from the NFL, a charge that would seem to be supported by the indisputable fact that the Redskins were the last NFL team to integrate, and not until 1962. Marshall allowed African Americans to play for the Redskins only under pressure from the administration of President John F. Kennedy.

Battered and bruised, physically and mentally, the Seahawks left Cleveland without paying the bills they'd incurred during their visit. McBride quietly took care of Hester's creditors to enable the AAFC to avoid a blotch on an otherwise glorious opening night. The Miami franchise would be an embarrassment to the AAFC for the rest of the season.

On the same day the Browns polished off the Seahawks in the AAFC opener, the Brooklyn Dodgers announced that quarterback Glenn Dobbs had suffered a chipped bone in his throwing hand on the final play of the exhibition loss to Cleveland in late August. Head coach Mal Stevens, who, as a practicing surgeon, doubled as the team's doctor, said the only cure was rest. Stevens said Dobbs could run with the football, but couldn't throw it, and would be used sparingly until the injury healed.

The day after the Browns and Seahawks inaugurated the AAFC, the city of Buffalo greeted its Bisons with a welcoming parade. World War II hero Admiral William (Bull) Halsey was the grand marshal, and commissioner Crowley, making the short trip from Cleveland, was in attendance. The Dodgers spoiled the party the next day, September 8, conquering the Bisons, 27–14, in Civic Stadium before a gathering of 25,489. Brooklyn led, 14–0, after three periods. The two teams combined for four touchdowns in the final quarter, with Dobbs connecting on passes of 50 yards to Joe Davis and 31 yards to Saxon Judd to cement the victory. So much for being used sparingly and being unable to throw.

In San Francisco on that second Sunday in September, the 49ers lost to the New York Yankees, 21–7. The Associated Press estimated the crowd at Kezar Stadium at 35,000 fans; the United Press reporter said the crowd was 40,000. Either way, the first major league football game in California (or the first since 1937, if the second American Football League can be considered a major league) capped off a rousing opening weekend for the AAFC.

The Browns returned to Bowling Green State University after their opening game victory. They didn't break training camp until September 11, two days before they were scheduled to help the Chicago Rockets open their home season at Soldier Field on Friday, the 13th. That would prove to be an omen for the Rockets. Advance ticket sales forecast a crowd of 70,000 in the stadium that could accommodate 100,000 spectators. Cleveland, despite its impressive opening game, was a solid ten-point underdog. The odds makers thought the Rockets' duo of Hunchy Hoernschmeyer and Crazylegs Hirsch could handle the Browns.

The predicted attendance proved to be overly optimistic, and so did Las Vegas. Still, owner John Keeshin was satisfied with the crowd of 51,962, even if he wasn't satisfied with the outcome of the game. The Browns kept Hirsch and Hoernschmeyer in check and won, 20–6. It was the last time the Browns would enter a game as an underdog until November of 1948.

Although college football was far more popular than the professional game in 1946, the AAFC wasn't afraid to venture into the domain of the collegians and schedule games on Saturdays. On September 14, the Yankees opened their home schedule with a 21–10 victory over a plucky Bisons team that entered the contest a three-touchdown underdog. Buffalo led, 10–7, before surrendering a pair of fourth quarter touchdowns to their hosts. The game attracted 40,606 fans to Yankee Stadium.

Three thousand miles to the west, the Dons attracted 19,500 fans to the Los Angeles Memorial Coliseum to watch them defeat the Dodgers, 20–14. The next day, the 49ers wrapped up the AAFC's second week of action with a 21–14 win over the Seahawks. San Francisco's Dick Renfro put smiles on the faces of 25,000 Kezar Stadium patrons with touchdown runs of eight, five, and four yards. It isn't known if Hester tried to leave San Francisco without paying his team's hotel and restaurant bills.

Angelo Bertelli and the Boston Yanks lost their court fight against the Los Angeles Dons and the AAFC the second week of September. A judge ruled the contract Bertelli signed in February to play for the Dons was valid, and ordered him to play for Los Angeles or no one in 1946 and '47. Ted Collins was determined to keep Bertelli away from the AAFC, and offered him a $10,000 contract to simply serve as a scout for the Yanks. Bertelli considered it, then decided he wanted to play and left his home in West Springfield, Massachusetts, for the west coast on September 17. "I've been out of football for two years now," Bertelli said as he departed. "I can't afford to miss another season."[2] The AAFC had chalked up another victory over the NFL.

The older league enjoyed a couple of victories as well. On September 20, the Browns announced they wouldn't go to court to enforce the valid contracts Vince Banonis and Ted Fritsch had signed with them earlier in 1946. Banonis never reported to Cleveland's training camp; Fritsch did but quickly sought release from his contract. The Browns granted his request. "We are not interested in the type of player who would not fulfill a legitimate contract that was signed in good faith," said Paul Brown. "I don't feel that court hearings and lawsuits add much to our game of football. I have a happy and wholesome squad and I'm satisfied to keep it that way. We want men who really want to play for us."[3] Brown knew he had assembled a team that would win without Banonis and Fritsch. Fritsch had to returned to Green Bay with Cleveland's blessing. To go to court to force Banonis to play for the Browns would've been an unnecessary waste of energy and money. It would also have been a potential distraction, and Brown hated distractions.

By design, the AAFC got the jump on its rival, starting its season three weeks before the NFL. The AAFC's third weekend began on Friday, September 20, in Chicago, where the Rockets tied the Yankees, 17–17. A crowd just half the size of the previous week's (estimated at 25,000) watched the home team gain the deadlock on a 36-yard pass from Walt Williams to Bill Boedeker with 55 seconds remaining. In Los Angeles, the Dons dispatched the Seahawks, 30–14. The Dons scored three second half touchdowns after trailing, 14–10, at the intermission. There was an estimated crowd of 23,000 in the Coliseum to watch the action.

On Sunday, September 22, the Browns posted their second shutout in three games, beating the Bisons in Buffalo, 28–0, before a crowd of 30,202. According to the United Press' observer, there were 30,000 people in Kezar Stadium to cheer on their 49ers to a 32–13 victory over the Dodgers. San Francisco put the game away in the middle periods, scoring 12 points in the second and 13 in the third. Earlier reports that the 49ers would play all of their home games on Friday nights had been erroneous.

The Browns returned home after their two-game road swing. They'd host the Yankees, and ticket sales were brisk. Cleveland's newspapers predicted a crowd of 70,000. Attendance through the AAFC's first three weeks had been promising.

Arch Ward had envisioned the Chicago franchise as being the centerpiece of his new football league. John Keeshin had been an activist owner, signing two of college football's brightest stars in Hirsch and Hoernschmeyer, and hiring a coach with track record of success in Dick Hanley. But the Keeshin/Hanley partnership soured quickly. Hanley didn't appreciate Keeshin's meddling, and before the season's third game submitted his resignation.

Hanley called the Rockets' situation "simply a case of incompatible personalities." Of his former boss, Hanley said he'd never gotten "so much front office advice. For somebody who knows nothing about football, Keeshin had more coaching advice than anybody I ever knew." Hanley said Keeshin told him that if the Rockets didn't beat the Bisons in Soldier Field on September 25, he and the players "might as well jump in the lake." Hanley's response was "if you think you can get somebody to do a better job, go ahead."[4] Keeshin did.

In announcing his coach's resignation after just two games on the job, Keeshin said Hanley had been whining since the opening of training camp. "Within the past several weeks, Dick Hanley has repeatedly submitted his resignation. On the last occasion, today, I accepted it. I am sorry Dick's relationship with the Rockets terminated in this fashion. As far as I am concerned, we part as friends."[5] Keeshin told Hanley's assistants, Pat Boland and Ernie Nevers, to report to his office on September 26 to discuss their status. For the game against Buffalo, he took the unusual step of placing three of his players in charge of the team. "Wee" Willie Wilkin, Ned Mathews, and Bob Dove served as "tri-coaches," and led the Rockets to their first victory, 38–35. Steve Nemeth's 13-yard field goal with five seconds to play was the game-winner. The contest was viewed by 20,678 confused fans.

As for Hanley, he and his assistants watched the game, but from where isn't clear. The Associated Press game story claimed Hanley, Nevers and Boland took in the action from the Soldier Field stands. The United Press reported that the three men watched the game from the Rockets' bench. The battle between Hanley and Keeshin had just begun.

Nevers and Boland met with Keeshin the following day and were kept on the Rockets' payroll. Their duties weren't defined. Keeshin was so pleased with his club's first victory that he decided to retain Wilkin, Mathews and Dove as his coaches for the foreseeable future. "The boys will be on their own for a while—elect their own officers and coaches—until we get the best football brains in the country to guide a potentially great team."[6] Keeshin said Wilkin, a 30-year-old, six-year veteran of the NFL, would serves as spokesman for the tri-coaches.

On September 29, with Wilkin, Mathews and Dove at the helm, the Rockets defeated San Francisco in Chicago, 24–7. It was their most impressive performance of the season. Hoernschmeyer was the star of the afternoon, throwing three touchdown passes and scampering on runs of 71 and 56 yards. A crowd of 26,873 (including Hanley) got a glimpse of the team Keeshin thought he had assembled. After the game, the players scrawled on a blackboard in the dressing room, "This game for our boss, Mr. J.L. Keeshin. Signed, The Boys."[7]

Although there were obvious dangers to allowing the inmates to run the asylum, the Rockets would play their best football of the campaign for their fellow players-turned-coaches, at least early on. After the upset of the 49ers, Chicago's record was 2-1-1. It was the first of only two occasions in the team's history it would be above the .500 mark. While record books and other reference sources credit Hanley with a 1-1-1 record as a professional coach, giving him credit for leading the Rockets to the victory over Buffalo, newspaper accounts made it clear Hanley watched that game strictly as a spectator. His record as a professional coach should read 0-1-1.

While the Rockets were showing signs of life, if briefly, the Browns improved their record to 4-0 with a 24-7 victory over the Yankees in Municipal Stadium on September 29. The crowd failed to exceed 70,000 as had been anticipated, but was still an impressive 57,084. The gate receipts of $138,673.73 were the largest ever for a regular season professional football game. In Buffalo, the Bisons and Dons played to a 21-all tie before 18,163.

As of the final weekend of September, the AAFC no longer had the stage all to itself. The NFL opened its season on the 29th of September, and many eyes were on Los Angeles, which, in 1945, had no major league football. In 1946, it had two clubs, sharing the same stadium. After drawing nearly 90,000 for an exhibition game, the Rams and owner Dan Reeves had to be bitterly disappointed by the turnout for the team's first regular season game. Just 30,000 watched the defending NFL champions lose to the Philadelphia Eagles, 25–14. The Eagles had been the only team to defeat the Rams during their championship season of 1945. While disappointing, the crowd was slightly larger than the attendance at the Dons' first two home games.

The AAFC standings after the first month of competition:

Eastern Division

New York	2-1-1	66-58
Brooklyn	1-3-0	54-66
Buffalo	0-4-1	80-135
Miami	0-3-0	28-95

Western Division

Cleveland	4–0–0	116–13
Los Angeles	2–0–1	71–43
Chicago	2–1–1	85–79
San Francisco	2–2–0	67–72

The AAFC's strongest teams were in the west, and that wouldn't change as the season progressed. The Browns alone would win three more games (12) than the Dodgers, Bisons and Seahawks combined. The 49ers (nine) would win as many as those three teams combined.

The "best football brains" Keeshin wanted to coach the Rockets belonged to an active player performing at Wrigley Field for the Chicago Bears. On September 30, Keeshin met with Bears quarterback Sid Luckman for two and a half hours in an effort to convince him to retire as a player and accept the Rockets' head coaching job. Keeshin offered Luckman a salary of $20,000 per season. The length of the contract wasn't specified. Keeshin said Luckman wanted the job but didn't think George Halas would release him from his contract with the Bears, and he was right. After meeting with Keeshin, Luckman had a meeting with Halas, then informed Keeshin that he'd stay with the Bears. Essentially repeating what he'd said when previously offered a contract with the AAFC, Luckman said, "As long as I'm playing football, I am going to remain with the Bears."[8]

Keeshin criticized Halas for refusing to let Luckman out of his contract. The quarterback was less than two months short of his 30th birthday, "and Halas should realize Luckman's years as a player are limited."[9] Luckman was far from retirement, playing through the 1950 season, but his final year as the Bears' starting quarterback would be 1947. Keeshin called Halas "selfish" for not allowing Luckman to move on to the next phase of his football career by taking the Rockets' coaching job. The feisty Halas didn't see it that way.

In Papa Bear's opinion, Keeshin's effort to lure Luckman to the Rockets constituted "a subversive effort to tear down the Bears. It is what I would call hoodlum tactics and does not belong in sports. I can assure you these tactics will not pay off. Any feeling that we in the National Football League might ever have had toward co-operating with the new league is now permanently and irrevocably abandoned." Halas added that the incident signaled "the beginning of the end" of the AAFC. That analysis proved to be highly premature.

Halas' use of the phrase "hoodlum tactics" didn't sit well with Keeshin, and he filed a libel lawsuit against the Bears' owner on October 1, seeking $250,000 in damages. Halas wasn't worried. "Lawyers get more important in the business every day. I had considered the Luckman case a closed incident after Sid turned down the offer and said he was sticking with the Bears. Now, however, I may file a suit against the Rockets for attempting to get him to breach his contract."[10]

Keeshin responded, "Talk and a loud mouth will never damage the All-America Conference."[11] He repeated his challenge to the Bears to meet the Rockets on the gridiron, with the proceeds given to charity.

"I'd caution Mr. Keeshin about talking too loud about playing the Bears, or we might surprise him and accept,"[12] sneered Halas. His response indicated that he and his fellow NFL owners didn't believe the AAFC was serious about taking on the NFL on the field, and issued their numerous challenges as a mere public relations gesture, secure in the knowledge they'd be ignored. The Bears were in the process of winning the NFL's western championship and would likely have made quick work of Keeshin's team in an exhibition match. Then again, who can be certain?

Having lost Luckman, Keeshin briefly considered re-instating the deposed Dick Hanley as head coach. He took the unprecedented step of polling his players, who voted 33–1 against Hanley's return. Keeshin said he'd abide by their decision, and announced the three-player triumvirate of Wilkin, Mathews and Dove would continue to coach the Rockets.

As early as the fourth weekend of the season, concern was expressed that the Browns were poised to make a shambles of the AAFC championship race. The concern came, ironically, from Cleveland, where newspaper columnist Gordon Cobbledick told his readers on September 29 that "if the Browns do what they have been threatening to do—make it a one-team race—the effect on the league could be damaging in the extreme."[13]

Paul Brown, while aware that a new entity like the AAFC needed competitive balance to attract fans, wasn't about to apologize for the powerhouse he'd built. "What do they want us to do, lie down and let the other guys run over us? I never heard anything so ridiculous. I don't believe the league is as un-balanced as some people believe, but if there are a few clubs that haven't measured up to major league standards, that becomes a problem which requires only time to remedy. It's certainly foolish to expect a brand new league like ours to produce eight evenly-matched teams."[14] Commissioner Crowley had been wrong when he'd said before the season that he expected all of the AAFC's teams to be strong contenders. Brown was right in saying such a thing wasn't possible (in any league, established or new), but he was wrong about the lack of balance in the AAFC. It would prove to be just as un-balanced at season's end as it appeared to be after its first month of competition, particularly in the eastern division, where no one could challenge the Yankees. The Browns dominated the west, but San Francisco and Los Angeles posted winning records and waged a spirited fight for second place. Chicago would lose just one more game than it won.

Following the Keeshin-Halas fracas, which ultimately turned out to be much ado about nothing, the month of October passed without any major skirmishes between the AAFC and NFL. The Yankees kicked off the first weekend of the month with a 21–13 victory over their in-state rivals, the Bisons, in Buffalo on Friday, October 4. The new league had no qualms about providing competition for high school football, and 17,101 fans chose to attend the professional game rather than support the high school of their choice. A crowd of 43,713 sat in Municipal Stadium to watch the Browns defeat the Dodgers, 24–7, on Sunday the 6th. Miami's home opener, scheduled for Monday the 7th, was postponed as a precaution because a hurricane was bearing down on south Florida. The storm changed course, as hurricanes often do, and spared Miami and environs. The Seahawks played their first home game on Tuesday, October 8, and disappointed a crowd of 7,831 by losing to San Francisco, 34–7. Miami's record fell to 0–4. The Seahawks, at Harvey Hester's request, then hit the road for four consecutive games. When they returned to Miami in early November, they'd completed their road schedule for the season.

The United Press reported on October 8 that Jerry Lynch, president of the Detroit All-Stars football club, had applied for membership in the AAFC. The matter would be taken up by the owners at the league's December meeting.

The Seahawks started their four-game road trip in Buffalo on Friday, October 11, and earned their first victory of the year. Johnny Vardian's 38-yard field goal lifted Miami to a 17–14 victory. It was the only game Miami would win with Jack Meagher as head coach. In Brooklyn, the Rockets rallied for a 21–21 tie with the Dodgers. With the ball at Chicago's 36 yard line and less than two minutes to play, Hunchy Hoernschmeyer passed to Ralph Heywood, with "tri-coach" Ned Mathews trailing the play. Heywood startled Brooklyn's defenders by tossing a lateral to Mathews at the Dodgers' 23 yard line, and Mathews lugged the ball the rest of the way.

Two days later, in a rainstorm in Yankee Stadium, the Browns edged the Yankees, 7–0. A 33-yard pass from Otto Graham to Dante (Gluefingers) Lavelli provided the game's only score. The Browns remained undefeated at 6–0, and on top of the AAFC's western division.

Miami's one-game winning streak was snapped by the Rockets in Soldier Field, 28–7, on Friday, October 18. Chicago's rushing defense smothered the visitors, holding the Seahawks to minus 28 yards on the ground. The embarrassing performance proved to be more than Meagher could stand. Meanwhile, the record of Wilkin, Mathews and Dove as the Rockets' "tri-coaches" improved to 3–2–1 while 20,172 watched. It would also be the trio's last victory. The 49ers game at Buffalo was postponed by inclement weather. It was played on Saturday, and the Bisons won, 17–14, before a pitiful crowd of just 6,101. Buffalo's enthusiasm for its AAFC team appeared to be waning rapidly.

In Cleveland on Sunday, October 20, the Browns concluded the first half of their season a perfect 7–0 with a 31–14 whipping of the Dons. The game

The Browns defeated the Dons in the Los Angeles Coliseum, 31–14, on Thanksgiving Day of 1948 in front of a less-than-sell-out crowd. It was Cleveland's 12th victory without a loss in what became an historic undefeated, untied championship season (Michael Schwartz Library, Cleveland State University).

was witnessed by 71,134 spectators, the largest crowd for a regular season professional football game in history. The crowd was only 6,000 less than the total number who'd paid to watch all of the Rams' regular season home games in Cleveland in 1945. The gate was $158,186.32, the second-largest in pro football history. That same afternoon 2,500 miles away, the Rams and Lions drew 30,111 to the Coliseum.

From the "department of where are they now," the *Cleveland Plain Dealer* reported on October 20 that Sam Cordovano, the construction magnate who'd resigned as head coach and general manager of the Buffalo Bisons and sold his stock in the team before training camp started, to pursue opportunities outside Buffalo and outside football that he couldn't turn down, had been seen in Toledo, Ohio, promoting harness races.

The AAFC experienced its second head coaching change in late October. Jack Meagher resigned following the Seahawks' 21-point loss to the Rockets in Chicago, the game in which Miami's rushing attack had been stuffed to the tune of minus 28 yards. He was replaced by former Bears player Hampton Pool, who was one of Meagher's assistants. Meagher left with a 1–5 record and never served as a head coach in the professional ranks again. More coaching changes would follow before October ended.

Despite George Halas' claim that John Keeshin's attempt to lure Sid Luckman from the Bears to the Rockets had irrevocably and eternally destroyed any chance of co-operation between the AAFC and NFL, Browns owner Mickey McBride had a proposition for the old league on October 22. It was an offer McBride, and the rest of the AAFC, had to know the NFL could and would refuse.

With his Browns riding high with a 7–0 record, McBride challenged the NFL's champion, whoever it would turn out to be, to a best-of-three playoff for the championship of professional football. "If the Browns win the championship, we'll be willing to play the National League champion any place and anytime," McBride said. "We'll play 'em on a winner take all basis, or we'll even play 'em for nothing, with all the profits going to charity. We'll leave it up to them to decide."

"Personally," he went on, "I'm in favor of a two-out-of-three game series, with the players getting 70 percent [of the proceeds] of the first two games. To my way of thinking, the ideal set-up would be to have the first two games played on the home fields of the contending clubs, with the third game, if necessary, being played in a neutral city like New Orleans. Everybody in our league is willing to get together with the National League. We don't believe in squabbling with those fellows at the expense of the public. The football fans are anxious for the champions to meet, and they are entitled to see for themselves which league has the strongest team. If anybody is so small that he doesn't want to play the game, he doesn't belong in football."[15]

Bert Bell was that small. His response to McBride was a terse "out of the question. Our season ends with the regular play-off between the eastern and western winners. The winner of that game is the only world champion we recognize."[16] McBride undoubtedly mentioned a 70 percent cut of the pie for the players in order to entice the NFL players to pressure the owners to agree to the play-off. NFL salaries were small, and the players would've welcomed a chance to augment them by participating in a championship series with the AAFC. And McBride undoubtedly mentioned the desire of the fans to see a championship series as another way to pressure the NFL, or at least to paint Bell and the NFL owners as the villains for the rejection he surely knew was coming.

Hampton Pool's first game as Miami's head coach was Dr. Mal Stevens' last game as Brooklyn's head coach. Or it may have been Tom Scott's first game. According to wire service accounts, Stevens submitted his resignation to Dodgers owner Bill Cox just hours before Brooklyn hosted the Seahawks at Ebbets Field on October 25. Stevens told Cox that practicing medicine and coaching football didn't mix. Those wire service stories said Cox immediately placed Scott, a Stevens assistant, in charge of the team. But the website pro-football-reference credits Stevens with a 2–4–1 record as the Dodgers' coach, which would include their 30–7 victory over Miami.

Cox hired Fred Linehan to coach his team, only to have Linehan quit without so much as conducting a practice, citing a lack of time due to outside business interests. Coaching was a part-time profession in most cases, with Paul Brown in Cleveland being a notable exception. Cox put Scott back in charge while he went shopping for another head coach, and came up with former Boston and Washington Redskins running back Cliff Battles. Battles had no head coaching experience, but had been an assistant at Columbia University for five seasons starting in 1938. The two-time NFL rushing champion and future Hall of Famer took the reins on November 1 in Chicago, where the Dodgers were scheduled to play the Rockets. The game was postponed by bad weather. The Dodgers made Battles' debut a successful one the following night, beating Chicago, 21–14. Although newspaper accounts of Battles' hiring said nothing about him sharing the head coaching duties with Scott, pro-football-reference claims the two men spent the rest of the 1946 season as "co-coaches," a common practice in that era.

The Browns suffered their first defeat on Sunday, October 27. San Francisco quarterback Frankie Albert connected on 14 of 21 passes, three of them for touchdowns, to befuddle Cleveland's previously almost impenetrable defense and lead the 49ers to a 34–20 victory before 70,386 stunned fans in Municipal Stadium. The Browns had allowed just 34 points total through their first seven games. The Dons lost to the Yankees, 31–17, with just 15,000 watching the action in Los Angeles. In Buffalo, the Bisons torched the Rockets, 49–17, in front of a gathering of 15,758. The beating convinced Keeshin that the concept of multiple head coaches, all of whom doubled as players, wasn't working.

Two days after the debacle in Buffalo, Keeshin re-instated former assistant coach Pat Boland and put him in charge of the Rockets for the rest of the season. Although Willie Wilkin, Ned Mathews and Bob Dove had compiled a record of 3–2–1, Keeshin decided his team needed "an older, more experienced head."[17] He also restored Ernie Nevers to his previous position as backfield coach. Boland's first game was the seven-point loss to the Dodgers on November 2 that was Battles' first game as Brooklyn's head coach. That concluded the AAFC's coaching carousel for its first season. Four of the original eight head coaches (Sam Cordovano, Dick Hanley, Jack Meagher and Mal Stevens) didn't make it halfway through the season. Cordovano didn't even last until his team's training camp.

The AAFC standings after its second month of games:

Eastern Division

New York	5–2–1	149–105
Brooklyn	2–4–1	122–141
Buffalo	2–6–1	173–204
Miami	1–6–0	66–201

4. 1946

Western Division

Cleveland	7–1–0	200–68
San Francisco	5–3–0	172–130
Los Angeles	3–3–1	137–143
Chicago	3–3–2	160–177

November opened with the 49ers defeating the Bisons, 27–14, in San Francisco on Saturday the 2nd. A sparse crowd of 12,500 shifted nervously in their seats as Buffalo took a 7–0 lead into the locker room at halftime. The 49ers tied the game in the third quarter and pulled away in the fourth by scoring three touchdowns.

About 400 miles to the south, the Dons handed the Browns their second straight loss on Sunday. Joe Aguirre's 11-yard field goal with 18 seconds to play lifted the Dons to a 17–16 victory. The upset was witnessed by 24,800 fans in the Coliseum. Angelinos weren't storming the gates of the 100,000-seat stadium to watch either of their teams in action. Suddenly, there was a legitimate race for the AAFC's western division championship. The following Sunday, the Browns would invade Kezar Stadium to take on the 49ers. Cleveland's record was 7–2. San Francisco's was 6–3. One of those six victories had been at the expense of the Browns. Another victory would result in a first-place tie with four games remaining.

Also on November 3, the Yankees topped the stubborn Seahawks, 24–21, before a crowd of 18,880 in New York. The Yankees pulled out the victory on a 14-yard touchdown pass from Clarence (Ace) Parker to Jack Russell with 26 seconds left on the clock. The loss was Miami's final road game of the season. The Seahawks returned to south Florida to begin a season concluding six-game stand in the Orange Bowl. Hardly anyone noticed or cared.

John Keeshin hadn't appreciated George Halas referring to his attempt to hire Sid Luckman as the Rockets' head coach as "hoodlum tactics," and sued Halas for libel. After Luckman turned down the offer, Keeshin asked his players if they'd be willing to play for deposed coach Dick Hanley again. Thirty-three of the Rockets' 34 players said no. Keeshin made the result of his poll of the players public, and Hanley didn't appreciate that, so he sued Keeshin for libel in Illinois Superior Court on November 6. The suit asked for $100,000 in damages, claiming Keeshin's comments upon firing Hanley had damaged the ex-coach's reputation, particularly the fact his former players had voted 33–1 against his return. Hanley said making that information public had created the impression that he was an incompetent coach, and was making it hard for him to find another coaching job. As for the question of whether Hanley quit or was fired, Keeshin continued to claim the former, Hanley continued to claim the latter. The battle between the two men over whether Keeshin owed Hanley the remainder of his salary on his contract would rage long after Keeshin sold the Rockets and got out of football.

Integration, however minimal, had come to professional football in 1946 with the signings of Bill Willis and Marion Motley by the Browns, and Kenny Washington and Woody Strode by the Rams. In college football, a number of teams in the north and west had African American players, and that led to the cancellations of some intersectional games in the fall of 1946. Penn State was scheduled to travel to Gainesville, Florida, to take on the Gators. The Nittany Lions had African American players, and Florida law prohibited Caucasians and blacks from opposing each other in athletic events. The Penn State athletic department was informed that the law would be strictly enforced, and the game was canceled.

The University of Nevada also had African American players and had scheduled a visit to Starkville to play Mississippi State in November of 1946. Negotiations between the two schools' athletic departments failed to result in an agreement to allow the African Americans to play, so Nevada backed out of the game.

Paul Brown hadn't signed Willis and Motley with the intention of being a crusader for civil rights. He'd signed them with the intention of winning football games, which he was certain Willis and Motley would help the Browns do. Brown announced on November 8 that when the Browns visited Miami in early December, Willis and Motley would remain in Cleveland. "When I signed the boys last summer, I made an agreement with the league that I wouldn't use them in Florida," Brown explained. "I won't do anything that might embarrass the boys."[18] Brown made the announcement three weeks before the game so as to diffuse the potential controversy over whether the Browns would challenge the Florida law. That would've been a major distraction, and Brown despised distractions. It helped that Brown knew his team could whip the Seahawks without Willis and Motley.

The Seahawks made some news of their own on November 8. Harvey Hester announced that Hampton Pool would coach the team in 1947. Little did anyone realize at the time the Seahawks would barely make it through the rest of the 1946 season. The same day, the NFL's owners, meeting in Pittsburgh, voted to re-affirm the league constitution which prohibited post-season games (meaning after the league's championship game.) That squashed any infinitesimal possibility that may have existed for an AAFC-NFL championship clash for 1946.

The showdown for first place in the west drew a crowd of 41,061 to Kezar Stadium on November 10. The Browns scored touchdowns in each of the first two periods, then left matters in the hands of the defense. After being burned for 34 points in Cleveland two weeks earlier, the defense kept the 49ers off the scoreboard until the fourth quarter. Quarterback Frankie Albert picked up a teammate's fumble and returned it one yard for a score. The Browns' 14–7 victory improved their record to 8–2 and dropped the 49ers to 6–4. Cleveland was back in firm control of the western division.

In New York, the Yankees squeezed past the Dons, 17–12. Running back Eddie Prokop scored what proved to be the winning touchdown on a 77-yard punt return in the third quarter. The attendance at Yankee Stadium was 30,765. Across town in Ebbets Field, the Dodgers lost to Buffalo, 17–14. The crowd was 12,820.

Almost a quarter of a century before the NFL experimented with a weekly Monday night football game, the Seahawks played most of their games on the first workday of the week. On November 11, Miami lost to Chicago, 20–7, in front of an intimate gathering of 7,438 fans. Watching from the Orange Bowl's press box, and undoubtedly concerned by some 72,000 empty seats, were commissioner Jim Crowley and league vice president Eleanor Gehrig.

The United Press reported on November 11 that University of Minnesota football coach Bernie Bierman would resign his post to take over the Rockets in 1947. It was no secret that Keeshin wanted a big-name coach for his team. He'd failed in his first attempt (Sid Luckman), and Bierman was one of college football's most successful coaches. Bierman's 1936 (7–1), 1940 (8–0) and 1941 (8–0) Golden Gophers had claimed national championships, but his 1946 team would finish at 5–4, and it was thought he'd be open to trying his hand at coaching in the professional ranks. He wasn't.

The AAFC may have been rebuffed in every effort to meet the NFL on the field, but the new league was racking up victories against its rival in court. Or, in this case, out of court. It was announced on November 13 that the Dons and the AAFC had reached an out-of-court settlement with Ted Collins and the NFL over Collins' attempt to get Angelo Bertelli to break his contract and play for the Boston Yanks. After a judge ruled that Bertelli's contract with the Dons was valid and he'd have to play for Los Angeles or sit out the 1946 and '47 football seasons, the AAFC sued Collins for damages. Collins agreed to pay what was termed "a substantial cash settlement" to the AAFC. The suit also asked that Collins be prohibited from trying to sign any other AAFC players.

Dan Topping's decision to desert the NFL for the AAFC paid dividends. Not only could his Yankees play their home games in Yankee Stadium, but they were one of the league's powerhouses, after years of Topping's Dodgers bringing up the rear in the NFL in Brooklyn. On a rainy Sunday, November 18, in New York, the Yankees beat San Francisco, 10–9, to clinch the eastern division championship and a berth in the first AAFC title game on December 22. A crowd of 18,695 watched the Yankees drive 76 yards in the fourth quarter to wipe out the 49ers' six-point lead. Ace Parker's 26-yard pass to Eddie Prokop provided the winning points. New York was 8–2–1 with three games to play. No other eastern division team had a winning record. No other eastern division team had won more than three games.

The same rainstorm that held the crowd to under 20,000 in Yankee Stadium kept Dodgers fans away from nearby Ebbets Field. Los Angeles beat Brooklyn in the slop, 19–14, as just 7,500 customers watched.

In Cleveland, the Browns moved closer to taking the western division crown with a 51–14 walloping of Chicago, witnessed by 60,457. In Miami on Monday night, the Seahawks picked up their second victory of the season, both at the expense of Buffalo. Only 5,592 were on hand as the Seahawks dusted the Bisons, 21–14.

For the weekend of November 17, attendance at the NFL's five games was a healthy 179,001. The AAFC's four games attracted just 92,244 patrons, almost two-thirds of them in Cleveland. What had started out promisingly was petering out rapidly, aided no doubt by the lack of a race for the division title in the east, where the Yankees had dominated from the opening kickoff of the season's first game. The Browns had been seriously threatened only briefly by the 49ers in the west, and that threat had been eliminated.

Among those not impressed with the AAFC was influential *Cleveland Press* sports columnist Franklin (Whitey) Lewis. Before the AAFC's first month of games was finished, Lewis expressed the opinion that the upstarts had no hope of achieving parity with the NFL. He was certain the NFL would welcome the Browns with open arms, and thought the older league would also be glad to add the 49ers and Yankees for the 1947 season. In late November, Lewis again took aim at the AAFC, the headline above his column on the 20th proclaiming the league was doomed. He was particularly perplexed by the mess in Miami and pondered "what they are using to pay their players with is the mystery of the month." It would be learned shortly after the season ended that the Seahawks' players weren't being paid. Harvey Hester had run out of money, but his players kept showing up for practices and games anyway.

While it was being organized, commissioner Crowley said the AAFC would be divided into northern and southern "regions," rather than the traditional eastern and western divisions, like the NFL. Crowley also said the southern region's champion would host the league's first title game on December 22. That plan was scrapped somewhere along the way, and the league's owners voted on November 21 to award the championship game to the winner of the western division. There had been some sentiment to play the game in New York, the nation's media and publicity capital, and there was some talk of moving the game ahead a week to December 15, in order to avoid the distraction of the Christmas holiday. But the NFL's championship game would be played on December 15, and the eastern division champion Giants would host it in the Polo Grounds. The AAFC didn't want its first championship game competing directly with the NFL's title game, with the two contests being played at the same time in stadiums barely a mile apart, so the championship game was awarded to the western division winner. The date for the game remained December 22. The AAFC, in spite of its bold talk and constant issuing of challenges, would rather compete with Santa Claus than the NFL.

The match-up for the AAFC's first title game was set on Sunday, November 24, when Cleveland clinched the western championship with a 42–17 trouncing of Buffalo in Municipal Stadium. The pre-Thanksgiving crowd of 37,054 was the smallest of the home season for the Browns, but still larger than any gathering the Rams had ever attracted. The Bisons gave the Browns a tussle, trailing just 14–10 midway through the third quarter. Cleveland pulled away with a touchdown pass from Otto Graham to Mac Speedie and rushing touchdowns by Marion Motley, Al Akins and Bud Schwenk for the blow-out victory. The Browns, with a pair of games remaining on the road, were 10–2.

With the Browns and Yankees having punched their tickets to the championship game, the rest of the AAFC's 1946 schedule was contested for fun and exercise. In New York, the Rockets surprised the Yankees, 38–28. The 21,270 fans in Yankee Stadium were aghast (and, with the division title clinched, possibly amused) by the sight of their heroes fumbling nine times and losing six of them. In Brooklyn, the 49ers, looking to finish a strong second in the west, beat up the Dodgers, 30–14. The crowd was 15,100. On Monday in Miami, the Dons whipped the Seahawks, 34–21. The crowd of 9,987 in the Orange Bowl was the largest the Seahawks would attract during their brief existence.

The AAFC wasn't about to cede the Thanksgiving day football spotlight to the NFL. In Detroit, the woeful Lions hosted the Boston Yanks and lost, 34–10, in a match-up of teams that would win three games between them for the year. The game was viewed by 13,010 fans. The Dodgers hosted the Yankees on November 28 and lost, 21–7. A crowd of 16,240 delayed their holiday repast to visit Ebbets Field and watch the action. Although it was a larger crowd than the Dodgers were accustomed to at home, it was disappointing because both teams fervently hoped to start a rivalry that would equal the red-hot baseball rivalry between the Dodgers and New York Giants. That wouldn't happen.

In Kezar Stadium on November 30, the 49ers blanked the Rockets, 14–0. The crowd was estimated at just 12,000. With their team out of contention, the football fans of the bay area had turned their attention to other amusements. But the 49ers stayed focused. They set their sights on second place, and the small share of the championship game receipts that would go with it.

With November in the books, the AAFC standings showed:

Eastern Division

New York	9–3–1	239–192
Brooklyn	3–8–1	192–242
Buffalo	3–9–0	235–308
Miami	2–9–0	137–293

Western Division

Cleveland	10–2–0	323–123
San Francisco	8–5–0	259–182
Los Angeles	6–4–1	219–211
Chicago	5–6–2	246–298

The Dons had a lot of seats to fill in the Coliseum, and they hadn't enjoyed much success doing it. In an effort to increase the crowd for their game with Buffalo on Sunday, December 1, management dropped the price for 60,000 general admission seats to a dollar. Seats between the 35 yard lines cost two bucks. Angelinos weren't impressed, and only 22,822 took advantage of the bargain seating to watch the Dons set an AAFC single-game scoring record in a 62–14 whomping of the Bisons. The offensive outburst broke the record of 51 points set by the Browns just two weeks earlier. The Dons' record wouldn't even hold up that long.

Heavy rain in Miami postponed the Seahawks' game with the Browns until Tuesday night, December 2. Even without stalwarts Bill Willis and Marion Motley, the Seahawks were no match for the Browns and lost, 34–0. The game was witnessed by just 9,083 football aficionados. In two games against a Cleveland team that stood no chance of competing in the AAFC because it lacked southern players, in the opinion of Miami's disgraced owner, Harvey Hester, the Seahawks scored exactly zero points while allowing 78.

Two weekends remained in the AAFC's regular season. The division champions had been crowned, but second place was up for grabs in the western division. Actually, second place was up for grabs in the east as well, but the fans of the Dodgers, Bisons and Seahawks could hardly be blamed if they weren't excited about a three-way battle for second place among teams that had won a combined eight games.

The game between the 49ers and Dons in Kezar Stadium on December 8 would determine the runner-up in the western division. The 49ers entered the game with an 8–5 record, the Dons were 7–4–1. The winner would claim second place and a sliver of the championship game financial pie. To the delight of 25,000 fans, the 49ers dominated from the opening kickoff, bludgeoning the visitors, 48–7.

On the other side of the continent, the Browns couldn't have been blamed if they'd waltzed through their final regular season game against the Dodgers in Brooklyn. They'd won the western division and had home-field advantage for the championship game. But Paul Brown's teams didn't waltz through games, even if, by playing their regulars, they risked serious injury that could jeopardize their chance to claim the league championship. The Browns thrashed the Dodgers, 66–14, breaking the Dons' week-old league record for points in a single game. Brown regarded the contest as a final tune-up for the title game two weeks hence, and he was thrilled with the performance and attitude of his players.

"I would say this was our best all-around exhibition," Brown said in the Ebbets Field dressing room. "We started to click, and all our plays worked with a certain smoothness that was beautiful for a coach to watch. But the thing that made me happy was the desire the boys had. After every touchdown, they came back chanting 'let's get another,' and that went right up to the last minute of the game. The long season hasn't taken the enjoyment out of the game for them."[19] The long season would only get longer for the Dodgers and their fans, of which 14,600 showed up to watch the Browns embarrass their team. Brooklyn had one game left on its schedule.

The weekend's Monday night game featured the Yankees and Seahawks in the Orange Bowl, and the visitors barely broke a sweat in beating the bedraggled Miamians, 31–0. The Seahawks played like a team which hadn't seen a paycheck in more than a month. The mismatch was witnessed by 7,090 fans.

In spite of his team's miserable record, Dodgers star rookie quarterback Glenn Dobbs showed his confidence in his team, and in the AAFC, by signing a five-year contract on December 11. Dobbs' performance had earned him first-team recognition on the Associated Press' combined NFL-AAFC all-pro squad. Joining Dobbs from the AAFC on the first-team were halfback Orban (Spec) Sanders and offensive lineman Frank (Bruiser) Kinard of the Yankees, and offensive lineman Bill Radovich of the Dons. Cleveland fullback Marion Motley and offensive end Dante Lavelli were named to the second team.

The Seahawks played their final game on, appropriately enough, Friday the 13th of December. A "crowd" of 2,340 (in the 80,000 seat Orange Bowl) provided enough inspiration to push the home team to a 31–20 victory over Brooklyn, in spite of Dobbs' heroics. Dobbs passed for 187 yards to give him 1,886 for the season, surpassing Cleveland's Otto Graham, who threw for 1,833 yards. But Graham's team was going to the AAFC championship game. Dobbs' team was going home to begin the off-season. The bewildered Seahawks wondered where they'd be playing in 1947. It wouldn't be in Miami.

The Associated Press announced its all–AAFC team on December 14, one day before the league's final regular season game. Only an offensive squad was selected. The choices were Cleveland's Otto Graham at quarterback, left end Mac Speedie and halfback Marion Motley; New York's tackle Bruiser Kinard and halfback Spec Sanders; all-purpose back Glenn Dobbs and tackle Martin Ruby of Brooklyn; guard Bill Radovich and center Bob Nelson of Los Angeles; and San Francisco guard Bruno Banducci and right end Alyn Beals.

The Dons and Rockets wrapped up the AAFC's first regular season in Los Angeles on Sunday, December 15. The two teams battled to a 17–17 tie, the Rockets' third deadlock of the year. The attendance was 22,515. The final AAFC standings:

Eastern Division

New York	10-3-1	.769	270-192
Brooklyn	3-10-1	.231	226-339
Buffalo	3-10-1	.231	249-370
Miami	3-11-0	.214	167-378

Western Division

Cleveland	12-2-0	.857	423-137
San Francisco	9-5-0	.643	307-189
Los Angeles	7-5-2	.583	305-290
Chicago	5-6-3	.455	263-315

The AAFC west had produced something resembling a race for the championship through the season's first nine games. The winner of the east had never been in doubt. The Dodgers and Bisons posted the worst records for second-place finishers in the history of professional football. In spite of the chaos in Chicago, where five head coaches were employed in 14 games, the Rockets finished a mere three points from a highly respectable 8-6 record. On the other hand, they also finished a mere three points from a not-so-respectable 5-9 record.

When the AAFC owners met on December 20 in Cleveland, two days before the league's first championship game between the Browns and Yankees, the first order of business was to clean up the colossal mess left by Hester in Miami. The Seahawks were declared in default, and the franchise, which had failed to draw a five-figure crowd to any of its seven home games, was terminated. Hester was removed from the AAFC's executive committee and replaced by Ben Lindheimer of the Dons. The league had filed charges against Hester and the Seahawks for violating the AAFC's indebtedness clause. Commissioner Crowley issued $60,000 in checks on the league's behalf to pay Miami's players, who hadn't seen a paycheck from Hester since the middle of October. Crowley said the league would assume the Seahawks' debts for which the owners felt morally responsible. How "moral responsibility" would be determined wasn't specified.

There was no shortage of applicants to replace the Seahawks. Representatives from Dallas, Baltimore, Boston, and Philadelphia attended the meeting. So did a group from Miami, which hoped to convince the owners to allow them to take over the franchise from Hester and keep the team in south Florida. Their plea fell on deaf ears. The AAFC wanted nothing more to do with Miami.

Baltimore, which was supposed to have been a charter member of the AAFC before voluntarily surrendering its franchise in January of 1946, was the front-runner to replace Miami. Attorney Robert Rodenberg of nearby Washington led the Baltimore contingent and said his group had reached an agreement with the Baltimore Park Board to lease Memorial Stadium for

$5,000 per game, if the games were played in the daylight. For night games, the board wanted 20 percent of the gross receipts, after taxes. Seahawks general manager Jack Espey, who was expected to remain with the organization if it re-located to Baltimore, said the team would ask that all of its home games be scheduled on Sundays, meaning they'd be played in the afternoon. Rent for seven afternoon games would be $35,000.

According to Rodenberg, he had a contract with the park board to use Memorial Stadium in 1947, with an option to renew the lease for four years. He said his group, which hadn't yet been granted a team, was already looking for a head coach. Those being considered included Harvard University head coach Dick Harlow; University of Maryland head coach Clark Shaughnessy; and Rip Miller, the Naval Academy assistant who would've been Baltimore's coach in 1946 if there had been a Baltimore team for him to coach.

No decision was made on Baltimore's bid at the meeting. The owners did decide to remove Rockets owner John Keeshin from the executive committee and replace him with Dan Topping. Keeshin denied rumors that he was trying to sell his team. "My club is not for sale,"[20] he insisted. Bill Cox of the Dodgers kept his seat on the executive committee. Cox acknowledged that his team hadn't made any money in 1946, but said the Dodgers would return in 1947.

The final order of business was conducting a draft of eligible college players. The two biggest names in college football, Glenn Davis and Felix (Doc) Blanchard of Army, were selected by the Dodgers and 49ers, respectively. Now it was up to both teams to out-bid the NFL for their services. Davis had indicated he'd forego playing professional football and make a career of the Army.

The Browns were 13½ point favorites to win the AAFC's first championship, and Yankees head coach Ray Flaherty thought the spread was about right. "We lost twice to the Browns during the regular season, and those 14-points they are spotting the Browns probably is correct. But we can't be counted out. This won't be the first time a team I have been with entered a play-off under similar circumstances. Back in 1934, our New York Giants dropped a couple of close games to the Chicago Bears, but we won the eastern division title and walloped the Bears good in the play-offs."[21]

Flaherty's memory of the 1934 season was a bit faulty. The Bears whipped the Giants good, 27–7, the first time the teams met, in Chicago. The Bears prevailed in the re-match in New York, 10–9. The rest of his recollection was accurate. The Bears entered the championship game undefeated at 13–0. Flaherty's Giants (8–5) weren't given much of a chance to derail the Bears, even though the game would be played in New York's Polo Grounds. An ice storm descended on New York the evening before the game, and footing was treacherous for both teams. The wintry conditions severely hampered both offenses, and the Bears were just 15 minutes away from concluding an historic season as they took a 13–3 lead into the fourth quarter.

Flaherty, showing the kind of thinking that would make him a successful head coach, suggested to Giants boss Steve Owen that the players might get better traction on the icy field if they wore sneakers rather than football spikes. A team employee was dispatched to find sneakers and returned with nine pair borrowed from the men's basketball team at nearby Manhattan College. Taking advantage of the improved traction, plus the fact the field had begun to thaw after being used for three quarters of football, the Giants outscored the bewildered Bears, 27–0, in the fourth period for a 30–13 victory and the NFL championship.

If the Yankees were going to upset the Browns, they'd need a big effort from a player who would much rather have worn a Cleveland uniform on that December 22 afternoon. Eddie Prokop had been a high school football star in Cleveland, then matriculated to Georgia Tech, where he earned All-America honors as a halfback in 1945. He signed with his hometown team, only to be plucked from their roster by the Yankees when Dan Topping had demanded that each AAFC team allow him to select two of their players to guarantee his club's success. The other teams were permitted to protect only three players, and Topping had his pick of the rest. As much as Paul Brown wanted Prokop on his team, he couldn't justify making him one of the three players the Browns would declare off-limits to the Yankees. Many players would have been thrilled by the chance to strut their stuff in the Big Apple. Prokop wasn't one of them. He spent much of the 1946 season sulking.

"Eddie really wanted to be playing for the Browns the last time we were here," said Flaherty of his team's 24–7 loss in Cleveland in late September. "But he has a completely different outlook now, and is anxious to make a good showing in his hometown this time." Flaherty thought Prokop would have a big impact on defense. "We were weak on passes in both games [against Cleveland] and Prokop should make a difference. He is a fast man and will have a better chance of keeping some of those speedy Browns covered."

As for the showdown with the NFL that the AAFC coveted, Flaherty said, "I think either the Browns or Yankees could lick the Bears [who'd won the NFL title game the week before] or the Giants. Since they won't play with us, all we have to do is claim we're the best."[22]

The numbers favored the Browns, who scored 423 points to the Yankees' 270, and allowed just 137 to New York's 192.

For a team that had drawn two crowds of better than 70,000 and two other crowds in excess of 60,000 during the regular season, the attendance of just 41,181 for the championship game was disappointing to the Browns and their owner, Mickey McBride. Without the heroics of halfback Edgar (Special Delivery) Jones, the game's outcome would've been disappointing as well.

The Yankees scored first, on an 11-yard field goal by Harvey Johnson in the first quarter. The slim advantage for the visitors held until two minutes remained in the first half. Bruising Browns fullback Marion Motley bulled over from the one yard line, capping a 70-yard drive and giving Cleveland a 7–3 lead at the half. New York marched 80 yards in the third quarter to regain the lead on a two-yard run by Spec Sanders. Johnson missed the extra point. The score stayed 9–7 until late in the fourth period, when the Browns took possession on their 24 yard line. On third-and-nine at the New York 35, with the season hanging in the balance, a rushed Otto Graham found his two favorite targets, ends Dante Lavelli and Mac Speedie, both covered. Flushed out of the pocket, he threw a low pass that Jones, streaking across the middle of the field, somehow managed to grab by his fingertips, just inches off the ground. He fell to the turf at the 16 yard line. From there, Lavelli managed to shake off Prokop's tight coverage to haul in the winning touchdown pass with less than a minute on the clock. Lou Groza converted the extra point, and the Yankees were left without enough time to retaliate. The Browns were 14–9 victors, and champions of the AAFC.

"Worried?" said Brown in the winners' dressing room, repeating a reporter's question. "You bet I was worried. I didn't stop worrying until it was all over, and then I got worried that I might not get off the field in one piece." As Brown made his way across the field to exchange the traditional post-game handshake with Flaherty, his jubilant players put him on their shoulders and carried him to the locker room.

Of those players, Brown said, "They were all great. Played a marvelous game. It was really a team triumph. Of course, we missed a lot of opportunities. Groza's injury could have cost us the game, but our strategy of short, bullet passes when the Yankees were expecting long ones finally paid off."[23] Groza missed field goals of 20, 42 and 48 yards. Chet Adams missed a boot from 37 yards. Had all those attempts been converted, and field goal kickers weren't nearly as accurate in 1946 as they are today, the Browns would've had a 19–9 lead, and Jones' heroics wouldn't have been necessary. The Browns would've been trying to run out the clock rather than scrambling for the winning score.

"It just wasn't our day again," moaned Flaherty, referring to the Yankees' two regular season losses to Cleveland. "The outcome may have been different had the field been dry. As it was, neither Sanders nor Prokop could break loose. Prokop gambled on the touchdown pass and lost. He had a choice of either going for the ball, or hitting Lavelli after he made the catch, took a chance on reaching the ball and just missed. We certainly didn't get the breaks today."[24]

Adding to the Yankees' disappointment was the size of the checks they got for their share of the championship game receipts. The victorious Browns earned $931.57, while the vanquished Yankees received $645.88 for their efforts.

The Browns were also attendance champions, not only of the AAFC but of all professional football. Cleveland established a new professional record by attracting 399,962 fans to its seven regular season home games. Add the crowd at the only exhibition game, played just down the road in Akron's Rubber Bowl, and the crowd for the AAFC title game, and the number increased to 477,107.

The rest of the attendance figures for the AAFC:

New York	194,600
Chicago	193,677
San Francisco	185,561
Los Angeles	144,315
Buffalo	117,954
Brooklyn	97,671
Miami	49,151

According to the attendance numbers provided by the website pro-football-reference, the AAFC drew 1,382,991 fans to its games in 1946. That averaged out to 24,696 per game. Cleveland had been a bonanza. New York, Chicago and Los Angeles had held their own against their NFL competition. Buffalo's attendance was cause for concern, as was Brooklyn's. Miami had been a disaster but would trouble the league no longer.

The AAFC's maiden voyage was in the books. No sooner did the gun sound ending the championship game in Cleveland than preparations for season number two began.

5

Exit Crowley, Enter Ingram

It wasn't going to be a merry Christmas in New York.

The Associated Press reported on Christmas Eve that several Yankee players weren't happy with their head coach, Ray Flaherty, or their owner, Dan Topping. Topping denied any knowledge of dissension within the ranks.

"This is the first I've heard of any dissension," said Topping. "We will study the situation ... all I can say is, Ray Flaherty was hired to win ball games, and a championship if possible. I must say he did win games, and came close to the title." Topping then added ominously for his dissatisfied players, "How he did it doesn't particularly concern me."[1]

How Flaherty did it did concern quarterback Ace Parker, end Perry Schwartz, halfback Clarence (Pug) Manders, and tackle Bruiser Kinard. Before the AAFC title game, Flaherty had gone out of his way to praise his veteran quarterback. "You wouldn't think it possible for a fellow who has been playing the game as long as Ace has to get excited about a game, but he does, and the whole team then reacts the same way."

"I remember the time we left for our first game in Cleveland," he continued. "The day before, Ace had been ordered to report for an x-ray examination because of the injury he received during training camp. It disclosed the broken vertebra, and Ace was left at home. He came down to the airport to see us off, and the guy, tough as he is, actually had tears in his eyes because he was going to miss the game."[2] Parker didn't share the same high opinion of Flaherty.

"I wouldn't play again under such a set-up if I were given 60 percent of the receipts of the entire conference," he said. "Topping and Flaherty had no consideration for the players at any time, and we were burned out before we met the Browns. This is the first successful but unhappy season I have ever had."[3]

Topping responded to speculation his displeased players might bolt for the NFL by saying, "As to reports some of the players plan to desert the team for the National League, I can say we consider the nucleus of the 1947 ball club already is signed."[4] Manders and Kinard were under contract for 1947; Parker and Schwartz weren't. Flaherty had predicted that the AAFC championship game would be Parker's last, and Cleveland newspapers reported that he had announced his retirement the night before the game. Parker denied those reports after blasting Flaherty and Topping, but he did wind up retiring before training camp began. The Yankees had a more than capable replacement for him at quarterback in Spec Sanders. Manders, the NFL's 1941 rushing champion with Topping's Brooklyn team, was also at the end of the line. He played just three games for the Dodgers in 1947 before retiring. Flaherty would survive the alleged insurrection.

Brooklyn quarterback Glenn Dobbs, who would've been the AAFC's "Rookie of the Year" had there been such an award, expressed confidence his team would be improved in 1947. He also expected improved fan support in Ebbets Field. "Of our seven home games, four were played in the rain. Still, we had an average attendance of 12,000. We need about 19,000 to break even. Give 'em a winning team and they'll back you just as they do the baseball Dodgers."[5] The 1946 baseball Dodgers had lost the National League pennant to the St. Louis Cardinals in the sport's first ever best-of-three playoff. They drew 1,796,824 fans to lead the league in attendance.

On December 28, the International News Service reported an NFL owner it didn't identify was preparing to "bolt" the older league and hook up with the AAFC. Speculation was that owner was either Alex Thompson of the Eagles, or Ted Collins of the Yanks. Collins was a close friend of AAFC commissioner Jim Crowley, and had hired Crowley as his coach before Crowley accepted the commissioner's post. Thompson was said to be frustrated with the power wielded by George Preston Marshall, Curly Lambeau, George Halas and the Mara family in the NFL.

Also on December 28, Crowley announced that the AAFC owners had unanimously accepted Baltimore's bid to replace Miami for the 1947 season. Bob Rodenberg's five-man group paid $100,000 for "contractual rights" to the defunct franchise, and promised to post a $250,000 bond for capitalization at the AAFC's winter meeting in January. Rodenberg's partners were introduced as his brother Bill; businessman and former college football player J.C. Herbert Bryant; realtor Karl Corby; and furniture store executive Mrs. Agnes Shevlin. After signing the necessary documents, Rodenberg departed for New York, where he said he'd start contract negotiations with "one of the nation's leading coaches."[6]

Crowley had another announcement to make on December 30. He was resigning as AAFC commissioner and taking over as principal owner and head coach of the Chicago Rockets. The purchase price wasn't revealed. Crowley said departing owner John Keeshin had asked him to step down as commissioner and take the Chicago coaching job after Dick Hanley resigned (or was fired, that was still being argued about) in September. Crowley declined the offer.

Keeshin spent the ensuing months trying and failing to lure a high profile coach to assume control of his team. He was thwarted in his attempt to sign Bears quarterback Sid Luckman when Halas refused to release him from his contract. It was reported that Keeshin had offered the job to University of Minnesota coaching legend Bernie Bierman. If those reports were true, Bierman wasn't interested. Keeshin then turned to another college coaching icon, Frank Leahy of Notre Dame.

Keeshin opened talks with Crowley at the league's pre-championship game meeting in Cleveland after Leahy rejected his offer to coach the Rockets. Events moved quickly, and the sale was negotiated and completed in a week. Crowley's partners in the deal were Bill Toohey, a manufacturer from Chicago, and businessman John Brogan of Green Bay. Both were high school teammates of Crowley's in Green Bay. Toohey would be the Rockets' team president. Crowley was vice president and head coach. Brogan's duties weren't specified. Keeshin retained a tiny token ownership in the team he'd founded.

"John Keeshin left the Cleveland meeting December 20th with the intention of obtaining Frank Leahy of Notre Dame to coach and direct the enterprise," said Browns owner Mickey McBride. "Failing in that, he has relinquished complete control to Crowley and his associates. I believe Jim Crowley will be very successful as coach and owner of the Chicago Rockets. Crowley is a good coach ... coaching is his life, and I know he prefers that to an administrative position. He likes the action of an active coaching career."[7] Crowley stepped down as commissioner with four years and $100,000 remaining on his contract. He said he'd stay on until a replacement could be hired. Speculation began immediately as to who that replacement would be, and some unlikely candidates were mentioned. How seriously some of these "candidates" were considered is anybody's guess.

Rumor had it some AAFC owners shed no tears over Crowley's departure. The unidentified owners felt Crowley hadn't been aggressive enough in the battle against the NFL. Others believed he'd bowed too easily to the demands of certain influential clubs.

Baltimore was officially in the fold, and the as yet unnamed team would get the rights to all of the players under contract to Miami, plus rights to an unspecified number of players from the seven other AAFC teams. As excited as the fans of Baltimore were about getting a major league football team, without reinforcements, they'd have a hard time sustaining much enthusiasm for what had been the worst team in the AAFC in 1946. The Seahawks averaged barely 12 points per game, and been out-scored by 211 points.

One day after Crowley resigned, it was reported that one of his Notre Dame teammates was a candidate to succeed him. U.S. District Attorney Don Miller, himself one of the famous "Four Horsemen" of the 1924 Fighting Irish, said, "This is the first I've heard of it. I'd listen to a proposition if it were made to me, but right now I can't say that I'd take the job. There are a lot of things to consider, and I'd have to await the actual offer."[8] The fact that Miller was surprised by the story indicates many of the names mentioned as possible successors to Crowley were probably tossed around by sportswriters looking for a something to write about during the slow period between the end of the football season and baseball's spring training.

The Browns signed offensive end Horace Gillom of Nevada on January 3, 1947. Gillom had played for Paul Brown at Massillon, and Brown called him the best athlete he'd ever coached. Gillom was one of the African American players on the Wolfpack team whose presence led to the cancellation of a game at Mississippi State in November of 1946. Mississippi law prohibited Caucasians and blacks from playing against each other in sporting events. Negotiations between the two schools' athletic administrators went nowhere. Gillom would be Cleveland's third African American player. With Miami no longer in the AAFC, he wouldn't have to worry about being barred from any league games, as Marion Motley and Bill Willis had been in 1946 when the Browns played in south Florida.

The AAFC office released its first all-league squad on January 4. As with the Associated Press all-league team, only offensive players were honored. The quarterback was Cleveland's Otto Graham; fullback Motley of the Browns; ends Dante Lavelli of Cleveland and Alyn Beals of San Francisco; halfbacks Glenn Dobbs of the Dodgers and Spec Sanders of the Yankees; guards Willis of Cleveland and Bruno Banducci of the 49ers; tackles Bruiser Kinard of the Yankees and Martin Ruby of Brooklyn; and center Bob Nelson of Los Angeles.

In the winter of 1943–44, the American Association, baseball's highest classification of minor league, came forward with a plan to put football teams into its cities. Nothing came of it. The idea was revived in January of 1947, when NFL commissioner Bert Bell arranged to meet with Frank Lane, president of the American Association. They were to discuss the leasing of Association ballparks for use by minor league football teams, to be sponsored by the NFL. "We are interested in getting ballparks and establishing minor football leagues,"[9] said Bell. What Bell didn't say was that a minor league system modeled on major league baseball's would give the NFL a place to send players who didn't make their team's roster to hone their skills, rather than releasing them and making them available to the AAFC. When needed, the minor leaguers could be called up by the parent club, just as baseball teams did.

One such minor league already existed. The Pacific Coast League apparently decided to move its season to the winter months so as not to compete with the NFL and AAFC. Both leagues had placed teams in Los Angeles, and the AAFC had a franchise in San Francisco, but the PCL continued to operate clubs in both cities. A game between Los Angeles and San Francisco resulted in the suspension of a pair of 49ers players for signing on as "ringers" with the San Francisco Clippers.

49ers head coach Buck Shaw announced on January 8 that tackle John Woudenberg and end Eddie Ballati had been suspended indefinitely and fined the curious sum of $236.36 for participating in a PCL game with the Clippers, using assumed names. Woudenberg played under the name Courtney Thorell. Ballati's fake name wasn't revealed. The amount of the fine represented the amount from the AAFC championship game players' pool that each 49er had received for finishing second in the western division. Each player, according to the Associated Press, had a clause in his contract preventing him from playing football for another team "until August 1st of the following season."

Rufus Klawans was president of the PCL and had no use for the AAFC. Klawans had spoken to the NFL owners in the spring of 1946 and proposed declaring the AAFC an outlaw league, slapping a five-year ban from organized football on any player who cast his lot with the new league. Klawans would hold a hearing on the Clippers' use of the two "ringers," at which Clippers owner Frank Ciraolo, general manager Gil Dowd, and head coach Bill Howard would be asked to testify. Howard said he saw no reason why Woudenberg shouldn't suit up for the Clippers. "We felt it was perfectly okay to use him, because he wasn't on the outlaw list provided by the National League, with which we have a working agreement,"[10] said the Clippers' coach. Klawans didn't agree and ordered the game forfeited to Los Angeles. The Clippers had won, 24–19.

The punishment for Woudenberg and Ballati, in addition to their fines and suspensions, would be determined by the next commissioner of the AAFC. It was anticipated that the owners would choose Crowley's successor at their winter meeting in late January. Published reports said the list of candidates the league's executive committee would consider included, but wasn't limited to attorney Don Miller; Columbia University head coach Lou Little; Navy head coach Tom Hamilton; former Democratic senator Jim Mead of New York; former Democratic Ohio governor Frank Lausche; Postmaster General Robert Hannegan; and two sportswriters: Warren Brown of the *Chicago Herald-Tribune*, and Whitey Lewis of the *Cleveland Press*. Lewis' name was submitted by Browns owner Mickey McBride, who obviously held no grudges, since Lewis had been a frequent critic of the AAFC, didn't think much of the quality of play, and had predicted its demise in a column written in November of 1946. Or, perhaps, McBride had a keen sense of humor.

The International News Service tried to put an end to the speculation on January 24, when it stated categorically that Major General Leslie R. Groves had been approached by at least one AAFC owner, and possibly two, about the job and would be hired by the end of the month.

It appeared in mid-January that the Yankees had scored another coup for the AAFC in the battle for college stars turning professional. Charley Trippi was an All-American halfback from the University of Georgia who'd been drafted by the sad-sack Chicago Cardinals and the Yankees. He wanted to play both football and baseball, and the Yankees offered him the opportunity to do both for one organization. Trippi was an outfielder and shortstop who hit .475 for the Bulldogs in the spring of 1946. He was negotiating baseball deals with the Chicago Cubs and Boston Red Sox. By signing with the Yankees, he could play for a baseball farm team from April until August, when he'd report to football training camp.

"I don't think we will have much trouble reaching an agreement," Trippi said on January 16. "The Yankees definitely gave me the best offer I have received, and I simply want to talk to Wally Butts, my Georgia coach, and several other people before signing up."[11] Unfortunately for Dan Topping, who owned both the baseball and football Yankees, one of the other people Trippi spoke with was Cardinals owner Bill Bidwill.

Topping had offered Trippi a four-year football contract for $60,000, and a two-year baseball contract for an unspecified amount. Bidwill countered with an offer of a four-year contract for $100,000 and said he'd use his influence with Cubs owner Phil Wrigley to get Trippi a contract with Chicago's National League team. Topping heard of Bidwill's offer and put a four-year, $105,000 football contract, plus bonuses, on the table. Topping still wanted to sign Trippi for his baseball team for two years, with a proviso: after two years, Trippi would have to choose between football and baseball as his career. Bidwill wouldn't ask Trippi to make a decision after two years, but he had a good idea which way Trippi was leaning.

"Actually, I don't know how good of a baseball player he is, and neither does Charlie," said Bidwill. "I think, though, his heart is in football."[12]

Said Trippi, "I would like to play both sports and find out for myself just which one suits me best."[13] He accepted Bidwill's offer. The red-faced Yankees had to cancel the press conference they'd scheduled for January 18 to announce Trippi's signing.

Signing Trippi took most of the sting out of losing another player the Cardinals though they'd out-bid the AAFC for. Tackle Jack Carpenter of the University of Michigan was drafted by both the Cardinals and the Browns. Wire services erroneously announced that he'd signed a contract with Chicago. He signed with Cleveland on January 21 and said he had no idea where the wire services had gotten their information.

Where was the cash coming from to sign players like Trippi to $100,000 contracts? It certainly wasn't coming from the profits racked up by professional football teams in 1946. The *Press* revealed on January 17 that the Browns, who led all of pro football in attendance the previous season, averaging an un-heard of 57,000 per home game, had a gross income of $1,262,461.27 for the year. After expenses, McBride had made a profit of only $5,739. It was still a far better financial showing than most of his fellow owners.

The *Press* also claimed, echoing a wire service report from late December, that an NFL owner was ready to abandon the old league and join fellow deserter Topping in the AAFC. Bob Yonkers, who covered the Browns for Cleveland's afternoon newspaper, said the AAFC would liquidate the Brooklyn franchise and replace it with Alex Thompson's Philadelphia Eagles. According to Yonkers, the Dodgers had lost $125,000 in 1946, and some of Bill Cox's fellow owners blamed him for the financial beating he took. The un-named owners reportedly didn't think Cox had put much effort into building a competitive team in 1946, and they didn't think he was doing much to improve his club for the coming season. And Cox, according to Yonkers, wasn't looking forward to a second season of sparse crowds at Ebbets Field. Thompson, meanwhile, was tired of the NFL being dominated by owners George Preston Marshall of the Redskins, George Halas of the Bears, Curly Lambeau (representing the people of Green Bay, who owned the Packers) and the Mara family, owners of the Giants. Yonkers admitted the story was only a rumor.

With Charlie Trippi under contract to the Cardinals, the next big-name collegian the NFL and AAFC would try to entice into their ranks would be halfback Claude (Buddy) Young of the University of Illinois. Young had finished fifth in the Heisman Trophy balloting in 1944, and quit the football team after the 1946 season. The reason was money. Young was married and had a family to provide for. He said he'd be open to "any offer that pays more than $90 a month."[14] Having lost the Trippi sweepstakes, the Yankees figured to make a big pitch for the speedy, shifty running back. But New York denied having signed Young days after he quit the Illini football team.

Friction in the front office of the Los Angeles Dons was reported in mid–January. Head coach Dudley DeGroot and general manager Ed (Slip) Madigan had feuded throughout the 1946 season, while DeGroot was coaching the team to a 7–5–2 record and third-place finish in the western division of the AAFC. The Dons' board of directors would try to iron out the differences between the two men. If that failed, either DeGroot or Madigan would be fired. After leading the Redskins to the 1945 NFL championship game, DeGroot had resigned due to disagreements with management. History was repeating itself 3,000 miles to the west.

When the NFL owners met to piece together the league's 1947 schedule, which would be expanded to 12 games, they'd give preference to the teams fighting with the AAFC for fans and their money. The Bears, Rams, Cardinals and Giants all shared their cities with AAFC teams. The Giants shared New York with two AAFC competitors, the Yankees and the Dodgers. The league would give those clubs favorable dates, and favorable opponents, at home in order to try to lure patrons away from the AAFC. That announcement was made by NFL public relations director George Strickler, who also revealed that the AAFC had made yet another peace overture toward the establishment. Strickler said the AAFC, growing weary of the rapidly escalating cost of doing business (in other words, signing players), wanted to negotiate what he termed "secret deals" with the NFL regarding college players drafted by both leagues. Strickler said there was no need to go into detail because the proposal had been turned down flat by the NFL owners.

The AAFC owners had a good reason for wanting to control the cost of signing college players. The players were in the rare position of being in the driver's seat in contract talks, at least the star players. They played both leagues off against the other, knowing that the power in negotiations would revert to the owners soon enough, when the two leagues merged, or when the AAFC went out of business. Some enjoyed their new-found leverage to the hilt, trying to drive up the price further by claiming they were seriously considering going into some other line of work. Les Horvath, Ohio State's 1944 Heisman Trophy winner, said he might hang out his shingle after graduating from dental school rather than play professionally. He listened to what the Rams and Browns offered, and signed with Los Angeles.

Glenn Davis and Doc Blanchard, the "Mr. Inside" and "Mr. Outside" of Army's powerful teams of the mid–1940s, both said they'd fulfill their military commitments rather than seek deferments to turn professional. And Buddy Young, days after quitting Illinois' football team to find a job, said, "I might not play professional football at all. I don't know whether I'm ready for professional football, I mean mentally ready." It wasn't mentioned whether or not Young was smiling coyly when he added, "Of course, if some professional club offered me a contract, I'd have to look at it. It's up to the professional teams to decide if I'm ready."[15] Young wasn't an All-American, but he was among college football's best players, and he knew he'd be offered a contract for 1947. It was nice to be in demand.

While the NFL owners didn't enjoy the bidding wars any more than the AAFC owners did, they saw no reason to agree to any proposal that might ease the burden on both sides. As far as the NFL was concerned, no one had forced Arch Ward to start a new football league. The AAFC was responsible for the astronomical rise in salaries, and their owners could stew in their own juices. As one unidentified NFL executive put it, "They were the fellows who were going to give the poor players what they had coming. Now let them meet our prices."[16] Like all new leagues, the AAFC's sales pitch had been one of economics: hook up with us and make more money. The bidding wars were hitting the NFL in the wallet, too, but their owners were enjoying watching the AAFC squirm. They were convinced the new league wouldn't last much longer. They weren't about to throw it a life preserver by agreeing to any "secret deals" with drafted players.

The differences between DeGroot and Madigan in Los Angeles proved to be irreconcilable. Madigan resigned on January 24, leaving the Dons' front office in disarray.

As the AAFC owners began their winter meeting, the NFL owners concluded theirs. They couldn't come up with a schedule, so they dropped the matter in commissioner Bell's lap. It would be up to him to schedule a dozen games for each of the league's 11 teams.

Bill Daley was a run-of-the-mill professional football player. Daley was a fullback who'd spurned the NFL to sign a two-year deal with the Brooklyn Dodgers in 1946. The Dodgers traded Daley to Miami during the season, and between the two teams he played in just three games (two with the Dodgers, one with the Seahawks), carrying the ball 14 times and gaining 63 yards. But he was about to become the latest point of contention between the AAFC and NFL.

The Pittsburgh Steelers still wanted Daley. They'd made him the seventh overall pick of the 1943 draft when they were the Phil/Pitt Steagles. Daley was an All-American in 1943, and had finished seventh in the Heisman Trophy balloting. His main claim to fame, however, was that he played for four different colleges in four years. The Steagles had drafted him out of Columbia University. The Steelers still owned Daley's NFL rights, and they were making noises about wanting to sign him, even though his AAFC contract ran through the 1947 season.

"We expect to respect the contracts of others," said Topping when the AAFC's winter meeting began in Chicago on January 29. "But we also expect to defend our own contracts, and our legal battles with the other league will start all over again if Daley signs with Pittsburgh."[17] The AAFC had fared well in court against the NFL so far. Angelo Bertelli's contract with the Dons had stood up in court, and Bertelli would be back with Los Angeles in 1947. The court had ruled that Chet Adams' contract with the Cleveland Rams had been voided when the team moved to Los Angeles, and Adams spent 1946 with the Browns. There's little doubt the contracts Ted Fritsch and Vince Banonis signed with the Browns would have been upheld in court had the team chosen to pursue the matter. But the Browns had an abundance of talent without Fritsch and Banonis, and Paul Brown didn't want players who didn't want to play for him.

When the Seahawks went belly up at the end of the 1946 season, commissioner Crowley decreed that the contracts of their players became property of the league. The league then awarded those contracts to the Baltimore franchise when it replaced Miami. And that would form the basis of the Steelers' argument if they signed Daley. It was the NFL's contention that the contracts of Miami's players were automatically voided when the team folded, making all of the former Seahawks free agents. It would be a difficult argument to make since former NFL commissioner Elmer Layden, upon declaring the Brooklyn Tigers franchise vacated after Topping defected to the AAFC, had ruled that all the Tigers' contracts became the property of the NFL, and then subsequently awarded them to the Boston Yanks. To argue the opposite in Daley's case would have been contradictory.

Brooklyn's Glenn Dobbs was voted the AAFC's most valuable player at the league's winter meeting. The voting was done not by the press, but by the league's head coaches. The coaches couldn't vote for their own players. Dobbs got five votes. His coach, Cliff Battles, cast his ballot for Otto Graham. San Francisco's Buck Shaw didn't attend the meeting. Baltimore didn't yet have a head coach.

Once they'd graduated from West Point, Glenn Davis and Doc Blanchard were entitled to four-month furloughs before their military commitment began. Both players asked that the furloughs be deferred until the fall, so they could use their time off to play professional football. Davis had been drafted by the Dodgers and Blanchard by the 49ers in the AAFC. The furlough request was denied by the Army on February 1. In order to turn pro, Davis and Blanchard would have to resign from the Army. It was a course neither was expected to pursue.

On February 10, Bob Yonkers, the same reporter who'd told readers of the *Cleveland Press* that the Philadelphia Eagles would probably replace the Brooklyn Dodgers in the AAFC, told his readers that Davis and Blanchard had signed three-year contracts with the 49ers. Brooklyn had traded Davis' draft rights to San Francisco for the good of the AAFC. It was assumed "Mr. Inside" and "Mr. Outside" wanted to continue playing together in the pros, and it was also assumed they'd rather play for a strong team in a glamorous city like San Francisco than for the bedraggled Dodgers in dingy Brooklyn. Yonkers said Davis and Blanchard had each received a $100,000 contract, plus signing bonuses of $10,000 apiece. If the report was true, it was a major victory for the AAFC, assuming Davis and Blanchard resigned from the Army to turn professional, which both men had sworn they wouldn't do.

From San Francisco, 49ers general manager John Blackinger immediately denied Yonkers' story. Yonkers stood by his reporting. He said he'd expected Blackinger's denial, and told his readers to ignore it. The deal with Davis and Blanchard was done.

Baltimore Colts principal owner Bob Rodenberg got his man on February

10. Rodenberg signed Purdue University head coach Cecil Isbell to a five-year contract to coach the Colts, with financial terms not disclosed. Isbell may have insisted on the long contract. He took a look at the roster he'd inherit from the wreckage of the Miami franchise and told Rodenberg he'd need a few seasons to build a contending team.

Isbell spent five years quarterbacking the Packers (1938–1942) before returning to his alma mater as head coach. His record at Purdue was mediocre (15–14) in his three seasons on the job. Nonetheless, he said he'd received five coaching offers from the professionals, "but this one was just too good to pass up."[18] He and his new boss set to work beefing up Baltimore's roster immediately.

"We will leave in a few days in a station wagon for California," said Rodenberg. "We'll go out by the southern route and come back by the northern, and we intend to contact players at every major college and university in the country."[19]

Although his colleague, Bob Yonkers, had written that Davis and Blanchard would resign from the Army and play for the 49ers in 1947, the *Press'* college football writer, Jack Clowser, begged to differ. Clowser said he didn't think the two stars would try to wiggle out of their obligation to the Army, then got verification straight from the horse's mouth. "Doc and I have definitely made up our minds not to resign," Clowser quoted Davis. "We'll stay in the regular Army."[20]

Pro football was fought in the trenches in the 1940s. But the AAFC, due mainly to the forward thinking of Paul Brown, had made much more effective use of the pass than the NFL did. The new league's passers established a professional record by completing 48.4 percent of their tosses in 1946, breaking the mark of 45.6 percent set by the NFL the year before. The AAFC threw 2,225 passes and completed 1,091 for 15,073 yards and 133 touchdowns. Just 8.3 percent of the passes attempted in the AAFC were intercepted.

A name no one had mentioned as a candidate for the AAFC commissioner's job was hired on February 27. The league's executive committee selected four-star admiral Jonas Ingram to succeed Crowley, who was free to concentrate on his job as head coach of the Rockets. Ingram, who was to retire from the Navy just days after his appointment, had been commander of the Atlantic fleet in World War II. But his football roots ran deep, and he proclaimed it to be the sport he'd always loved. Ingram played for Navy in 1905 and '06, and was the academy's first All-American. He returned to the academy as its head coach in 1915, serving for two seasons and posting a record of 9–8–2. His teams lost to Army both seasons, 15–7 and 14–0.

The 60-year old Ingram said he'd meet with Crowley to discuss the transition in the commissioner's office on March 15. But he saw his chief responsibility as reaching a peace accord with the NFL. "I knew Bert Bell when he

Paul Brown, who dragged professional football into the modern era, on the Cleveland sideline during an AAFC night game (Michael Schwartz Library, Cleveland State University).

was in knee pants," cracked the new AAFC leader. "I expect I'll be seeing him real soon. We both have our problems, and we should talk them over. There is no reason why the two leagues can't work out their problems in a businesslike and amicable way. I'll meet 'em halfway."[21]

Ingram was offered a five-year contract, the same length Crowley had signed. He rejected the offer, settling instead for a one-year pact at $30,000. Ingram wanted to offer both sides a chance to walk away from the marriage after a year if it wasn't working. He told his new employers, bluntly, that, within 12 months, there was every possibility they would decide they didn't like him. Or he may decide he didn't like working for them.

Bell had no comment about Ingram's hiring. That would have constituted an acknowledgment of the AAFC's existence, which the NFL was still trying to avoid.

The AAFC's coaches and owners gathered in Chicago on March 11 to piece together a 56-game season schedule for 1947. Paul Brown expressed confidence attendance would rise for the league's second season. "All of our owners started with the understanding they would lose money for the first couple of years," Brown said. "From the lessons learned last year, and the inevitable increase of fan interest, we're bound to do better around the league."[22] Brown didn't explain why he thought an increase in fan interest was inevitable.

Crowley said his Rockets would play most of their home games on Friday nights. He backtracked from the position, taken when he purchased the team, that he was anxious to go head-to-head with the Bears and Cardinals on Sunday afternoons.

Commissioner Ingram hired an assistant on March 20. Ingram enlisted Commodore Oliver O. (Scrappy) Kessing as his deputy, even though the league's constitution didn't call for one. Ingram said his 56-year-old naval comrade would allow him to do a better job. Kessing had played football for Navy, and served as graduate manager for athletics while Ingram was athletic director, from 1926 to 1929.

"He will represent me wherever he might be, and he knows my stand on every subject that might develop in the commissioner's office,"[23] said Ingram, adding that he hired Kessing with the full approval of the league's owners. Kessing was hired for one year, and his salary wasn't specified.

Speaking in Baltimore on March 24, Ingram addressed reports that Crowley's resignation hadn't been entirely voluntary. Reports circulated that some of the AAFC's less influential owners weren't happy with his performance, claiming he pandered to the "haves" at the expense of the "have-nots." And the AAFC had plenty of "have-nots." Ingram made it clear who would be in charge of the AAFC.

"The owners of the league don't own me," he said, adding, "I can be as tough as Judge Landis."[24] Ingram was referring to Kenesaw Mountain Landis, the federal court judge hired in 1921 to clean up baseball after it was alleged eight members of the Chicago White Sox had conspired with gamblers to throw the 1919 World Series to the Cincinnati Reds. Though the eight players were acquitted by a jury, Landis barred them from baseball for life anyway.

Before accepting the commissioner's job, Landis demanded and received virtually dictatorial power over major league baseball, and he wielded it for the next 23 years, long after the stench of the "Black Sox" scandal had subsided, and many owners questioned whether they'd ceded too much authority to the commissioner.

Ingram's reference to Landis was also a reference to a gambling scandal his NFL counterpart, Bert Bell, was struggling with. The day after the Bears beat the Giants, 24–14, for the 1946 NFL championship, it was revealed that gamblers had offered Giants fullback Merle Hapes and quarterback Frank Filchock $2,500, plus off-season jobs paying $15,000, to throw the game to Chicago. A notorious gambler by the name of Alvin Paris had bet the Bears would win by 11 points or more. Bell, New York City mayor Bill O'Dwyer, police commissioner Arthur Wallander, and Giants co-owner Tim Mara learned of the bribe and met to discuss the situation in O'Dwyer's office. They called in Hapes and Filchock and confronted them with the accusation. Hapes admitted being approached by the gamblers, Filchock denied it. Hapes wasn't permitted to play in the game, Filchock was and endured a horrid afternoon, completing just nine of 26 passes and throwing six interceptions. Fans could hardly be blamed for believing Filchock had been on the take. Bell and the NFL were still dealing with the fallout from the scandal in March of 1947. Both players were suspended by Bell for "actions detrimental to the welfare of the National Football League." Filchock played one more game in the NFL, with Baltimore in 1950. Hapes' career was over.

According to testimony in the trials of Paris, and three other men involved in the bribery attempt, Hapes was more than willing to help throw the game. Filchock thought it over, then refused, though his performance in the Polo Grounds that mid–December afternoon might indicate otherwise. Then again, would a player attempting to throw a game be so blatant about it? One of the trial judges claimed Filchock had been an innocent victim of circumstance.

Ingram had a warning for AAFC players, and any gamblers who might try to tempt them: gambling wouldn't be tolerated by the new commissioner.

There would be no need for the AAFC to go to court to force Bill Daley to honor the contract he'd signed with Brooklyn in 1946. The Colts, who inherited Daley's contract from the defunct Seahawks, traded Daley to the Rockets for halfbacks Billy Hillenbrand and Don Griffin in late March. Although Daley had a year left on his original deal, he agreed to a two-year pact with the Rockets on March 25. Terms weren't released. Daley missed most of the previous season after breaking his ankle while practicing with the College All-Stars for their game against the Los Angeles Rams.

The AAFC's owners spent much of March arguing among themselves about the 1947 schedule. Ingram's voice reportedly could be heard through

5. Exit Crowley, Enter Ingram

the closed door of the room the owners were meeting in on March 31 as they tried to resolve the matter. "They wanted a man to run this league who could get tough," the commissioner thundered. "Well, you've got him, and I mean business! We'll stay here until we get this schedule thrashed out, and I don't care if it takes three days!"[25]

One of the disagreements dealt with travel to the west coast. The Browns wanted to make just one trip to California to play both the 49ers and Dons. That was fine with the Dons, but not the 49ers, who protested that such an arrangement would require them to make four trips east during the season. Owner Tony Morabito wasn't concerned that his players would get jet-lagged. He was concerned about the cost of four cross-country trips. If the schedule couldn't be fixed, Morabito planned to insist that the other seven teams, the Browns included, chip in to pay his travel expenses. The 49ers prevailed, and the Browns made two trips to the west coast in 1947. It did take the owners three days to forge a schedule everyone could accept. The owners ratified the fourth draft of a schedule on April 2. The last games of the regular season would be on Sunday, December 7, and there would be only a week for the eastern and western champions to prepare for the title game on December 14.

Buddy Young and Dan Topping had no comment on a report that surfaced on April 2 that Young would sign with the Yankees. Actually, the report re-surfaced, since it had been rumored in late January, just after Young quit Illinois' football team, that he'd signed with New York. All Topping would admit to was that he was "willing to talk contract" with Young, but was "making no effort to contact Buddy."[26]

Topping would need special permission to sign Young since his class wouldn't graduate until the spring of 1948. Young quit the Illini to make money to support his wife and child, some of which he hoped to earn by playing in an all-star game between collegians and professionals that had been scheduled for January 12 in the Los Angeles Coliseum. The game was canceled, but it cost Young his amateur standing. He was declared ineligible for all amateur athletic events by the Amateur Athletic Union shortly afterward, although the connection between the AAU and the NCAA wasn't made clear.

If Young signed with the Yankees, he wasn't expected to ever suit up for them. Speculation was Topping would bow to pressure from his fellow owners to immediately trade Young to the Rockets for the good of the league. Young was from Chicago and would've given the Rockets a big-time drawing card in their battle for fans with the Bears and Cardinals.

Cecil Isbell's search for talent had taken him and Colts owner Bob Rodenberg to Texas, where Isbell signed two-time Longhorns All-American end Hubert Bechtol on April 2. The problem was Bechtol had already signed a contract with the Pittsburgh Steelers. Isbell said the contract with the NFL was void because Bechtol wasn't yet 21 years old when he'd signed it. Given that reasoning, Isbell didn't explain how Bechtol's contract with Baltimore could be valid since Bechtol still wasn't 21 years old. He wouldn't turn 21 until April 20. Isbell also said if the Steelers wanted to fight for Bechtol, the Colts were ready and willing to stake their claim to him in court.

Ingram visited Cleveland in early May to speak at Paul Brown's annual clinic for high school football coaches. The *Cleveland Press* expected him to touch on a number of topics pertaining to the AAFC when he addressed reporters, most notably the status of Young. According to the newspaper, Young had signed with the Yankees. Ingram said nothing about the former Illinois star. He did say a Texas businessman he declined to identify was negotiating with the AAFC to obtain a franchise for Dallas, which would begin play in the fall of 1948. The newspaper speculated that if Dallas was given a team, it would replace Brooklyn.

After months of rumors that dated back to the middle of January, Young signed with the Yankees on May 16. Crowley immediately said his club would "make overtures to the Yankees to get him for the Rockets."[27] First, it had to be determined whether Young was eligible to play in the AAFC. He was not eligible for the NFL, because his college class wouldn't graduate for another year. That should also have disqualified him for the AAFC. Ingram said he'd examine Young's contract as soon as it was submitted to his office for approval. According to the Associated Press, Ingram had responded on May 15 to a letter from Bill Murray, head coach at the University of Delaware, expressing concern over the possibility that Young would sign with the AAFC. Murray, speaking on behalf of all college football coaches, was afraid that allowing Young to join the Yankees would open the floodgates to a stampede of college players trying to abandon the amateur ranks and play for pay before their classes had graduated. The league had signed several players who still had college eligibility remaining, but their classes had all graduated. Ingram's response wasn't noted, but it's reasonable to assume he assured Murray that college football had nothing to fear from the AAFC.

Or did it? Dan Topping claimed Ingram had already approved Young's contract. But the United Press reported on May 23 that the contract was still being "examined" by the commissioner, and that his deputy, Scrappy Kessing, had been sent to Illinois to investigate Young's collegiate status. Nothing more was reported about the matter.

The Buffalo Bisons wanted to create their own identity. After one year of sharing the nickname "Bisons" with the city's minor league hockey and baseball clubs, management sponsored a name the team contest in the late spring of 1947. The entries receiving the most votes were the Blue Devils (third runner-up), the Nickels (second runner-up) and the Bullets (first runner-up). The winning entry was Bills, in honor of the famous wild west entertainer and frontiersman "Buffalo Bill" Cody. The entry was submitted by James F. Dyson, who received $500 for his creativity. The nickname was so well-received that Buffalo's team in the American Football League would adopt it beginning in 1960.

On July 12, commissioner Ingram received an angry letter from W.A. Alexander, the athletic director at Georgia Tech. Alexander accused the New York Yankees of using "a slick approach to tie up football players, still eligible for college competition, to the Yanks."[28] Specifically, Alexander was upset that a contract calling for a salary of one dollar for the 1947 season had been mailed to guard Bill Healey of the Yellow Jackets' football team. Healy was a junior athletically, meaning he had two years of eligibility remaining. Alexander thought the Yankees were trying to trick Healey into signing and giving up that eligibility.

Alexander's letter to Ingram said the contract was a standard AAFC player contract, and the envelope included a letter signed by Yankees head coach Ray Flaherty. The letter explained that "in order to hold you on our reserve list, it is necessary to send you a contract for the 1947 season. Enclosed is a contract for $1 which will complete our obligation to stay within league rules."[29] Alexander noted that had Healey signed the contract, he would have forfeit his remaining college eligibility.

Deputy commissioner Kessing responded quickly to Alexander's protest and absolved the Yankees of any wrongdoing. Kessing pointed out that Healey had started classes at Georgia Tech in the fall of 1942. His education, and his athletic career, were put on hold by the war. Healey's class graduated in the spring of 1946, making him eligible to turn professional. He'd indicated that he planned to return to school and finish his education before considering professional football.

"In order to retain him on their reserve list and prevent other clubs of our conference from tampering with him, it was necessary under our rules for the Yankees to submit a contract to the player on or before August 1st," Kessing explained. "This was done that the Yankees might fulfill their obligation, but the player was told not to sign if he intended to continue in college athletics. Healey's receipt of the contract does not make him a professional, nor can it make him ineligible for college competition."[30] As far as the AAFC was concerned, any football player whose college class had graduated was fair game, regardless of how much college eligibility he may have. Players knew that signing a contract would put an end to their college careers, and the decision was theirs. Did they want to keep playing for nothing, or did they want to get paid?

A week after Alexander's protest, and Kessing's response, were made public, the NFL's owners met in a special single-day session to address the problem of signing players with eligibility remaining. The result was a resolution declaring that no player could be signed by an NFL team if that player had college eligibility left, even if that player's class had graduated, provided that player had registered for classes for his school's fall quarter. If, however, the player hadn't enrolled in classes, and indicated that he didn't intend to return to school, he was free to sign an NFL contract, as long as he obtained written permission from his college coach.

AAFC teams began their training camps in mid-July. The first team to report was the Rockets, who opened their camp in Two Rivers, Wisconsin, on July 15. New owner/head coach Jim Crowley welcomed 61 players and started putting them through two-a-day workouts. The last team to begin training was the Browns, who started defense of their AAFC championship in Bowling Green, Ohio, on July 29. Paul Brown invited only 47 players to camp, the fewest of any AAFC team. Of course, as defending champions, the Browns needed less help than any other club. But that didn't mean Brown was standing pat. Twenty of the players in their camp hadn't been with the Browns in 1946.

On August 11, Bert Bell ended the NFL career of former Green Bay guard Fred Vant Hull by invoking the rule prohibiting players from jumping their contracts to join AAFC teams. Vant Hull last played for the Packers in 1942. He enlisted in the Navy and contacted Packers head coach Curly Lambeau after his discharge. Lambeau told him Green Bay had no room on its 33-player roster for him, so Vant Hull signed with the Dons, but never suited up for them. Bell's banishment meant Vant Hull was ineligible to play for any team in the NFL or the minor Dixie, American or Pacific Coast leagues for five years. He never played professional football again.

The AAFC opened its second season with the exhibition match-up of the Yankees and Bills in Newark's Ruppert Stadium on August 18. A crowd of 11,000 watched New York smother Buffalo, 29–7. Four days later, the Baltimore Colts debuted and lost to the Bills in Hershey, Pennsylvania, 29–20.

While the Colts and Bills were playing a game that didn't count in a small town in southeastern Pennsylvania, the nation's sporting attention was on Chicago, where the annual college all-star game was played in Soldier Field. An overflow crowd of 105,840 watched the collegians stun the NFL champion Bears, 16–0. Leading the all-stars was hometown hero Buddy Young, who set up his team's two touchdowns with runs of 31 and 40 yards through the vaunted Bears defense. Young had cast his lot with the AAFC and would return to the Yankees' training camp after the game. A deal with the Rockets, to take full advantage of Young's drawing power in his hometown, couldn't be reached.

The Dons' quarterback Angelo Bertelli tore a knee ligament in an exhibition game against Brooklyn in Portland, Oregon, late in August. Estimates were that he'd miss at least two weeks. It was the start of an injury-plagued season for the former Notre Dame signal-caller. Without Bertelli, the Dons still managed to defeat the 49ers, 14–7, in an exhibition game on August 24. The crowd in Kezar Stadium for the practice game was estimated at a robust 40,000.

After opening their exhibition season in Oregon, the Dodgers stayed out west and tangled with the Rockets in Salt Lake City. Brooklyn quarterback Glenn Dobbs shattered the professional football record for longest punt when he kicked a 97-yarder from his own two yard line. The ball reportedly traveled 77 yards in the air, hit on the Rockets' 20, and bounced into the end zone. The previous record had also been held by a Brooklyn Dodger, also against a team from Chicago, but of the NFL variety. Ralph Kercheval had boomed a punt 86 yards in a game against the Bears in 1935.

As the regular season approached, commissioner Ingram made another attempt to convince the NFL to allow its champion to meet the AAFC's champion on the field of battle in late December. "Last Thursday [August 21] at a meeting in Chicago of the owners of the All-America Football Conference," said a written statement issued by the league's public relations office, "I was authorized to issue the following challenge through the commissioner of the National League to its owners: the 1947 championship team of the All-America Conference challenges the 1947 championship team of the National League to a game to determine the world's championship of professional football, the entire net proceeds to be contributed to an outstanding national charity or outstanding national cause in the interest of the American people, or the entire net proceeds go to the winner, to be distributed as said winning ball club may decide." Ingram and the AAFC owners hoped to win the battle of public opinion by pledging to donate the proceeds to charity. Ingram estimated that an AAFC-NFL championship game would produce a $250,000 gate.

Ingram left no doubt as to who he believed would win such a showdown. "We feel we have four teams better than anything they've got,"[31] said the commissioner. Those four teams were the defending champion Browns, plus the Yankees, 49ers andCed Dons.

On behalf of the NFL's owners, Bell's response was brief and to the point: not interested.

Before the Browns launched the defense of their AAFC championship with an exhibition game against Baltimore on August 29, head coach and general manager Paul Brown talked about the financial future of professional football in less than glowing terms. "We haven't come down to Earth yet in professional football," Brown said. "Hence, we're not a substantial business operation. I don't mean only our conference, either. Take Pittsburgh and Washington in the National League. They sell out regularly, yet they don't make any money. This is because their parks are too small and their costs of operation are too high. All the clubs must level out before you can say that professional football is sound financially. Salaries are sky high, and they probably won't come down until the cut-throat bidding of the two professional leagues, the All-America and the National, get together on some kind of an agreement regarding drafted players. Then all of us will have a chance to make money."[32]

Although nothing mattered more to Brown that winning football games, as a minority owner of the Browns, he was aware of the bottom line. As general manager, it was his job to negotiate contracts with the players he also coached. Even though the Browns had shattered all existing professional football attendance records in 1946, drawing almost 400,000 fans to their regular season home games, they managed a meager profit of barely more than $5,000. Brown, and the rest of the AAFC, would continue to plead with the NFL to agree to a common draft. The pleas would fall on deaf ears.

6

1947

Never one to mince words, Paul Brown had a message for the 47 players who reported to the Cleveland Browns' training camp at Bowling Green State University in late July.

"We're no longer champions," he reminded them. "Today, we start all over."[1]

After as much as six weeks of preparation for some teams, like the Chicago Rockets, the AAFC opened its second regular season on Friday, August 29. Less than a week earlier, more than 105,000 spectators had filled Soldier Field to watch the annual college all-star game. Less than half that number were on hand for the kickoff to the AAFC's second season, but the gathering of 41,182 was more than satisfactory to the new owners of the Rockets. The outcome of the game left something to be desired.

Jarring John Kimbrough's fourth quarter touchdown lifted the visiting Los Angeles Dons to a 21–17 victory over the Rockets, spoiling the debut of Chicago's new part owner and head coach, Sleepy Jim Crowley. With new, and supposedly financially stable ownership, plus new players and a head coach with an outstanding record (86–23–11) compiled in college, big things were expected from the Rockets in 1947. Big things were anticipated from the AAFC as well, at least in the opinion of an unidentified correspondent for the United Press, who wrote after watching the Dons-Rockets donnybrook: "The All-America Football Conference, which struggled for existence last year, was off to a terrific start today, and is apparently ready to challenge the National League in every respect this season." Initial observations, at least as far as the Rockets were concerned, were highly deceiving.

The rest of the AAFC's opening weekend saw the Bills upset the Yankees in Buffalo, 28–24, and the 49ers beat the Dodgers, 23–7, in San Francisco. A record crowd of 32,385 in Civic Stadium watched rookie quarterback George Ratterman toss a four-yard pass to rookie running back Chet Mutryn on a fourth down play in the fourth quarter to steal Buffalo's victory from the favored Yankees. New York's rookie running back, Buddy Young, carried the ball 13 times for 81 yards in an impressive professional debut. At Kezar Stadium, the Dodgers scored three minutes into the game, then didn't score again. The 49ers tallied in every period to post an easy victory before 31,874 onlookers.

As had been the case in 1946, the AAFC started its season several weeks before the NFL. The older league invaded AAFC territory by scheduling an exhibition game between the Bears and Boston Yanks in Akron's Rubber Bowl for Sunday, September 7. That was two days after the Browns opened their season at home against Buffalo. An advertisement for the contest on the front page of the *Cleveland Plain Dealer*'s sports section touted the Bears as "the greatest team in pro football" and noted their seven world championships, including 1946. These were fighting words in northeastern Ohio. Reserve seats for the game sold for $3.60, the same price as the most expensive seat to a Browns game in Municipal Stadium.

George Halas brought his Bears to northeastern Ohio early and was among the 63,263 spectators at the Browns' opening night game against the Bills on Friday, September 5. Cleveland wasn't impressed by Buffalo's upset of the Yankees and cruised to a 27–0 lead at halftime. The Bills staged a mild second-half rally but succumbed, 30–14. Ratterman, the Bills' quarterback, wanted to play for the Browns but was snubbed by Paul Brown, who reportedly declined to offer him a contract because he left Notre Dame with a year of sports eligibility remaining. That hadn't stopped Brown from signing many other players in the same situation.

Said Brown of his team's first game in defense of its league title, "We got up a good head of steam and took a commanding lead in the first half, and then let down and looked bad in the last two periods. I started the kids in the second half and Buffalo almost tore them apart. That just goes to show you the difference between an experienced player and one just breaking in."[2]

The Bills had out-scored the Browns, 14–3, in the second half, leading head coach Lowell (Red) Dawson to say, "Once we did get going, we gave them a battle. I think we were down a bit after our victory over New York." Dawson then sounded an ominous note for the rest of the AAFC. "Cleveland is a much-improved club over last year."[3] That was all the AAFC needed.

Halas spoke to reporters after the game. He refused to compare the NFL to the AAFC, but conceded that "the Browns certainly have a fine team, and Paul Brown is doing an excellent job."[4] That was as much as the writers could wring out of Papa Bear.

The Bills didn't leave Cleveland empty-handed. They lost the game, but gained a player. Guard Floyd Konetsky, a former Cleveland and Los Angeles Ram who was the last player to be released by the Browns following their training camp in 1947, accepted an offer to play for Buffalo. The offer was made just two days after Konetsky had signed a contract as an assistant coach at Cleveland's Western Reserve University. The school voided his contract to allow him to resume his playing career.

While the Browns were polishing off Buffalo in their home opener, the Yankees celebrated their first home game of the season by whipping the Rockets, 48–26. A Yankee Stadium crowd of 37,777 watched as Bob Kennedy ripped off the longest run from scrimmage in AAFC history, a 78-yard touchdown scamper. Harvey Johnson's six PATs for the Yankees were also a league record.

In San Francisco on Sunday, September 7, the 49ers edged the Dons, 17–14, before a gathering of 31,298. The 49ers sprinted to a 14–0 lead before the visitors fought back. Joe Vetrano's 12-yard field goal provided the winning points.

Two thousand miles to the east on that Sunday afternoon, the Bears and Yanks attracted 11,237 to their exhibition game in Akron. The Bears won, 37–20.

On Monday, September 8, the Baltimore Colts debuted before a crowd of 37,418 in Memorial Stadium. That was approximately 12,000 fewer fans than their predecessors, the Miami Seahawks, had drawn to their seven home games in 1946. The fans were treated to an unusual play on the game's opening kickoff. Brooklyn's Elmore Harris returned the kick to his team's 22 yard line, then was hit by Baltimore's Hubert Bechtol and fumbled. Brooklyn's Harry Buffington picked up the loose ball. Buffington described the action that followed. "I threw a good block and was spun around. And when I stopped spinning, there was the loose ball in front of me. I grabbed it and started for the goal. I didn't realize I was going in the wrong direction until I was about two strides from the goal line. I was going so fast, I couldn't stop. I saw [teammate] Mickey Collmer in the clear and tried to pass to him. The ball was knocked down, and Jimmy Castiglia of Baltimore fell on it for a touchdown."[5] The Colts also scored on the second half kickoff, which Billy Hillenbrand returned 98 yards for the touchdown. Baltimore won, 16–7.

With the AAFC and the NFL at war, a proposition for another professional league was put on the table on September 8. The odd suggestion came from John Taylor, the president of the University of Louisville. Taylor was tired of the hypocrisy of college football and wrote a letter to the presidents of 14 universities, which weren't identified in the Associated Press story, suggesting they start a collegiate professional league. Under Taylor's plan, colleges would hire football players the same way they hired professors. The players would represent the school that hired them on the gridiron, but they wouldn't be students, and they'd be paid for their efforts. The AAFC and NFL had nothing to fear from Taylor's revolutionary idea.

With the 1947 season barely a week old, the AAFC's first blockbuster trade was announced on September 8. The Dodgers traded their star quarterback,

Glenn Dobbs, to the Dons, who sent their injured quarterback, Angelo Bertelli, to the Rockets, who traded their star tailback, Hunchy Hoernschmeyer, to Brooklyn.

"I know I am giving up an edge in kicking by trading Dobbs," said Dodgers coach Cliff Battles, "but Hunchy will give us a superior field general. Dobbs made several strategical [sic] mistakes this fall. In addition, Hoernschmeyer is five years younger than Dobbs."[6]

Perhaps the worst strategic mistake Dobbs made, according to published reports, was being a pain in the butt to his coach, the Dodgers' front office, and his teammates. Although he said the right things, such as the optimistic statements about the Dodgers' future after signing a five-year contract in December of 1946, Dobbs was alleged to be more concerned about his personal statistics than the team's performance. One writer referred to him as "a one-man show." He refused to listen to instructions from Battles or the front office, yet his trade was met with a near-rebellion by Dodger fans.

The Dodgers hosted the Browns in their first game without Dobbs, and Paul Gould of the *Brooklyn Daily Eagle* predicted, "I wouldn't be surprised if the crowd is under 10,000. The fans liked Dobbs, although most of them were aware of the friction between him and the front office. Last year, Bill Daley squawked because Dobbs didn't let him play more, so Cox got rid of Daley for stirring up trouble."[7]

Added Dan Parker of the *New York Mirror*, "Bill Cox, co-owner of the Brooklyn football Dodgers, once threatened to move the club to Dallas if Brooklyn didn't support it. Having parted with Glenn Dobbs, the only player on his team who meant anything to the box office, William had better start looking around for a landing place farther away than Dallas—just in case."[8]

Ironically, the trade of Dobbs had just the opposite effect at Ebbets Field's ticket window—but only briefly, and for the wrong reason. The largest crowd to watch a football game in Brooklyn since 1942—18,876—showed up for the visit by the Browns. The vast majority, however, paid their money to jeer the home team. No one could abuse the home players like Brooklyn fans, and the Dodgers gave them plenty to jeer about. Cleveland scored three touchdowns in the game's first five minutes and plastered the Dodgers, 55–7.

That same evening in Los Angeles, the Yankees refused to be intimidated by the largest crowd ever to watch an AAFC game and beat the Dons, 30–14, in Memorial Coliseum. For the record, the throng of 82,675 was the largest ever to witness a regular season professional football game.

On Sunday, September 14, the Bills beat the Rockets in Buffalo, 28–20. Another record crowd (for Civic Stadium) of 33,648 was on hand. In San Francisco, the 49ers battled the elements and the Colts for a 14–7 victory. A crowd of 25,787 peered through the fog that enveloped Kezar Stadium to watch fullback Norm Standlee score both of the home team's touchdowns.

San Francisco's Norm Standlee is tackled by Cleveland's Alex Kanter in the Browns' 14–7 victory at Kezar Stadium in November of 1946. Lou Saban (66) and John Yonakor (50) close in to assist (Michael Schwartz Library, Cleveland State University).

The Bills kicked off the fourth weekend of competition by kicking around the Rockets in Soldier Field, 31–14, on Friday, September 19. The game started promisingly for Chicago with quarterback Sam Vacanti connecting with Crazylegs Hirsch on a 76-yard touchdown catch and run for an early 7–0 lead. That was the high point of the evening for the Rockets and the 22,865 people in attendance. Ratterman torched the Chicago secondary for 18 completions in 31 attempts, good for 294 yards and four touchdowns. Buffalo may have been the most improved team in the AAFC.

Two days later, the Yankees concluded their two-game California road trip with a 21–16 victory over the 49ers. A sell-out crowd of 52,819 at Kezar Stadium groaned as the visitors took a 21–3 lead in the third quarter. The 49ers fought back, but not far enough. In Cleveland, the Browns made quick work of the Colts, scoring three touchdowns in their first 12 offensive plays. The defense took it from there, and Cleveland posted a 28–0 victory in front of 44,257 fans.

Attendance figures at most of the AAFC's games in September had been impressive, but that didn't silence the critics who insisted the league would be hard-pressed to make it through the 1947 season. Former commissioner Jim Crowley had a message for the pessimists. Although his winless Rockets were having problems, he believed the AAFC as a whole was faring nicely.

"The league is healthier now than it ever was," Crowley said. "And what's more, it's here to stay. Anybody who thinks it's on the verge of folding up is way off the beam. In fact, I think we're in healthier condition than the National League. They're harder up for players than we are. I don't know how long it will take for the leagues to get together, but I do think there will be peace sooner than a lot of people think."

Crowley then assessed the status of the AAFC one month into its second campaign. "Already you can see a marked improvement in Buffalo, San Francisco, Los Angeles, and even in New York and Cleveland. Baltimore is a healthy franchise, too. I don't know what's going to happen in Brooklyn. That just doesn't seem to be a good football town. And as far as we're concerned, we can't go any place but up."[9]

That upward movement didn't start when the Rockets hosted the Browns on Friday, September 26. Cleveland took a 27-0 lead into its dressing room at halftime and toyed with Crowley's bunch in the second half, winning 41-21. The attendance at Soldier Field wasn't keeping pace with that of other AAFC cities, with the exception of Brooklyn. Only 23,067 paid to see the Rockets do battle with the defending league champions.

Baltimore fans needed just two home games to obliterate the 1946 attendance figures of the Miami Seahawks, which, admittedly, didn't require much effort. The Colts drew a mob of 51,563 to their second home game on Sunday, September 28. The patrons left unhappy as the Yankees defeated Baltimore, 21-7. More people saw the Colts on that late September afternoon than paid to see all of the Seahawks' home games in 1946. The Colts had drawn 88,981 to their first two games in Memorial Stadium. The Seahawks drew 49,000 to their seven games in the Orange Bowl.

In Buffalo, a crowd of 36,099 watched the 49ers overcome a 17-point deficit to crush the Bills, 41-24. San Francisco scored 20 points in the fourth quarter to win going away. Buffalo had drawn franchise record crowds to each of its first three games. With four home games remaining, the Bills were within 16,000 of equaling their 1946 attendance.

After one month of the 1947 season, the AAFC standings:

Eastern Division

New York	4-1-0	144-91
Buffalo	3-2-0	125-132
Baltimore	1-3-0	30-80
Brooklyn	0-4-0	42-142

Western Division

Cleveland	4-0-0	154-42

San Francisco	4-1-0	111-73
Los Angeles	2-2-0	100-89
Chicago	0-5-0	102-172

As had been the case in 1946, the AAFC's strongest teams were still in the west.

It remained to be seen if the 49ers and Dons could challenge the Browns, and if the Bills had improved enough to give the Yankees a run for their money in the east. Buffalo had the offensive firepower, thanks largely to the efforts of George Ratterman, its new quarterback. But the Bills' defense was suspect. Only the league's two winless clubs, Chicago and Brooklyn, had given up more points than Buffalo.

On the other end of the spectrum, the Colts had scored just 30 points through four games, averaging barely a touchdown per contest. Baltimore needed offense, and hoped a former NFL MVP could provide it. The Colts signed Frank Sinkwich on October 3, after he'd been placed on the Yankees' retired list. Sinkwich was the NFL's 1944 MVP while playing for the Lions, and his signing had been a coup for the AAFC. But he played in just four games for New York in 1946, carrying the ball seven times for 20 yards. He'd seen limited action in 1947, playing in three games and picking up 33 yards on 16 carries. The Yankees claimed Sinkwich decided to call it quits due to a knee injury. But his friends back home in Georgia said Sinkwich was fed up with being a benchwarmer. The Colts asked the Yankees for permission to talk to him, and a doctor assured them Sinkwich's knees were fine. His presence was expected to strengthen Baltimore's offensive backfield.

Brooklyn stretched Chicago's losing streak to six on October 3 with a 35-31 victory in Soldier Field. Most of the scoring was done in the fourth quarter. The Rockets led, 17-14, entering the final 15 minutes. The two teams then combined for five touchdowns in the last period, with Brooklyn tallying three of them. The attendance was 16,844. As the Rockets' futility grew, their fan support, minimal to begin with, steadily decreased.

Fan support was not an issue for the Browns. Predictions early in the week were that 70,000 would storm the gates of Municipal Stadium for Cleveland's clash with the Yankees on October 5. On the morning of the game, that prediction grew to 80,000. The Browns had 17,000 seats to sell on game day. The weather was perfect for an early autumn Sunday, and those tickets were gobbled up quickly by football-hungry fans. Ten thousand potential patrons were turned away empty-handed. The attendance of 80,067 resulted in a gate of $168,000. It was the second-largest crowd in AAFC history, surpassed only by the gathering of better than 82,000 in the Los Angeles Memorial Coliseum for the Dons-Yankees game a few weeks earlier. Just like their baseball namesakes, the Yankees drew a crowd wherever they played.

Also like their baseball brethren, the football Yankees projected a certain swagger and played with an attitude befitting the champions Dan Topping intended for them to be. That attitude didn't endear Ray Flaherty or his team to Paul Brown, who remembered what Flaherty said to his team after their first game against the Browns, a 24–7 loss in Cleveland in September of 1946.

"You ought to be ashamed of yourselves," Flaherty snarled, "losing to a Podunk team with a high school coach."[10] Brown never forgot the slight, and there was no AAFC coach he enjoyed beating more than Flaherty.

Of the match-up on October 5, Flaherty said, "Speed will determine the outcome of this game. These are the two fastest teams in the league, and I think the Browns are a little faster than we are. But we're much faster than a year ago, with Buddy Young in our backfield. In fact, we're a better club all around."[11]

Brown agreed. "They're a better ball club than last season. Sanders is an improved ballplayer, and Young has stepped up the offense."[12] Improved or not, the Yankees still couldn't beat the Browns in front of a packed house on Cleveland's lakefront. Flaherty's team suffered its fourth straight defeat at the hands of the Podunk team and its high school coach, 26–17.

Elsewhere in the AAFC on October 5, the Colts scored almost as many points in one game as they'd scored all season as 29,556 watched in Baltimore. The Colts took a 28–14 lead in the third quarter, only to have the 49ers rally to tie the game in the fourth. San Francisco drew to within a touchdown on a pass from Frankie Albert to Alyn Beals, who lateraled to running back John Strzykalski. The visitors tied the score on a 38-yard pass from Albert to Earle Parsons. The game ended in a 28–28 deadlock.

In Los Angeles, the Bills edged the Dons, 27–25. Checking the game's statistics will reveal a "4" in the line score for Los Angeles in the fourth quarter. Trying to protect a 27–21 lead, Bills quarterback Ratterman took the unusual step of giving the Dons a pair of intentional safeties by purposely stepping out of the end zone. The odd tactic worked, disappointing a crowd of 36,087. Newly-acquired Glenn Dobbs split the Dons' quarterbacking duties with Charley O'Rourke.

It had been rumored that more than one Detroit group expressed an interest in an AAFC franchise to compete with the Lions. On October 6, commissioner Ingram was reported to be in Detroit, talking with Walter Briggs, the owner of baseball's Tigers and the stadium they played in, about joining the AAFC in 1948. After the discussion, Ingram said he was optimistic, but gave no indication which existing team a Detroit club would replace. The rumor mill said a Detroit AAFC team would have the city all to itself, because Briggs was angry with Lions owner Fred Mandel and had already informed him that the Lions' lease at Briggs Stadium wouldn't be renewed for 1948. Since there was no other suitable place in Detroit for the Lions to play, Mandel would either have to fold the team or re-locate it.

Detroit wasn't the only new venue the AAFC was looking at. The United Press reported on October 8 that the league was considering three cities for the 1948 season, but didn't identify them. As for the present, Ingram said, "all of our clubs will finish 1947 play where they are now, and if any change is made, it will be before the 1948 or 1949 season. All of the teams are making money now, and it's no secret the Brooklyn Dodgers and Chicago Rockets have the hardest road."[13] The claim that all of the AAFC's teams were making money was met with widespread skepticism, if not outright disbelief.

With Dobbs in his line-up, the Dons' coach Dudley DeGroot knew the time had come to diversify his team's offense. When he arrived in Cleveland for his team's October 12 game with the Browns, DeGroot told reporters, "I had a long time to study the conference statistics on my way here. I noticed we have attempted fewer passes than any other team in the league. In fact, we aren't even close to our nearest rival. That's not good for a pro team. All teams in this business have to throw a lot if they expect to go places, and we haven't been doing that."[14] Through five games, the Dons had thrown 89 passes, an average of 18 per contest.

Los Angeles had given the Browns trouble in 1946, administering one of their two defeats. Paul Brown went on record mid-week as warning the fans to expect another defeat the following Sunday. "We're ripe for picking," said a disgusted Brown. "I can tell by our attitude. We'll get licked by the Dons as sure as I'm standing here and making that prediction three days in advance. We were in just such a frame of mind last year when San Francisco came in here and blew us off the map. We thought we were too good for them."[15] It isn't known if Mickey McBride and the folks in the Browns' ticket office, with 18,000 ducats available for the game, appreciated the coach's candor.

Being a master psychologist, Brown may have made his stinging comments knowing his players would read them in the city's evening newspaper and raise their dander. Or he may have accurately gauged the attitude of his team. Or both. Those who took his remarks to heart and bet on the underdogs won big. As 63,124 looked on, the Dons beat the Browns for the second time in three meetings, 13–10. Ben Agajanian's 23-yard field goal with less than three minutes to play proved to be the game-winner. Agajanian took advantage of a second chance to be a hero after missing a 28-yard attempt because the Browns were penalized for having 12 players on the field. Cleveland lost three fumbles in the game, and Los Angeles converted each turnover into points.

Radio and film star Don Ameche, a co-owner of the Dons, watched the game with McBride in the Browns' owner's private box. He enjoyed the outcome much more than his host did. "I don't have the time to make all the trips with the Dons, but I had a hunch this might be a good game," said Ameche. "I'm glad I didn't miss it."[16]

Controversy erupted at the conclusion of the Bills-Colts game in Civic Stadium. With 13 seconds remaining in the contest, and the Bills on top 20–15, Red Wright of Baltimore recovered a Bills fumble on Buffalo's 39 yard line. With seven seconds showing on the clock, Colts quarterback Bud Schwenk threw a pass to Lamar Davis, who tight-roped down the sideline and appeared to score the winning touchdown. Field judge Eddie Tryon, however, ruled that Davis had stepped out of bounds inside the one yard line, and umpire George Simpson fired the gun ending the game. The Colt players and coaches protested, insisting that Davis had remained in bounds and scored the winning points. Failing to win that argument, they said if Davis had stepped out, the clock should have stopped and the Colts should have been allowed to run one more play. Both arguments were rejected. Some of the 27,345 fans swarmed the field after the game, and police were needed to disperse them. Colts co-owner Bob Rodenberg immediately sent a wire to the league office, protesting the game's outcome.

Things were quieter in San Francisco, where the 49ers kept the visiting Rockets winless, 42–28. San Francisco led, 42–7, after three periods, and the defense rested in the fourth. The Rockets were generous guests, losing six fumbles and throwing four interceptions. Attendance was 23,300. The Rockets weren't much of a draw, even if their presence virtually guaranteed a victory for the home team. In Yankee Stadium, the Associated Press correspondent was almost apologetic about New York's 31–7 dusting of Brooklyn, explaining that even though "the Dodgers never crossed the mid-field stripe under their own power ... the game wasn't anywhere near the lop-sided way it seemed." In an effort to prove his point, the unidentified correspondent said that hardly any of the 21,822 spectators departed until the game was over.

All was not well in Ebbets Field, where the departure of Glenn Dobbs and the arrival of Hunchy Hoernschmeyer hadn't changed the fortunes of the woeful Dodgers. At a press conference on October 15, Bill Cox denied that he had discussed the possibility of moving the team to Dallas with majority owner Gerald Smith. Cox also denied approaching Branch Rickey, part owner and general manager of the baseball Dodgers, and asking about Rickey's interest in operating both teams. He didn't deny that the Dodgers might not return in 1948.

"We lost more than $100,000 last year," Cox confessed. "I don't think I'd want to take a beating for years and years. If we can keep it going, we certainly want to."[17] So much for Ingram's assertion that all AAFC teams were making money.

Rodenberg had several differences of opinion with the officiating in his team's October 12 loss to Buffalo. The wire he sent to commissioner Ingram at AAFC headquarters immediately after the game detailed four mistakes, all of which contributed to Baltimore's defeat.

(1) Field judge Eddie Tryon was wrong when he ruled Lamar Davis had stepped out of bounds inches short of the goal line on what turned out to be the game's final play. Rodenberg insisted Davis had scored.

(2) If Davis had stepped out, umpire George Simpson erred by firing the pistol signifying time had expired, ending the game. Rodenberg claimed the clock should've stopped when Davis stepped out of bounds, and the Colts should've had time to run one more play.

(3) The officials made a mistake when they flagged a Colts player for a personal foul in the fourth quarter. Rodenberg said the unnecessary roughness call was unwarranted.

(4) The officials were incorrect when they awarded Buffalo's Chet Mutryn a touchdown on a two-yard run that cut Baltimore's lead to 12–7 in the second period. Rodenberg said his defense had stopped Mutryn short of the goal line.

Ingram denied all four protests. The Buffalo victory was official. It wouldn't be the last time the Colts would feel they had been robbed by the referees in a loss to the Bills.

The Colts left Buffalo with a defeat on the field, but they gained a new player. They signed Floyd Konetsky, who'd been released by the Bills before the game. Baltimore became the third team to employ Konetsky in 1947, following Cleveland and Buffalo.

In mid–October, Washington Redskins quarterback Slingin' Sammy Baugh became, in the words of the United Press, "the first NFL personality even to admit there was such a thing as the All-America Conference." Not only did Baugh acknowledge the AAFC's existence, he wanted a championship playoff between the two leagues.

"They've got some doggone good football players," said Baugh, "and while I haven't seen them play at all, they must be putting on a good brand of football."[18] Despite Baugh's stature in the NFL, his comments were ignored.

Brooklyn's Hunchy Hoernschmeyer enjoyed a record-setting night on October 17 in Ebbets Field. Hoernschmeyer's 86-yard touchdown run was the longest in AAFC history, as were his 179 rushing yards for the game, gained on just 19 carries. Hoernschmeyer shattered the previous single-game mark of 143, set by Marion Motley of the Browns in 1946. The new record wouldn't stand for long. Barely a week. The Dodgers and Bills fought to a 14–14 tie as just 9,272 watched.

Ingram announced on October 18 that the league had changed officiating assignments for the weekend's game between the Colts and Dons in Baltimore. Tryon and head linesman Bill Ohrenberger, who'd been involved in the disputed game in Buffalo the previous week, were re-assigned. They were replaced by field judge Bill Pritchard and head linesman Fay T. Vincent.

Sammy Baugh, the future Hall of Fame quarterback of the Washington Redskins, was among the few NFL players to defy the league's official policy and acknowledge the existence of the AAFC, and concede that it played some pretty good football (Library of Congress).

"We have every confidence in the integrity of Tryon and Ohrenberger," Ingram said, "but it would be unfair to them to send them into Baltimore at this time, although both expressed willingness to go."[19] The Colts were stomped by the Dons, 38–10, in a defeat that could in no way be blamed on the officials. That may help explain why Rodenberg tried so hard to convince Ingram to overturn the result of the loss in Buffalo. Victories for the Colts were few and far between. Baltimore hadn't won a game since opening day. A crowd of 36,852 in Memorial Stadium saw Ben Agajanian of the Dons set a new AAFC record with a 53-yard field goal, breaking Lou Groza's previous mark of 51 yards. New AAFC offensive records were being established almost each week.

In Cleveland, the Browns out-lasted the Rockets, 31–28, in a game that wasn't as close as the score indicated. The Browns led, 31–14, with four minutes remaining before Chicago rallied for two late, and meaningless, touchdowns. The victory, witnessed by 35,266 fans, kept the Browns in first place in the AAFC west, and launched them on a 29-game unbeaten streak that would stretch into the 1949 season.

President Harry Truman didn't attend any of the AAFC's games the weekend of October 24, despite the fact that, two days earlier, he'd been presented with a silver season pass. Why the league waited until the 1947 season was more than half over to present Truman with the pass isn't known. If Truman used the pass any time during the season, his presence wasn't noted in any newspaper game accounts.

Three days after the loss in Cleveland, the Rockets' eighth without a victory, assistant coach Hampton Pool resigned. Pool had suffered through Miami's 3–11 season in 1946, and joined the Rockets after the Seahawks folded. His coaching experience in the AAFC consisted of three victories and 19 defeats. Pool said he had been "considering for some time to resign to accept better opportunities. They have become available now and I feel I should leave at this time."[20]

Rumors abounded that Rockets head coach Jim Crowley was also about to step aside. "I don't know where that story started," responded Crowley's partner, Bill Toohey. "There is absolutely no foundation for it. Crowley is still our coach, and he will continue to direct the team as long as he wants to, as far as I'm concerned."[21]

Two days after Pool quit, the Rockets hosted the Yankees and lost, 28–7. New York mangled Chicago's defense for 395 yards rushing, 250 of them gained by Spec Sanders on 24 carries for an AAFC and professional football record. The NFL still does not recognize records set in the AAFC, which is why Sanders' amazing performance is nowhere to be found in the official record books. On the opposite end of the spectrum, the Rockets' rushing game was non-existent, losing 20 yards for the game. Chicago native Buddy Young thrilled his friends and relatives in the Soldier Field stands by returning the second half kickoff 95 yards for a score. A crowd of 20,310 watched Chicago lose its ninth straight.

On Sunday, October 26, the Browns made their first of two visits to the west coast and defeated their only serious rival for the western division title, the 49ers, by a count of 14–7. The game was witnessed by 54,325 fans. About 400 miles to the south, in Memorial Coliseum, the Dons destroyed the Colts, 56–0, in the second game of their coast-to-coast, home-and-home series.

Glenn Dobbs threw four touchdown passes to please a crowd of 27,000. Over the past two weeks, the Dons had overwhelmed the over-matched Colts, 94–10. Colts head coach Cecil Isbell knew what he was talking about when he told Rodenberg he'd need several seasons to build the remnants of the Seahawks into a contender.

In Civic Stadium, the Bills had no trouble with the out-manned Dodgers, 35–7. Brooklyn dressed only 30 players and lost linebacker Caleb (Tex) Warrington when he was thrown out of the game by head linesman Bill Ohrenberger, to the delight of 23,762 Bills fans. Warrington objected to being flagged for unnecessary roughness and chose to discuss the matter with Ohrenberger. Deputy commissioner Scrappy Kessing was in the press box and witnessed the incident. The league fined Warrington $500 and suspended him for the rest of the season.

The Dodgers achieved their first Ebbets Field victory of the season on Halloween night, topping the Rockets in a steady downpour, 7–3. Most Brooklyn residents preferred to stay indoors where it was warm and dry and hand out candy to trick-or-treaters. Just 2,960 attended the game.

At the conclusion of October, the AAFC's standings:

Eastern Division

New York	6–2–0	220–131
Buffalo	6–2–1	221–193
Brooklyn	2–6–1	112–256
Baltimore	1–6–1	83–212

Western Division

Cleveland	7–1–0	225–107
San Francisco	5–2–1	188–143
Los Angeles	5–3–0	232–136
Chicago	0–10–0	199–305

Heading into the final full month of competition, there were playoff races in both divisions. The Bills trailed the Yankees by just a half game in the east. The Browns and 49ers were battling again in the west, with the Dons within striking distance. Los Angeles' record, and its numbers, had been artificially inflated by its two-game cakewalk over the Colts.

The Bills had drawn record crowds to Civic Stadium all season, and the biggest crowd yet watched their heroes lose to the Browns, 28–7, on Sunday, November 2. There weren't enough seats to accommodate the 43,167 onlookers, so spectators spilled over onto the running track that surrounded the gridiron. Cleveland scored once in each quarter, including a pro football record 99-yard touchdown pass from Otto Graham to Mac Speedie in the third period. Graham faded back into his end zone to pass, and Speedie caught the ball at the goal line, then scampered 100 yards for the score.

Watching the game from the press box, Bills assistant coach Red Conkright was spotted wearing a tie clasp with the inscription CLEVELAND BROWNS 1946 WORLD CHAMPIONS. Conkright had been an assistant with the Browns the previous season, and the tie clasp, given by management to the players and coaches, left no doubt as to their opinion of their status. After the game, Conkright said that should Buffalo win the AAFC east championship, owner Jim Breuil would ask that the title game be played in Cleveland's huge stadium, assuming the Browns were the western winners. That comment provides insight into what was truly important to the men bankrolling the AAFC. Breuil, despite being a multi-millionaire whose team was attracting record crowds to almost every home game, was more than willing to turn his back on the fans who'd supported his team so well in 1947, as well as sacrificing whatever home field advantage his players might have enjoyed (there was the minor matter of trying to win the game) for the possibility of a big payday in a stadium with more than twice as many seats as Buffalo's. Of course, Breuil's players would have benefited from a bigger payday, too.

In New York, the Yankees took advantage of Buffalo's loss to pad their lead in the eastern division. Bruce Alford returned the game's opening kickoff 82 yards for a touchdown, and the home team was off and running. So was quarterback Spec Sanders, who carried 14 times and averaged ten yards per carry. In leading the Yankees to a 35–21 victory over Baltimore, Sanders set a new AAFC record in the category of "touchdowns accounted for." Sanders was responsible for 21 New York scores, 13 by rushing and eight by passing. That broke the record of 19 shared by Glenn Dobbs and Otto Graham. Sanders' 13 rushing touchdowns broke the record of 12 he'd set in 1946, and his 774 yards rushing established a new mark (for rushing yardage by a quarterback) breaking the record of 709 he set the previous season. With 21,174 watching, the Yankees moved a game and a half ahead of the Bills.

In Los Angeles, the 49ers essentially eliminated the Dons from the championship race with a 26–16 victory. San Francisco quarterback Frankie Albert threw four touchdown passes for the winners. For the losers, Ben Agajanian converted a 51-yard field goal, but missed an extra point for the first time in four years. Agajanian had kicked 31 consecutive extra points in 1947. A crowd of 53,716 in the Coliseum watched the 49ers stay within a game and a half of the front-running Browns. The Dons fell three games behind with five to play.

The Rockets ended their ten-game losing streak on Friday, November 7, defeating Baltimore, 27–21, at Soldier Field. It was Crowley's first win as a head coach in the professional ranks. Also his last. Although professional football history books and reference websites credit Crowley with an 0–10 record as head coach of the Rockets, my research disputes the claims that he'd resigned after Chicago's tenth game of the season. The newspapers researched for this book reported nothing about a resignation. They also said nothing about former assistant Hampton Pool returning to the team and taking over as head coach. The newspapers clearly stated that Crowley was still in charge of the Rockets through the season's final game, after which he resigned. The battle between the weakest teams in the AAFC attracted only 5,385 witnesses.

After drawing their smallest crowd ever at home, the Dodgers hit the road and drew the smallest crowd ever at Cleveland's Municipal Stadium for a Browns game. The 30,279 who expected to watch Paul Brown's gang run roughshod over the visitors on November 9 were stunned as the Dodgers nearly, and should have, pulled off the biggest upset in AAFC history. The Browns survived due to some spectacular ineptitude on the part of the Dodgers' special teams, and thanks to a good play by their own. Four touchdowns were scored, but only one extra point was converted. Brooklyn's Phil Martinovich may have endured the single worst kicking day in professional football history.

Mickey Collmer of the Dodgers opened the scoring with a four-yard run in the first period. Martinovich missed the extra point. Cleveland answered with a 72-yard pass from Otto Graham to Dante Lavelli. Lou Groza converted, and the score was 7–6 after one quarter. Graham connected with Mickey Mayne on a 15-yard scoring pass in the second quarter to increase the Browns' lead to 13–6. The usually reliable Groza flubbed the extra point. The Browns offense then went into hibernation. In the fourth quarter, Roy (Monk) Gafford's 79-yard touchdown bolt cut the Dodgers' deficit to 13–12. It remained that way when Horace Gillom broke through Brooklyn's protection and blocked Martinovich's extra point attempt. In the interim, Martinovich tried field goals of 29, 34, 43 and 46 yards. Each boot fell short of the goal post. The Browns escaped with a victory they didn't deserve.

The futility of the Dodgers' kicking game was typical. Martinovich attempted 20 field goals in 1947. He converted an anemic three of them, for a success rate of 15 percent. For his four-year career, including one season (six games) with the Bears and one (two games) with the Lions, Martinovich connected on 13 of 38 field goals, or 34.2 percent. He made 88 percent of his extra point tries in 1947. He retired at season's end.

Up the Lake Erie shoreline in Buffalo, the Bills took advantage of typical early November weather to shut out the Dons, 25–0, in the snow and mud of Civic Stadium. The inclement weather held the crowd to a disappointing 21,293 for the Bills' last home game of the season. The Bills drew 217,706 fans to their seven home games, nearly 100,000 more than 1946. The victory kept the Bills a game and a half behind the Yankees, who came from behind to defeat the 49ers in Yankee Stadium.

The New York—San Francisco tussle was dominated by special teams play, as the Cleveland—Brooklyn game was. Thanks to a recovered fumble and two blocked punts, the 49ers built a slim 16–14 lead in the fourth quarter. Harvey Johnson's 19-yard field goal put the Yankees on top, 17–16, with eight minutes to play. Bruce Alford sealed the deal when he recovered a blocked Frankie Albert punt in the San Francisco end zone for the final margin of 24–16. The crowd at Yankee Stadium was 37,342.

The awarding of home field advantage in the AAFC's championship game to the eastern division winner at a league meeting in mid–November was a formality. The western division winner had enjoyed home field the year before, so it was the eastern winner's turn. The Bills reluctantly agreed to host the game if they won the division, despite the small seating capacity of Civic Stadium.

The reason why the Bills (at least ownership) wanted to play the AAFC championship game on the road was on display Sunday, November 16, when the Browns clinched their second straight western division title by clobbering the 49ers, 37–14. It was the Browns' last appearance at home for the season, and 76,504 fans turned out to say farewell and thanks for another division title. The gate for the afternoon was $166,000. That was the kind of money Jim Breuil wanted to be able to split if his team won the eastern division title. Even a standing room only crowd in Civic Stadium couldn't generate that kind of payday.

"We really played a good football game," said Paul Brown in the Cleveland dressing room. "I feel good about it. We took advantage of every mistake they made and didn't commit any serious errors ourselves."[22]

"They just had too many fireworks for us," moaned 49ers coach Buck Shaw. "We don't have enough depth of material. This was the best game the Browns have played against us. That gets disheartening."[23]

In Brooklyn, the Dodgers won their second home game of the season, topping the Colts, 21–14. Another small gathering of 9,604 was in attendance.

Dudley DeGroot resigned as head coach of the Dons on November 18. In announcing the coaching change, team president Don Ameche said DeGroot's decision to quit was "best for all concerned."[24] DeGroot had beaten the Browns twice in three meetings, but he hadn't beaten the Dons' biggest rival, the 49ers. Nor had he been able to lead the Dons to a win over the Yankees. They had also lost their last three games after demolishing the woeful Colts in back-to-back games in late October. DeGroot, who had one year left on his contract, left a team with a 5–6 record. His overall coaching mark in Los Angeles was 12–11–2. But DeGroot wasn't entirely finished with the Dons. In order to earn the contract settlement he'd negotiated with Ameche, he was assigned to scout the Browns for their Thanksgiving day match-up with the Dons in Los Angeles. DeGroot's assistants Mel Hein and Ted Shipkey would serve as co-head coaches for the rest of the year. Co-coaches wasn't an uncommon practice in that era.

The 49ers shook off the disappointment of being eliminated from the western division championship race by bouncing the Rockets, 41–16, in Chicago on Friday, November 21. San Francisco piled up a 34–0 lead before halftime, then cruised. Only 5,791 Chicagoans had nothing better to do that night than pay their way in to Soldier Field to watch the carnage.

New York City was the place to be for football fans on Sunday, November 23. The Yankees, Giants and Dodgers were all playing at home at the same time. The Yankees were hosting the Browns in what proved to be a preview of the AAFC title game; the Giants took on the Packers in the Polo Grounds less than a mile away, and the Dodgers battled the Dons in Ebbets Field.

The Dons responded positively to their new head coaches, defeating Brooklyn, 16–12. An AAFC record five field goals were kicked in the contest, three by Ben Agajanian and two by Phil Martinovich, 67 percent of his successful field goal attempts for the season. A crowd of 11,866 people who couldn't get tickets to Yankee Stadium or the Polo Grounds attended the game.

Just a year after losing the NFL championship game to the Bears, the Giants hit the skids in 1947 and entered their game with the Packers winless. They stayed winless, tying the visitors, 24–24. The contest attracted 27,939 fans to the Polo Grounds.

At the same time, on the other side of the Harlem River, an epic battle between the two best teams in the AAFC unfolded. As 70,306 fans cheered, the Yankees pummeled the Browns until late in the first half. Four rushing touchdowns, three by Spec Sanders and one by Buddy Young, gave the Yankees a seemingly insurmountable 28–0 lead. Cleveland broke the shutout on a 34-yard pass from Otto Graham to Bill Boedeker just before the intermission. As the players headed for their dressing rooms, a few of the Yankees, notably Young, unwisely taunted the already angry Browns. A few defensive adjustments and a riled-up bunch of Clevelanders turned the tables in the second half, and the game ended in a 28–28 tie. The three games in New York had drawn 109,865 fans.

The tie with the Browns was costly to the Yankees as the Bills beat the Colts in Baltimore, 33–14. New York had blown a golden opportunity to stay a game and a half in front of Buffalo. Instead, as 19,563 fans watched and moaned, the Bills shaved a half game off their first-place deficit. The Yankees were 9–2–1, the Bills 8–3–1. A showdown loomed in Yankee Stadium the following week.

On November 24, commissioner Ingram said he wanted to know what the intentions of the owners of the Rockets and Dodgers were for 1948. Both were drawing pitiful crowds to their games, particularly the Rockets, who had attracted fewer than 6,000 fans to their last two home games in 100,000-seat Soldier Field.

"I expect to know shortly if Bill Cox intends to operate the Dodgers next year," said Ingram. "And Bill Toohey, [the] Rockets' owner, must declare his intentions."[25] Toohey didn't waste any time responding. He said the Rockets would remain in Chicago in 1948. Ultimately, however, Toohey wouldn't be the one to make that decision.

The Associated Press reported on November 25 that a Los Angeles city council representative had invited the AAFC champion to meet the NFL champion in a "charity game" to be played in the Coliseum on either December 27 or 28. Harold Harby was certain an AAFC-NFL championship game would pack the 100,000-seat arena. With tickets selling for five dollars, that would raise half a million bucks for the unidentified charity or charities. Harby sent the invitation to Ingram, who couldn't accept quickly enough. He said he would wait for Ingram's reply before issuing an invitation to Bert Bell. On behalf of the NFL, Bell wasn't interested.

For the second year in a row, the AAFC declined to concede Thanksgiving day to the Detroit Lions, who'd been playing at home on the holiday since 1934. In spite of DeGroot's scouting report, the Browns overcame an early 10-0 deficit and beat the Dons in Los Angeles, 27-17, in a contest attended by 45,009 fans. Despite the outcome, Paul Brown wasn't happy. He accused the Dons of playing dirty.

"There is no place in football for the dirty player," Brown sermonized. "Until he is eliminated, the game has a long way to go, and I blame the coach if his men play unfairly."[26]

The Dons' interim co-coach Mel Hein spent 15 seasons as a tough-as-nails center for the Giants from 1931 to 1945. His accomplishments made him among the first class of inductees in the Pro Football Hall of Fame in 1963. He wasn't about to take any lip from a balding, skinny coach who never played the game professionally.

"We played hard, tough football, and Brown doesn't like our style of gang-tackling the ball carrier. He went to the officials before the game and told them we played dirty football,"[27] scowled Hein. Los Angeles Rams head coach Bob Snyder, a former NFL player himself, watched the Browns-Dons game from the Coliseum stands. He was reported to be unimpressed by the defending AAFC champions.

On the day after Thanksgiving, representatives of the Bills were in U.S. District Court in Miami, filing a lawsuit against Harvey Hester, owner of the long-defunct Seahawks. The Bills wanted the $15,000 visiting team guarantee Hester owed them for their game in the Orange Bowl on November 18, 1946. Hester hadn't paid his players in a month by mid-November, and he also wasn't paying his fellow owners. In one of his last acts as commissioner, Jim Crowley had pledged the league would pay the bills Hester had accumulated which it felt morally obligated to pay. Either the league missed that one, or hoped Breuil would be willing to forget about it. Breuil wasn't.

If Buffalo was going to win the eastern division title, it would have to beat New York in Yankee Stadium on November 30. The young Bills weren't up to the task. With a crowd of 39,012 providing added inspiration, the Yankees pounded Buffalo, 35–13, to clinch the division crown and set up a rematch of the 1946 league championship game with the Browns. This time, the Yankees would have home field advantage. That, however, hadn't meant much a week earlier, when they'd blown a 28–0 lead and settled for a tie with Cleveland.

A slightly less significant game was played in Baltimore that same afternoon. The Colts were the only team the pitiful Rockets had beaten, and they got some revenge for the embarrassing setback, 14–7. Then again, a team that had won only twice, as Baltimore had, shouldn't have been embarrassed about losing to anybody. Not even to Chicago, which had won only once. Attendance at Memorial Stadium was 14,085, as the novelty for Baltimore fans of having a (supposedly) major league football team had been buried under an avalanche of defeats.

The New York Pro Football Writers Association hosted a meeting on December 1 and somehow managed to convince the commissioners of both the NFL and AAFC to attend. Bert Bell and Jonas Ingram certainly didn't share the dais, and there's no record of whether or not they even nodded to each other. Philadelphia Eagles owner Alex Thompson broke with NFL policy when he posed the question "should there be a common player draft between the two professional football leagues," and then turned and looked at the table where Bills coach Red Dawson was seated. Dawson stayed in town following his team's loss to the Yankees the day before to attend the meeting. He said he was in favor of a common draft. Thompson said he agreed. Professional football salaries had increased between 80 percent and 100 percent since the AAFC was born, and Thompson was tired of paying more than he felt he should have to for talent.

Thompson's comments weren't appreciated by Bell and Giants co-owner John Mara, who were seated at the same table as the Eagles' owner. Bell and Mara were asked the same question by the writers hosting the meeting and refused to answer. Ingram pounced on the opportunity to make another plea for a common draft, exhibition games between the AAFC and NFL, and a game between the two league's champions to determine the best team in professional football. Bell and Mara were unmoved. Thompson was in for a stern lecture as soon as Bell and Mara got him alone.

The AAFC's second regular season concluded with four games on Sunday, December 7. In Baltimore, the Browns tuned up for the championship game by destroying the Colts, 42–0. Cleveland's offense accumulated 559 yards even though most of the starters got the bulk of the afternoon off after building a big early lead. The defense never let up. The chance to watch the defending champs in action lured 20,874 fans to Memorial Stadium. Attendance-wise, 1947 had been a successful year for the transplanted Miami franchise. On the field, the product actually took a slight step backward.

The league's two runners-up, Buffalo and San Francisco, finished their seasons with a 21–21 tie in Kezar Stadium. After the defenses had dominated through the first three quarters, each team scored two touchdowns in the final period. The deadlock was viewed by 22,943 fans.

In Brooklyn, the Yankees blew a 17–3 lead before 14,166 fans, but rallied for a 20–17 victory over the Dodgers. Fourth quarter touchdowns by Hunchy Hoernschmeyer and Bill (Dub) Jones tied the score, but Harvey Johnson's ten-yard field goal with 32 seconds on the clock proved to be the game-winning points. However, in going all-out to win a meaningless game, Yankees head coach Ray Flaherty seriously damaged his team's chances to win the league championship the following week. Flaherty kept speedy scatback Buddy Young in the game in the fourth quarter in an effort to pull out the victory. Young suffered a sprained ankle. The ankle wouldn't sideline him for the championship game, but his effectiveness was curtailed.

In Los Angeles, the Dons spanked the Rockets, 34–14. What had begun with optimism slightly less than a year ago, when Jim Crowley resigned as AAFC commissioner to buy majority interest in the Rockets, ended with Crowley stepping down as the team's head coach after the game. Crowley had surrendered his duties as general manager mid-way through the season. He said he'd sell his 51 percent ownership share in the Rockets and retire from football. He had a job lined up with a manufacturing concern in New York City.

The game against the worst team in the league drew just 20,856 fans to the Coliseum. But overall, attendance had increased by over 160,000 at the Dons' home games in 1947. The AAFC was more than holding its own in the battle for Los Angeles.

The final AAFC standings:

Eastern Division

New York	11–2–1	.846	378–239
Buffalo	8–4–2	.667	320–288
Brooklyn	3–10–1	.231	181–340
Baltimore	2–11–1	.154	167–377

Western Division

Cleveland	12–1–1	.923	410–185
San Francisco	8–4–2	.667	327–264
Los Angeles	7–7–0	.500	328–256
Chicago	1–13–0	.071	263–425

Competitive balance improved in 1947. Five of the AAFC's eight teams had finished with records of .500 or better. The Bills had been in contention for the eastern division title until their 13th game. In the west, however, for the second straight year, the Browns were never seriously threatened even though the 49ers were strong again. The Dons put up a fight only through the first eight games, barely more than half the season.

The severity of the Chicago situation became public on December 8, the day after the season's final games. The Associated Press claimed the Rockets had lost more than $200,000, and owners John Brogan and Bill Toohey would sell their minority stake in the team. Crowley's 51 percent stake was already on the block, and word out of Chicago was that a deal had been reached with a group of unidentified businessmen whose net worth was approximately $33,000,000. Toohey and Brogan would retain minority shares in the team, and current minority stockholder R. Edward Garn would be named general manager. Garn had served as acting general manager since mid-season, when Crowley found that being majority owner, executive vice president, GM and head coach was more than he could handle.

The AAFC chalked up another victory in the player acquisition category in early December when the Browns signed quarterback Warren Lahr. Paul Brown and his staff had plenty of opportunity to watch Lahr in action as he was playing in their backyard at Cleveland's Western Reserve University. He wasn't drafted by an AAFC team, but had been selected by the Steelers in the NFL. Lahr chose to turn professional even though he had a year of college athletic eligibility remaining.

"I think he is one of the really good players in college football,"[28] Brown said.

When the numbers for 1947 had been tallied, the AAFC reported an attendance increase of 20.6 percent over the previous season's figures. The league's 56 regular season games had been viewed by 1,828,480 paying customers, an average of 32,651 per contest. Cleveland again topped all of professional football in attendance with 392,760 watching the Browns' seven games in Municipal Stadium.

Before the Yankees hosted the Browns in a re-match of the 1946 championship game, the AAFC's owners met in New York and, on December 14, went through the formality of terminating the Chicago franchise. Unlike the previous year, when the same owners terminated Miami's franchise with the intention of moving it to Baltimore, the Rockets weren't going anywhere. The league would run the team temporarily, which included conducting its draft on the day following the title game. Details were still being worked out regarding the transfer of ownership from the trio of Crowley, Toohey and Brogan to businessmen Daniel F. Rice and Colonel Henry Crown. Rice was a grain dealer and business partner of Ben Lindheimer, the majority owner of the Dons. Crown was president of Materials Service Corporation. After the Rockets were terminated, the meeting adjourned until December 16, when, in addition to conducting the league's draft, the matter of the future of the Brooklyn Dodgers would be addressed.

Said Paul Brown of his team's chances to successfully defend its AAFC championship in Yankee Stadium on December 15, "I wish we were in better shape. It's sure to be a bearcat of a game."[29]

Yankees coach Ray Flaherty sounded like a coach who believed he had the better team and was tired of losing to the Podunk team and its high school coach. "My club is up for this one just as it has been up for the other Cleveland games. We out-played them in one of the games, and held the lead for a long time in three others. I hope we can get a lead and keep it for once tomorrow."[30]

The Browns wasted no time making sure Flaherty's hope was frustrated. With 61,879 fans looking on, the Browns marched 67 yards for a touchdown in the first period. Marion Motley's 51-yard run put the ball on the New York 13, but the defense appeared to have denied the visitors when Bruce Alford intercepted Otto Graham's pass. The Yankees were flagged for defensive holding, and Graham made them pay for the mistake. He flipped a 12-yard pass to Mac Speedie that moved the ball to the one yard line. Graham sneaked the ball over for the score. Lou Groza, who hadn't been expected to play due to an injury, converted the extra point, and the Browns were up, 7–0.

The Yankees navigated to the Cleveland five in the second quarter. Three running plays gained one yard. On fourth down, Harvey Johnson booted a 12-yard field goal to draw New York to within 7–3. That was the halftime score.

In the third quarter, Browns defensive back Tom Colella intercepted a Spec Sanders pass at midfield and returned it to the Yankees' 41. Graham took advantage of the short field and handed off to Motley for a 16-yard gain. Passes to Edgar Jones for 11 yards and Mickey Mayne for eight moved the ball inside New York's 10. Jones scored from four yards out. Groza's injury had forced him out of the game, and linebacker Lou Saban kicked the extra point. Saban was no stranger to placekicking. With Groza on the sideline, Saban was a perfect four-for-four on extra points in the epic 28–28 tie with the Yankees three weeks earlier. The Browns had taken a 14–3 lead, and that was the final score.

It was a rough afternoon for Buddy Young, gamely gritting it out on a sprained ankle. Young personally killed two Yankee drives with costly fumbles, both of which the Browns recovered. The first was at the Cleveland 27. The second, in the closing minutes of the game, was lost at the Cleveland 19.

"It's nice to win," said Browns owner Mickey McBride. "I'm tickled to bring the championship back to Cleveland."[31]

"I guess we'll just have to keep trying," sighed Yankees boss Dan Topping. "This can't go on forever."[32] But Topping was mistaken. His Yankees would never defeat the Podunk team with the high school coach.

7

For the Good of the League

Possibly the craziest rumor to emerge from the four-year skirmish between the AAFC and NFL was floated during the owners' meeting in New York following the Browns' conquest of the Yankees. With the Dons looking for a new head coach, word got around that owner Ben Lindheimer's top choice to run his team was Curly Lambeau, the legendary head coach and general manager of the Green Bay Packers. Lambeau founded the Packers in 1921, when the NFL was known as the American Professional Football Association. He coached the Packers to six NFL championships, the most recent in 1944. The idea of Lambeau deserting the Packers to take over a team in the upstart AAFC was unthinkable, and Lambeau quickly denied the rumor. Lindheimer didn't. The story, ludicrous though it was, made for good publicity. And any added credibility it provided the AAFC was welcome.

Lindheimer said his next head coach would probably come from the Midwest (Lindheimer lived in Chicago), and that may have led to the Lambeau rumor. The Dons' next head coach would have ties to the Middle West, but his name wouldn't be Lambeau. Although Lindheimer refused to comment about the speculation regarding his team's next coach, he had something to say about the AAFC's Chicago situation. He said two groups of "stable and wealthy" investors were bidding for the remains of the Rockets, which the AAFC currently controlled. Whichever group won the bidding would be the third ownership in the Rockets' three-year existence. It would hire the team's third new coaching staff. Stability and the Rockets were rarely mentioned in the same breath.

As for the league's other trouble spot, the owners solved the Brooklyn problem by deciding they didn't have one. Commissioner Jonas Ingram declared on December 16 that "Brooklyn has fulfilled its financial obligations and therefore is a member in good standing."[1] That didn't stop reporters from asking Branch Rickey, the minority owner and general manager of the baseball

7. For the Good of the League

Dodgers, if he was interested in getting involved with the borough's football team. Rickey said he was considering investing in the football Dodgers, but he didn't think there would be a change in ownership since Bill Cox had met the club's financial obligation to the league. Rickey was nothing if not shrewd. He'd expressed an interest in getting involved with professional football three years earlier. He wasn't about to tip his hand too soon. Two days after the league meeting, Bob Yonkers, the professional football beat writer for the *Cleveland Press*, reported that Rickey would buy out Cox and majority owner Gerald Smith and take control of the Dodgers. The deal would be completed before the next scheduled owner's meeting in February. Yonkers also wrote that the AAFC was weary of making peace overtures to the NFL that were ignored, and no more such overtures would be forthcoming.

The AAFC owners decided their real problem continued to be a lack of competitive balance. The teams that had been strong in 1946 (Cleveland, New York, San Francisco and Los Angeles) were strong again in 1947. Buffalo had improved dramatically, more than doubling its victory total from three to eight. But Brooklyn had won just six games in two years, and the transplanted Seahawks were even worse in Baltimore than they'd been in Miami (2–11–1 compared to 3–11). The Rockets, who were just three points away from eight victories in 1946, had completely collapsed. What could be done about it?

Ingram was assigned the task of thoroughly studying each club's roster. It would then be determined how to fairly disperse the "unused talent" from the league's strong teams among its weak teams. Robbing from rich and giving to the poor, for the overall good of the AAFC. Competitive teams meant competition for the division championships, and that meant more fans. More fans, in turn, meant more revenue. With Ingram thus empowered, the meeting adjourned.

After a few months in the Army, Second Lieutenant Glenn (Mr. Outside) Davis decided he'd rather play football than serve his eight-year commitment to the military, which he'd agreed to when recruited to play for West Point. Davis filed an application to be relieved of his commitment shortly before Christmas. He revealed that information in a telephone conversation with 49ers owner Tony Morabito. He also revealed to Morabito that he planned to sign with the Rams, who owned his NFL rights. Provided the Rams agreed to match (or exceed) the deal he'd been offered by San Francisco. That was a deal an angry Morabito insisted Davis had already agreed to. The 49ers traded for Davis' draft rights after drafting his Army backfield partner, Felix (Doc) Blanchard, also known as Mr. Inside. Morabito thought he'd have a better chance of signing Blanchard if he could keep Blanchard and Davis together. If the 49ers could sign Blanchard, Morabito was confident Davis would jump at the chance to play in the same backfield with him professionally. Blanchard said he wouldn't ask to be released from his commitment to the Army, and he meant it. Davis had second thoughts. He promised Morabito he wouldn't sign with the Rams before consulting with the 49ers, but he also made it clear to Morabito he'd made up his mind. Davis grew up in the Los Angeles area, and he was going to play professionally for the Rams. Nothing Morabito could say would change his mind.

The Army had other ideas, and wasted no time denying Davis' application for release from his commitment. The rejection was personally approved by the Army's chief of staff, five-star general Dwight D. Eisenhower. Although the war had ended two and a half years earlier, the Army was still considered to be in a state of emergency, and it was determined Davis couldn't be spared. Not to play professional football, anyway.

The AAFC announced its all-league first team for 1947 in late December. As had been the case in 1946, only an offensive team was selected. Six players from the champion Browns were among the league's 11 best: quarterback Otto Graham, fullback Marion Motley, receivers Mac Speedie and Dante Lavelli, and guards Lou Rymkus and Bill Willis. Joining them were tailback Spec Sanders and tackle Nate Johnson of New York; center Bob Nelson of Los Angeles; guard Bruno Banducci of San Francisco; and Buffalo halfback Chet Mutryn.

With the AAFC's season over, the NFL took center stage for its 1947 championship game, which was pushed back a week due to the necessity for a play-off to determine the eastern division champion. The Eagles and Steelers tied for first place in the east, each with 8-4 records. Pittsburgh managed to win twice as many games as it lost despite being out-scored by 19 points on the year. The play-off was held in Pittsburgh's Forbes Field, and the Eagles won handily, 21-0. That set up a meeting with another former doormat in the title game. The Chicago Cardinals, losers of more games than any other team in the NFL, dating back to its formation in 1920, had captured their first western division championship with a record of 9-3. The Cardinals hosted the title game on December 28.

At a league meeting before the game, NFL commissioner Bert Bell proudly told reporters that his circuit's total attendance for 1947, including exhibition games, was 2.5 million. Despite the record attendance, four teams (Boston, Los Angeles, Detroit and New York) lost money. Bell said the Giants "almost broke even." He also vehemently denied the rumor that Lambeau would leave Green Bay to coach the Los Angeles Dons, and he confirmed that Fred Mandel would sell the Lions.

The older league's championship game, featuring two clubs that had never advanced that far before, drew only 30,750 to Chicago's Comiskey Park on the Sunday before New Year's. It was less than half of the attendance at the AAFC's championship game two weeks earlier. The Cardinals won their first, and, to date, their only NFL championship of the modern era, 28-21.

The Browns signed quarterback Yelberton Abraham (Y.A.) Tittle of Louisiana State on December 28. Tittle had completed 49 of 96 passes for the Tigers for 789 yards and 11 touchdowns during the 1947 season. Paul Brown planned to groom Tittle to be Otto Graham's successor, even though Graham was only 26 and would be entering just his third season in 1948. Brown never wanted to be caught unprepared. Tittle would never wear a Browns uniform, due to unusual circumstances.

As 1947 came to a close, a deal to sell the Lions fell apart. Lions owner Mandel, a furniture store owner from Chicago, had reportedly lost a half a million dollars since purchasing the team in 1940. Mandel's business couldn't sustain such a loss, and he was negotiating to sell the team to a group of Detroit businessmen which included Tigers owner Walter Briggs. The spokesman for the syndicate, Lyle Fife, announced on December 30 that the talks had broken down over Mandel's asking price of $300,000.

"Apparently we are too far apart in our thinking to consummate the deal," said Fife. "It is our final offer, and any re-opening of negotiations will be up to Mandel. We are in the professional football business, and it can be assumed we'll look into the All-America Conference."[2] Fife's syndicate held one significant bargaining chip in its negotiations with Mandel. Briggs owned the stadium the Lions played in, and had already told Mandel the team's lease would not be renewed for 1948. Mandel had little choice but to sell for whatever price he could get.

On New Year's Day, the International News Service confirmed Bob Yonkers' report that Rickey would buy the Dodgers from Cox and Smith. He'd purchase the club "at terms said to have been advantageous" since Cox and Smith were anxious to bail out following substantial financial losses in 1946 and '47. The report said Cox had been escorted to New Orleans on a private plane owned by Rickey's son. The cagey Rickey's only comment was that if the sale had already been completed, he wasn't aware of it.

The Yankees started the new year by signing fullback Lowell Tew of Alabama. Tew had been Washington's second round draft pick, and Redskins owner George Preston Marshall took the loss in stride. Never one to miss an opportunity to make fun of the AAFC, Marshall said "I think it is a good thing for Tew, who is only 20, to get experience in that W.P.A. project. In two years, Dan Topping will be tired of football."[3]

Yankees coach Ray Flaherty, who was Marshall's coach in Washington from 1937 to 1942, tried to tweak Marshall by acting as if the signing of Tew was no big deal. "It might be true," he conceded. "We had a couple of representatives down there."[4]

On January 7, Branch Rickey met the press as the new owner of the Brooklyn Dodgers. The Associated Press reported that the baseball Dodgers, which Rickey had been running since 1942, had purchased the football

Dodgers. Rickey said at the news conference that he hadn't yet decided if the football team would become part of the baseball team's operation, or would be incorporated by the baseball team as a separate entity. The purchase price wasn't announced, but it can be safely assumed the International News Service had been correct when it reported the terms were highly favorable to Rickey. The Dodgers' general manager was notoriously frugal, as the players who negotiated contracts with him in Brooklyn, and in St. Louis when Rickey ran the Cardinals in the 1920s and 1930s, would willingly attest. The United Press claimed the AAFC was so anxious to have an executive of Rickey's stature as a club owner, and so anxious to be rid of Cox and Smith (particularly Cox), that it gave the Dodgers to Rickey almost free of charge to run on a one-year trial basis. As strange as that sounds, it was given some credence by Rickey's comments at the news conference. "I understand there are people of responsible caliber who are interested in running the franchise. If they can guarantee continued football in Brooklyn, and prove acceptable to the league, I will give them one year free rent." The baseball Dodgers owned Ebbets Field. Rickey then dropped the responsibility for hiring the Dodgers' next head coach (Cliff Battles was out) into the lap of the assembled journalists.

"I am appointing you as a committee of the whole to agree on a coach. If you can agree on one man, I give you my word we will hire him."[5] It may have been a hollow gesture, since Rickey, who'd been dealing with the New York City media for better than half a decade, was probably certain the city's writers would never agree on a single candidate to coach the Dodgers—at least not a candidate who'd be interested in the job. New York's sportswriters were as fiercely competitive among themselves as Rickey's baseball team was with the New York Giants.

Said Commissioner Ingram simply, "I welcome the new ownership of the Brooklyn football club into the conference."[6] One problem solved, at least temporarily. One problem remained.

Negotiations between Fred Mandel and Lyle Fife's group resumed early in January and resulted in an agreement to take the Lions off Mandel's hands by the middle of the month. That obviously ended any talk of Fife's group hooking up with the AAFC.

According to the International News Service, a group of investors led by R. Edward Garn, a minority stockholder in the previous ownership group and the team's acting general manager since October of 1947, had made a deal to buy the Chicago Rockets. Garn's syndicate had reportedly made a significant contract offer to Johnny Lujack, Notre Dame's Heisman Trophy–winning quarterback. Although the Rockets offered Lujack more money, he chose to sign with the Bears instead. Garn admitted that while his group had made an offer, it couldn't have signed Lujack until the deal with the AAFC was completed, and that wouldn't happen for several more weeks. Lujack

7. For the Good of the League

chose to take the bird in the hand rather than waiting for two in the bush. He signed a four-year contract worth $18,000 per season, plus a $5,000 signing bonus.

While Lujack mulled over offers from the Bears and Rockets, the Yankees and Packers vied to get University of Wisconsin halfback Earl (Jug) Girard's name on a contract. Girard signed an $8,000 contract with the Packers, but his mother refused to counter-sign, and her signature was legally required because her son hadn't reached his 21st birthday. His father was deceased. The Yankees responded with an offer of $10,000 plus a minor league baseball contract—the same type of deal that appeared to have lured Charley Trippi, only to have Trippi change his mind and sign with the Cardinals. Curly Lambeau couldn't offer Girard a baseball contract, but he agreed to match the $10,000 the Yankees would pay him to play football. With her son just days away from becoming a legal adult, Mrs. Girard said the choice was his. After turning 21, he chose Green Bay.

Two of the AAFC's three coaching vacancies were filled before the end of January. The wire service stories reporting the hiring of Carl Voyles by the Dodgers made no mention of whether or not he'd been the choice of the city's sportswriters. Voyles was hardly a giant of the college coaching profession. His only winning season had been his first, when he led William & Mary to a record of 6–2–1 in 1940. That earned him the Auburn University job, and his five years in eastern Alabama were undistinguished. Voyles' Auburn teams were 15–22, and he resigned after his Tigers lost seven of nine games in 1947. Still, he had a supporter in Paul Brown.

"Brooklyn wasn't too bad last year, and this new coach ... will help them a lot. He's not known too well around here, but he has a darn good record down south, and he's well-respected. Dick Gallagher [Brown's assistant] knows Voyles very well and is certain he'll make a winner out of the Dodgers."[7] Brown's comments were curious to say the least. The Dodgers were terrible in 1947, although they should have beaten the Browns the second time the teams met. Voyles' overall coaching record wasn't "darn good." It was a less-than-mediocre 21–24–1. On the other hand, Brown was probably pleased (but couldn't say so) that a competitor had selected a coach who, based on his record, didn't figure to give Brown's team much trouble.

After introducing Voyles, whose only comment was that he was pleased to be in Brooklyn, Rickey bemoaned the Dodgers' loss of star college quarterback Charlie Conerly, who chose to sign with the Giants. "It really has me bewildered," said Rickey. "Never in my career in baseball have I made an offer to compare with Conerly's. Exclusive of the bonus, Conerly was offered $20,000 a year for four years. That would come to $100,000—the highest salary ever offered a pro football player—and still we lose him." Conerly, who played college football at Mississippi, said Rickey never made him a contract offer. Conerly said he did speak to Wid Mathews, who was a talent scout for the baseball Dodgers.

Rickey said Conerly's decision to sign with the NFL—and with Brooklyn's cross-town rival, no less—wouldn't stop him from putting the best possible team on the field. "The war is officially on as far as the Dodgers are concerned," he vowed. However, he said the salaries the NFL was paying to Conerly and Harry Gilmer, Alabama's star quarterback who spurned the AAFC to sign with Washington, amounted to "uneconomical methods."[8] And Rickey despised spending more money than was absolutely necessary.

After signing just about every high profile college star in 1947, the AAFC had lost just about every high profile college star in 1948. Browns owner Mickey McBride was asked if he was concerned. "I don't know what the trouble is," he answered. "I can only speak for my own team, and we're going ahead with plans for 1948. We'll go after whatever players we feel will help us. Some of them will cost us more than they're probably worth, but that's true of almost any commodity these days."[9]

Especially professional football.

Added Dan Sherby, McBride's partner in both his taxi cab business and his football team, "We're not running out of millionaires. The millionaires are running out of money."[10] Sherby claimed the days of lavishing big contracts on players coming out of college, or switching leagues, had run their course. He hastened to add that his comments weren't meant to suggest the AAFC was going bankrupt. But the bottom line was Harvey Hester's Seahawks had gone bankrupt midway through the 1946 season. John Keeshin had incurred a large loss and sold the Rockets after that season. Jim Crowley and his associates, the new owners of the Rockets, had been forced to sell after heavy losses in 1947. Bill Cox and Gerald Smith unloaded the Dodgers after losing a frightful amount of money in two seasons in the AAFC. Hester, Keeshin, Cox and Smith were among a group of owners that former commissioner Crowley had proclaimed to be worth approximately $200,000,000 back in 1945. That statement seemed questionable when Crowley made it. It seemed ridiculous by the end of the 1947 season.

Although the Rockets still didn't have an owner, they had a coach. Well-traveled college coach Ed McKeever was signed to a three-year contract on January 25. McKeever had been mentioned as a possible coach of the Rockets before Dick Hanley was hired more than two years earlier. McKeever was Notre Dame's interim head coach in 1944 (while Frank Leahy was in the Navy) and led the Fighting Irish to a record of 8–2. He took the head coaching job at Cornell in 1946, and the Big Red responded with a 5–3–1 season. McKeever spent 1947 coaching the University of San Francisco and had the team ranked as high as #20 (briefly) in the Associated Press poll. The Dons finished the season at 7–3. He brought a college coaching mark of 20–8–1 to Chicago. He'd be allowed to select three assistants with the Rockets.

Not long after one of his bosses had declared the days of spending big money on playing talent to be over, Browns quarterback Otto Graham signed a contract for 1948 worth $17,000. That placed him in the same financial bracket as star NFL quarterbacks Bob Waterfield of the Rams and Sid Luckman of the Bears. Graham, however, would be paid less than Johnny Lujack, who'd earn more money than Luckman, the quarterback he'd be backing up in 1948. Lujack hadn't yet thrown a pass as a professional, but would be paid more money than a pair of quarterbacks who'd led their teams to league championships.

The Army granted cadet Hank Foldberg's request to be released from his military obligation on February 7. Foldberg had played with Davis and Blanchard on Army's powerhouse teams of 1944–46. He asked to be released from his military commitment because, in the words of the Army's press release, "he desired to assist in alleviating family financial difficulties" by playing professional football. He'd been drafted by the Redskins and Dodgers and chose to sign with Brooklyn.

Commissioner Ingram appointed a committee of five head coaches to consider possible rule changes for the upcoming season. Paul Brown, Red Dawson, Ray Flaherty, Cecil Isbell and Buck Shaw were expected to suggest three changes:

(1) Teams be allowed to substitute more than one player during time-outs.
(2) The quarterback in a T-formation should be an eligible receiver.
(3) Plastic headgear should be banned and replaced by leather.

Ingram had made a favorable impression on the owners in his first season as commissioner. His contract was renewed for a second year, although he wasn't given a raise. His salary remained $30,000 annually. Deputy commissioner Scrappy Kessing, whose one-year contract had expired, was also re-hired, and elected treasurer of the league.

The AAFC's coaches voted Browns quarterback Graham the MVP of the 1947 season. Three of them did, anyway. Coaches could not vote for their own players. Graham received three votes, Spec Sanders of the Yankees got two, and George Ratterman of the Bills got one. Deposed coaches Cliff Battles and Dudley DeGroot weren't asked to vote. McKeever, not having coached in the AAFC in 1947, wasn't eligible.

The schedule for 1948 was hammered out during the winter meeting, and Branch Rickey made his presence felt during the discussion. Coming from a baseball background, with games played almost every day, Rickey firmly believed football players were capable of competing in two games per

Hall of Fame baseball executive Branch Rickey, managing the St. Louis Browns in 1915. Rickey dabbled in professional football in 1947, owning the AAFC's Brooklyn Dodgers. Rickey brought a baseball mindset to football, suggesting that the AAFC's schedule should be expanded to 29 games (Library of Congress).

week. Rickey suggested expanding the AAFC's schedule to an unprecedented 29 games for 1949, and to prove his point, he wanted one team to take on the task of playing three games within an eight-day period in 1948. The league's other owners were willing to humor Rickey, and they chose the AAFC's flagship franchise to be the guinea pig for his grand experiment. When Paul Brown and Mickey McBride got their team's schedule for 1948, it showed the Browns playing the Yankees in New York, the Dons in Los Angeles, and the 49ers in San Francisco in an eight-day span in late November. Just two days would separate the games in Los Angeles and San Francisco. Brown agreed to the schedule because it meant his team would make only one west coast trip. He hated visiting California twice.

The most important piece of business taken up during what the wire services described as an "uneventful" series of meetings was commissioner Ingram's "share the talent" plan. At least, newspaper accounts during the 1948 season gave every indication that it was solely Ingram's idea. It had been decided at the AAFC's post-championship game meeting in December that

7. For the Good of the League

something dramatic needed to be done to help the league's weakest teams: Chicago, Baltimore, and Brooklyn. Ingram was told to study the rosters of each team and formulate a plan to improve competitive balance. It isn't clear whether he was carrying out orders from the owners, or if the plan for the league's stronger teams (Cleveland, New York, San Francisco) to make some of their players available to the have-nots was strictly Ingram's idea. Whichever was the case, Ingram said help in the form of player transfers from the Browns, Yankees and 49ers would be on the way "as soon as the coaches can assemble their draft choices for the coming year."[11] Early indications were the strong teams would surrender 20 players to the patsies. Baltimore would get eight players, Brooklyn and Chicago would get six. And these wouldn't be benchwarmers. Each team would be allowed to draft a protected list of 15 players from their 33-player rosters. That would leave some good football players available to some teams who desperately needed them.

Ingram closed the meeting by saying "the determination and the unselfish co-operation of the representatives of the various clubs during the meeting was very impressive. They have made plans for 1948, 1949 and 1950."[12] Those plans included opening the 1948 season on August 29 and ending it on December 5, with the championship game set for December 12.

As for the "Chicago problem," Ingram said new ownership was in place and had been approved by the seven other clubs. The new owners of the Rockets would be introduced to the fans "at the proper time."[13]

On March 9, Bob Rodenberg, the Washington-based attorney who spearheaded the effort to re-locate the smoldering remains of the Miami Seahawks to Baltimore, turned the smoldering remains of the Colts over to the AAFC. Baltimore's football fans had responded enthusiastically to the Colts, attracting 199,661 patrons for an average attendance of 28,523. A crowd of better than 51,000 attended the team's second home game, against the Yankees. Still, the Colts managed to lose $166,000 for the year, and the team had been the AAFC's personal punching bag, losing 11 games and being outscored by an average margin of 27–12. Rodenberg's partners, including his brother Bill, didn't see any reason to believe 1948 would bring much improvement, and they decided to stop throwing good money after bad. Or they ran out of money. Rodenberg himself didn't have enough money to operate the Colts and handed the franchise back to the league.

Baltimore wasn't going to surrender the Colts without a fight, and mayor Thomas D'Alesandro presided over a meeting of a 16-member "Save the Colts" committee on the ninth of March. D'Alesandro's goal was to raise $400,000 to operate the Colts in 1948, and he placed hotel executive Howard Busick in charge of achieving the objective. Rumor had it that Bill Cox, until early January the co-owner of the Dodgers, was anxious to get back into football and investigated the possibility to sinking money into the Colts.

Commissioner Ingram, who attended D'Alesandro's meeting, assured Baltimore's football fans their team wouldn't be a ward of the league for long. On March 13, he said that "within a week, we expect to conclude all details of negotiations with a Baltimore group which is planning to take over the club's franchise."[14] Exactly one week later, the *Cleveland Press* reported that group would consist of 15 members and be led by Busick. It sounded like the "Save the Colts" committee had decided to save the Colts by themselves.

The deal to save the Colts came with an expensive catch for the league's strongest teams. Not financially, but on the field. The new owners of the Baltimore team insisted that Cleveland, San Francisco and New York give up three players from their rosters to fortify the Colts. Otherwise, they weren't interested in putting the same club that had been 2–11–1 on the field in 1948. Ingram told Mickey McBride, Tony Morabito and Dan Topping that strengthening the Colts was preferable to playing the 1948 season with just seven teams. They reluctantly agreed. Although Buffalo and San Francisco had identical 8–4–2 records in 1947, the Bills were exempt from the "share the talent" plan because they had been a miserable also-ran in 1946.

Browns assistant coach Fritz Heisler spoke to Cleveland's American Legion post 343 in mid–March and warned his audience not to expect another AAFC championship in 1948. Heisler said Ingram's "share the talent" plan (not just with Baltimore, but also Brooklyn and Chicago) would result in an across the board strengthening of Cleveland's competition, making the road to a third straight AAFC title much more difficult. At the same time the AAFC was artificially bolstering its weakest franchises, Heisler's boss, Paul Brown, was hard at work bolstering the Browns.

The AAFC's last head coaching position was filled in late March when the Dons hired Jimmy Phelan away from St. Mary's of California. Phelan had been Knute Rockne's starting quarterback at Notre Dame in 1917. He'd coached at Missouri, Purdue and the University of Washington before taking over the football program at St. Mary's in 1942. His 27 years as a head coach in college produced a record of 136–82–14. His 1936 Washington team ranked fifth in the Associated Press top 20 national poll. His 1945 St. Mary's squad was ranked seventh nationally.

"I will attempt to give the Dons the most colorful offense in the country," Phelan promised. "We will have football innovations that will startle the world. Although I am basically a single-wing coach, we will suit our system to our material and probably use some T-formation plays."[15] Phelan's material included tailback Glenn Dobbs, who had been the AAFC's 1946 MVP while operating in the single-wing in Brooklyn. Phelan said he accepted the Dons' job because they made him an offer he couldn't refuse.

If evidence was needed that the football war was growing increasingly expensive, it was provided on March 16. The Bears announced they were increasing their ticket prices for 1948 by an average of 10 percent.

As part of the deal to bring new, and hopefully properly financed, ownership to the Colts, the Cleveland Browns agreed to relinquish the rights to halfback Jake Leicht and quarterback Y.A. Tittle on April 14. Leicht had been an all–Pacific Coast Conference performer at Oregon who hadn't yet signed with the Browns and agreed to have his rights transferred to Baltimore. Tittle had signed with Cleveland in late December of 1947, but also agreed to the transfer. Paul Brown was loaded with running backs and didn't mind parting with Leicht, who wasn't a proven commodity as a professional. Tittle wasn't proven either, but Brown agonized over giving him up. Brown, a former quarterback himself, saw Tittle's potential and was counting on him to understudy Otto Graham in 1948. Losing Tittle to Baltimore was particularly galling to Brown since the Dons had decided to surrender one of their quarterbacks, Charley O'Rourke, to the Colts. With Dobbs under contract for the next four seasons, the Dons felt they could afford to let O'Rourke go. Or did they?

Two days after the announcement that Los Angeles had sent O'Rourke to the Colts, the Dons denied it. And that denial was one of several problems holding up the successful conclusion of negotiations between the AAFC, which still owned the Colts, and the group of Baltimore businessmen who wanted to take over the team. But only under certain conditions, which a spokesman for the group, who talked to the Associated Press on condition of anonymity, detailed.

According to the spokesman, Los Angeles hadn't sent O'Rourke to Baltimore. Two players supposedly released to the Colts by the Yankees, linemen Dick Barwegan and Pete Berezney, hadn't agreed to contracts yet. The 49ers had reneged on their pledge to give the Colts the draft rights to Fred Land. "We will not go ahead with our negotiations to restore the Baltimore franchise to financial health unless the league agrees to keep its promise and send four good men to Baltimore,"[16] the spokesman insisted. So far, only two players, Tittle and Leicht, had agreed to report to the Colts, and only Tittle was under contract—the deal he'd signed with the Browns. At that point, it was a stretch to call Tittle and Leicht "good players" since both were rookies who hadn't even put on a uniform yet. The owners-to-be of the Colts wanted more than that.

The negotiations continued, however, and on April 19, 20 businessmen officially incorporated themselves into the Baltimore Football Club. They pledged $200,000 to fund the team for 1948, and announced a sale of stock to the public to raise more money. The group hired Walter Driskill, the athletic director at Oklahoma University and formerly athletic director at the University of Maryland, as the Colts' general manager. A ten-year lease on Baltimore's Memorial Stadium was approved by the city's Board of Estimates on April 29. The agreement called for the Colts to pay $5,000 per game, or 15 percent of each game's gross receipts, in rent.

On April 30, the Dons finally sold Charley O'Rourke's contract to Baltimore. Before that, the Colts returned the contract of running back Frank Sinkwich to the Yankees. New team president Robert Embry said the club's agreement with the AAFC allowed it to accept or reject any contract it inherited from Bob Rodenberg's ownership, and it chose to reject Sinkwich's contract. Had the Colts kept the former NFL MVP and Heisman Trophy winning tailback, they'd have had to pay him $15,000 for the 1948 season, in addition to paying the Yankees $2,500 for keeping his contract. Sinkwich played in eight games for the Colts in 1947, gaining 208 yards on 55 carries and catching one pass. He had two bad knees. That kind of risk wasn't worth $15,000. Sinkwich's career was over.

There was one thing the owners in both professional football leagues could agree on: they were paying their players too much money. In an unattributed article on May 1, the *Cleveland Press* quoted several of those owners from both leagues. Curly Lambeau was reported to be furious when Green Bay's star running back, Tony Canadeo, walked out of contract negotiations with the coach and general manager. "The present situation is too cockeyed to be sound," Lambeau complained. "Re-adjustment is imperative and inevitable. Club executives [such as Lambeau] took cuts or held the line to weather the storm in pro football, but the players salaries continued to skyrocket. Club owners can no longer stand the strain."[17] The strain was being felt strongly in Green Bay, the last of the NFL's small-town franchises. The publicly-owned Packers would barely survive the war with the AAFC.

Lamented team president Ray Benningsen of the NFL champion Chicago Cardinals, "Last year with a championship team we made a negligible amount of money. We made a very, very small profit."[18]

In the AAFC, Ed Garn, speaking on behalf of the new ownership of the Rockets, which still hadn't been finalized and introduced to the team's fans, said it was club policy to award raises to players who deserved them. Garn said he didn't know how many of the 35 contracts the Rockets had mailed to their players contained raises. It can be safely assumed the answer was not many, since the Rockets had staggered to a 1–13 record the previous season. On the other hand, the defending AAFC champion Browns had given "substantial" pay increases to "most of our players"[19] according to head coach and general manager Paul Brown.

Tony Morabito, the lumber magnate who owned the 49ers, assessed the situation bluntly. He said if his fellow owners continued to be "foolish" and bid against each other for playing talent, the result would be the end of professional football within five years. Morabito said ticket prices in both leagues had reached their peak and couldn't be raised any higher. "I know a lot of ball players who are getting 2½ or three times as much as they are worth or should be getting,"[20] he claimed. A common player draft between the AAFC and NFL would have solved everybody's problem. But the NFL owners, who continued to hope that if they kept ignoring the AAFC it would go away, wouldn't consider the idea.

Commissioner Ingram told reporters covering the AAFC's winter meeting in mid–February that the new ownership of the Rockets would be introduced "at the proper time." The proper time finally arrived on May 19, when Garn said a group of more than 20 businessmen, sportsmen and professional men had formed the Football Club of Chicago. He identified only four of his partners, and they held impressive positions. Among the investors in the Rockets were Illinois Lieutenant Governor Hugh W. Cross; Major General Leo Boyle, the adjutant general of the state's National Guard; Illinois state senator Walter Butler, and Frank Burke, vice president of Chicago City Bank and Trust. Garn said the Rockets' new owners had decided to keep head coach Ed McKeever, and signed him to a long-term contract. Garn said the Rockets would "play, and play hard"[21] at Soldier Field.

Rumors never stopped swirling that Paul Brown would return to Columbus to rescue an Ohio State football program that had struggled without him. Late in May, Brown spoke to the Agonis Club of Columbus, and his words caused panic in the *Cleveland Press*' sports department, which printed a bold headline on the sports section's front page: "DOES BROWN PREFER OSU? READ BETWEEN THESE LINES!"

For those who were convinced Brown would never turn his back on Mickey McBride's money, which Ohio State couldn't match, he said "the most pleasant way to live is to have a job that you love; money is secondary." Brown said he'd driven past the home he and his family shared in the Columbus suburb of Upper Arlington. As if that piece of reminiscing wasn't frightening enough to the *Press*, Brown said of his three seasons at Ohio State, "I look back on my whole experience here as a happy dream." He counseled the high school football players in his audience, "If I were you, I would go to Ohio State. There is no finer institution."[22]

The other seven coaches in the AAFC could but hope that Brown would be enticed to return to college coaching. It's worth pondering if the league would've survived if he had.

Charlie Conerly signed with the New York Giants on June 15. He signed for five years, and the value of the deal was estimated at $80,000. Conerly verified that the Dodgers had offered him a five-year contract worth $100,000, "but they didn't go that high until after I told them I had decided to play with the Giants."[23] Conerly said he doubted the seriousness of Brooklyn's offer. He said he thought the Dodgers made the offer for public relations purposes, in an effort to save face with their fans, knowing that he was committed to the Giants and would have to turn it down.

Having lost out on Conerly, the Dodgers signed University of Michigan quarterback Bob Chappuis in late June. Terms weren't disclosed. Branch Rickey traded tailback Bill (Dub) Jones and the draft rights to Jay Smith and Bob Jensen to Cleveland for the draft rights to Chappuis. In Michigan's 49–0 romp over Southern Cal in the 1948 Rose Bowl, Chappuis completed 14 passes and accounted for 279 yards of total offense passing and rushing. Even though Paul Brown needed a back-up to Otto Graham, he was willing to part with Chappuis in exchange for Jones, who would become a star in Cleveland's backfield for several years. Jensen would be passed along to the Rockets. Smith wouldn't play professional football.

The effort by the new owners of the Rockets to improve the AAFC's worst team began on July 6 with the purchase of the contracts of running backs Eddie Prokop and Dewey Proctor from the Yankees. Prokop had averaged 4.3 yards on 76 carries in 1947. Proctor ran just 15 times and averaged only one yard per rush. Although the Associated Press story announcing the transaction said Chicago had bought the contracts of both players, stories later in the season suggested Prokop and Proctor had been given away as part of commissioner Ingram's "share the wealth" initiative. Whichever was accurate, the duo was expected to help strengthen a Rockets offense that would feature quarterback Angelo Bertelli and end Crazylegs Hirsch. That combination was expected to strike fear into the hearts of opposing defenses in 1948, but expectations and reality occasionally don't match, and that would be the case with the Rockets.

Looking for improvement anywhere they could potentially find it, the Rockets, possibly at the suggestion of their newly-acquired halfback, Prokop, signed his older brother, Joe, in early July. Also a running back, Joe Prokop had played college football at Notre Dame, but didn't enjoy the success his brother would at Georgia Tech, where Eddie was an All-American. Joe Prokop was attempting a football comeback, not having played in six years. He hadn't played since college.

Chicago was the first AAFC team to open training camp in 1948. New head coach Ed McKeever assumed he'd need as much time as possible to whip his squad into shape. Sixty-one players reported on July 18. Seventeen were rookies. Twenty players from the team that posted a 1–13 record for Jim Crowley in 1947 returned.

Yankees star quarterback Spec Sanders ended a brief holdout and signed a contract in late July. He received a raise in salary for two years of outstanding service to the Yankees. Owner Dan Topping wasn't among those magnates in both leagues moaning about the cost of player salaries in pro football, at least not yet. Topping could afford the astronomical salaries the hired help was getting. He may have been the wealthiest owner in professional football. His family owned the prosperous Anaconda Copper Company.

The two-time AAFC champion Browns reported to training camp in Bowling Green, Ohio, on July 26. As he'd done the previous season, Paul Brown started the process of seeking another league title by warning the players not to rest on their laurels. "As of today, we are starting a new season. We cannot afford to be thinking of ourselves in terms of champions. We've got a lot of work to do, and there are going to be seven tough teams gunning for us. It's up to us to be ready for them."[24] Brown would have his team more than ready for all comers in 1948.

The *Cleveland Press* told its readers what a typical day at training camp consisted of for the Browns: wake-up call at 7:00, followed by breakfast, lecture, practice, lunch, siesta, lecture, practice, dinner, recreation, and lights out at 10:30. That was the training regimen that would produce four AAFC champions.

With training camps in session, it's time to look at the results of Ingram's plan to distribute players from the AAFC's stronger teams to its less fortunate franchises, in hopes of improving competitive balance for the 1948 season. The league champion Browns lost quarterback Y.A. Tittle, defensive back Jake Leicht, running back Spiro Dellerba, receiver Mickey Mayne, and offensive lineman Ernie Blandin, all to the Colts. Of those players, only Blandin was a starter, and the Browns had a more than capable replacement in future Hall of Famer Lou Groza. Dellerba had averaged 6.1 yards per carry on 29 rushes in 1947, but was converted to linebacker by Baltimore. Mayne caught just six passes for Cleveland in 1947, but averaged nearly 40 yards per reception. He rushed 41 times and picked up just 75 yards. Tittle and Leicht were rookies who never wore a Browns uniform.

The Yankees lost all–AAFC offensive lineman Dick Barwegan to the Colts. Offensive lineman Nate Johnson went to the Rockets, along with running backs Prokop and Proctor. New York would keenly feel the loss of half of its offensive line during the 1948 season. If the purpose of Ingram's plan was not only to strengthen the weak teams but to weaken the strong teams and bring them back to the pack, it worked in New York.

As for the 49ers, they reneged on their agreement to assign the draft rights to Fred Land to the Colts. Owner Tony Morabito saw no reason why his team should subsidize the league's weak sisters and refused to participate in the "share the wealth" program. "We give nothing!" Morabito snarled when asked which players the 49ers would contribute. Ingram didn't have the authority to force the 49ers to co-operate. Land didn't help the 49ers much. His professional career consisted of two games.

Although the original plan had been for the Dodgers to receive reinforcements as well as the Colts and Rockets, there's no evidence Brooklyn participated in the give-away.

Joe Prokop's comeback didn't last long. He was cut on July 28. Even the Rockets weren't desperate enough to use a player who'd been away from the sport for six years. There was some interest generated by the team's new ownership and coaching staff, however. Nine thousand fans watched the team's intra-squad scrimmage in Yates Stadium on Chicago's South Side on August 15. The "Blues" defeated the "Whites," 33–13. In contrast, only 2,000 fans attended the Browns' intra-squad scrimmage.

Before the Rockets began their home season in Soldier Field, the huge stadium on the shore of Lake Michigan hosted the annual college all-star game on August 20. In front of a crowd of 101,200, the defending NFL champion Cardinals made quick work of the nation's biggest college football stars, 28–0. Controversy surrounded the contest over the refusal of Harry Gilmer, Alabama's star quarterback, to suit up for the all-stars after reportedly signing a binding contract to do so. Gilmer had been drafted by the Washington Redskins, and team owner George Preston Marshall didn't want his prize rookie to risk serious injury in a meaningless exhibition. An exhibition that didn't put a penny in Marshall's pocket. The collegians were paid to participate in the game, but Gilmer said he didn't think the insurance provided by the game's sponsor, the *Chicago Tribune*, was sufficient to cover potential lost salary if he suffered a career-threatening, or a career-ending, injury. It was widely assumed Gilmer bowed to pressure from Marshall, who wanted to see the all-star game canceled altogether. Aside from making a lot of money for charity, Marshall felt it served no purpose. There was talk of the NFL pulling out of its contract with the *Tribune*, and that was all the opening Jonas Ingram needed. It was no coincidence that the all-star game's founder was Arch Ward, who'd also started the AAFC, and was a sports columnist for the *Tribune*. Ingram said the AAFC's champion would be happy to meet the all-stars in the summer of 1949 if Marshall could convince his fellow owners to scrap the league's contract with the *Tribune* and end the NFL's affiliation with the all-star game. But he couldn't.

In temperatures hovering near 100 degrees, the Colts beat the Browns in an exhibition game at Scott high school in Toledo on August 27, the night four other AAFC teams were opening their regular season. The Browns dominated the Colts statistically but managed to lose, 21–17. The game is significant because it was the only one Cleveland would fail to win in 1948, and it was just an exhibition.

8

1948

The All-America Football Conference kicked off its historic third season on Friday, August 27. The season was historic because it marked the first time a challenger to the NFL had lived to open a third season. Red Grange's American Football League of 1926 folded after one year. The second American Football League of 1936–37 gave up after two years. So did the third American Football League of 1940–41. The AAFC was shaky, however, and commissioner Jonas Ingram would spend the autumn of 1948 denying rumors that it would either disband before the season was over, or at season's end.

Three new head coaches made their debuts on opening night. In Chicago, rookie head coach Jimmy Phelan, who'd promised fans in Los Angeles an offensive explosion in 1948, watched that offense, led by quarterback Glenn Dobbs, fall slightly short of the goal in a 7–0 victory over the Rockets, who were playing their first game for new head coach, Ed McKeever. Part of the reason for the lack of offense was the intense heat that enveloped the entire eastern United States from the Mississippi River to the Atlantic Ocean. Temperatures near 100 degrees, and the primitive methods of dealing with them that existed in the late 1940s, exhausted the players quickly. Most coaches, including, perhaps surprisingly, Cleveland's resident genius, Paul Brown, believed the worst thing players could do under such conditions was drink fluids, so water wasn't made available. At least, not in sufficient amounts. How football players survived the heat in those years defies analysis.

The Dons managed just 97 yards of total offense, most of it accumulated on their only touchdown drive. Fullback "Jarring" John Kimbrough punched the ball over from the one yard line late in the first half for the game's only score. Dobbs couldn't move the Los Angeles offense, but he made his defense's job easier with punts of 71, 62, 61, 60 and 57 yards. The Rockets marched 70 yards to the Dons' one yard line in the first quarter but failed to score. That proved to be their only threat, much to the dismay of 26,479 uncomfortable fans in Soldier Field.

The Rockets were led by former Dons quarterback Angelo Bertelli, who was reunited with McKeever, his former coach at Notre Dame. McKeever was an assistant with the Fighting Irish when Bertelli was establishing himself as one of college football's top quarterbacks. On that sultry late August night, Bertelli attempted 19 passes and completed just three. He threw two interceptions.

In Ebbets Field, the Yankees, the Dodgers, and a crowd of 16,411 sweltered in 90-plus degree heat. Trailing 3–0 in the third period, the Yankees rallied for three touchdowns, the last of which was an electrifying 94-yard punt return by scatback Tom Casey. New York won, 21–3, as Brooklyn lost its first game for new head coach Carl Voyles. Only one game had been played, but the early returns indicated not much had changed in Brooklyn or Chicago.

The AAFC completed its opening weekend on Sunday, August 29, as the 49ers trounced the Bills in Kezar Stadium, 35–14. San Francisco put the game away early, scoring three second period touchdowns. The 49ers hadn't lost any players to Ingram's "share the wealth" scheme, and it would show as the season progressed. The 49ers and Browns would stand head and shoulders above the other six teams in the league.

As had been its strategy since its first season, the AAFC got the jump on the NFL in 1948, opening its season three weeks before the older league. The two-time defending champions started the defense of their title at home on Friday, September 3. Phelan knew his Dons would have to generate more than 97 yards offensively to have a shot at beating the Browns for the third time, and they couldn't produce it. Touchdowns by halfbacks Ara Parseghian (a rookie) and Bill Boedeker (obtained in a trade with Chicago), a 51-yard Lou Groza field goal, and a sack of Dobbs in his end zone gave Cleveland a lead of 19–0 with half a minute remaining in the game. The Dons scored what seemed to be a meaningless touchdown with 30 seconds to play against Cleveland's reserve defenders. But then a fumble of the ensuing kickoff gave the ball back to the Dons, and the lead was cut to 19–14 with five seconds to go. The Browns covered the next kickoff and 60,193 fans exited having experienced more excitement than they'd cared to.

Dobbs promised a different result in the re-match on Thanksgiving day in Los Angeles. "It'll be a different story when we get those guys in our ballpark,"[1] he vowed in the losers' dressing room. Dobbs may have known that the re-match would be the second of three games the Browns would play in an eight-day period late in the season, all on the road, thanks to Branch Rickey's determination to prove that professional football teams could and should play twice a week. Regardless, Dobbs' backfield partner, Kimbrough, wasn't so sure.

"They'll be just as tough there, believe me,"[2] Kimbrough cautioned.

The Colts hadn't changed coaches during the off-season as the Rockets, Dodgers and Dons had. However, as an Associated Press writer noted in a preview of Baltimore's opening game on September 5, just about everything else was new. "After winning only two games their inaugural season ... the Colts threw out virtually everybody but coach Cecil Isbell and the water boy." Isbell, a star quarterback during his NFL career with Green Bay, knew a little something about quarterbacks. And he knew he had found one in Y.A. Tittle, the rookie the Browns had been forced to surrender as part of Ingram's effort to strengthen the AAFC's weak clubs, of which Baltimore had been the second weakest in 1947.

After scoring just 167 points, an average of less than a dozen per game, the previous year, the Colts opened 1948 by dropping 45 points on the Yankees in front of a disbelieving crowd of 31,800 in Memorial Stadium. Tittle completed 11 of 21 passes for an AAFC record 346 yards, including touchdown heaves of 20, 48 and 60 yards. He also scored on a quarterback sneak. Baltimore's Rex Grossman added a 53-yard field goal. New York's offense produced 28 points, but suffered a serious blow when halfback Buddy Young sustained cracked ribs and left the game in the first half.

In San Francisco, the 49ers polished off the Dodgers, 36–20. Frankie Albert pleased a Kezar Stadium crowd of 32,606 by duplicating Tittle's feat of throwing for three touchdowns and running for another.

Any thoughts that the close loss to Los Angeles in the season opener meant the new-look Rockets were on the right track were dispelled in a 42–7 shellacking at Buffalo on Monday, September 6. The Bills rang up six touchdowns even though quarterback George Ratterman's league-record streak of throwing a scoring pass in eight straight games ended. Halfback Julie Rykovich led Buffalo's attack with three touchdowns. The Rockets came within five seconds of being shut out for the second straight week. Dewey Proctor's one-yard touchdown run avoided a whitewash. A crowd of 25,816 watched the blow-out in Civic Stadium.

The Colts' upset victory over the Yankees would be the last game they'd play in Memorial Stadium. On September 8, the city's park board, which ran the stadium, voted to re-name it "Babe Ruth Stadium," in honor of the legendary baseball slugger who was born in Baltimore. The sports world was still mourning Ruth's passing on August 16, 1948, and looking for ways to honor him. The park board also reiterated that, in spite of the name change, the stadium was still dedicated to the memory of all the Maryland residents who'd given their lives in World War II.

When the Colts next played, they'd have Lu Gambino in their line-up. Gambino had led the Southern Conference with 16 touchdowns and gained 907 yards for the University of Maryland in 1947. For some reason, there had been a question about Gambino's eligibility to return to the Terrapins in 1948. Gambino had played two seasons for Indiana University, and two more for Maryland, and the Southern Conference correctly ruled that he'd used up his four years of college eligibility. Gambino dropped out of his classes at Maryland and signed with the Colts, even though he'd been drafted by the Browns in the AAFC. He wanted a three-year contract for $15,000 per season. He settled for a one-year contract for $9,000. Cleveland didn't contest Baltimore's right to sign Gambino, and he made little impact on the Colts' offense.

Chicago picked up its first victory for McKeever on Friday, September 10, fighting back for a 21–14 win over the Colts after blowing a two-touchdown lead. Baltimore tied the contest on a one-yard run by Tittle in the third quarter and a 47-yard pass from Tittle to Lamar Davis in the fourth. Rockets quarterback Sam Vacanti, who took over for an ineffective Bertelli, scored from a yard out with three minutes to play for the victory. The crowd at Soldier Field was just 14,642. After only three games, the fans had already begun to lose interest.

In Los Angeles on that same Friday night, the Dons beat the Dodgers, 17–7. The game was viewed by 35,246 fans.

A person described by the *Cleveland Press* as "a man close to the Buffalo situation" explained why the young Bills couldn't handle the Browns, who'd be visiting Civic Stadium on September 12. "Our trouble is that the boys just seem to fold when we play the Browns. We have so many who have been through it before, they don't look forward to the game."[3] The Browns had beaten Buffalo four times in as many tries in the regular season, and they made it five for five with a 42–13 romp before a gathering of 35,340 fans. The teams combined for five touchdowns in an 18-minute span of the first half, including a pair of long marches by the Bills against a Cleveland defense not accustomed to surrendering long scoring drives. The Browns stiffened and blanked the Bills in the second half. Browns receiver Mac Speedie set an AAFC record by catching ten passes for 151 yards. Marion Motley added 136 rushing yards on 17 carries.

After allowing the formerly offensively inept Colts to score 45 points the previous week, the Yankees gave up 41 points to San Francisco in a lopsided loss in Kezar Stadium. The 49ers scored on the opening kickoff, which New York's Bob Kennedy fumbled. Len Eshmont recovered the ball in the Yankees' end zone for the 49ers, and the rout was on. The Yankees couldn't score all afternoon, much to the delight of a sell-out crowd of 60,927.

Yankees head coach Ray Flaherty blamed his team's poor break from the gate on the talent lost thanks to Ingram's "share the wealth" initiative. New York lost a pair of starting offensive linemen, Dick Barwegan and Nate Johnson, and a pair of running backs, Eddie Prokop and Dewey Proctor. However, wire service reports at the time of the transactions claimed Johnson had been traded to the Rockets, and the contracts of Prokop and Proctor had been sold to Chicago. There's no question Barwegan had been given to the Colts with the Yankees getting nothing in exchange. And that didn't sit well with Flaherty.

"We had to give away seasoned players, and all Cleveland gave up was a tackle they didn't want and a rookie quarterback they never had in uniform,"[4] Flaherty grumbled. Paul Brown didn't agree.

"Flaherty doesn't have his facts straight," Brown shot back. "We wanted to keep [tackle Ernie] Blandin, but if we had kept him, we would have had to give the Colts either Lou Rymkus or Lou Groza. We also wanted Tittle and knew he could help us, but if we didn't part with him we would have had to sacrifice Otto Graham or Cliff Lewis. And that wasn't all we gave up. Flaherty seems to have forgotten that we gave the Colts a pretty fair halfback in Jake Leicht and a kid they are using as a first-string halfback in Spiro Dellerba. We also gave them Mickey Mayne and Marshall Shurnas."[5] Brown had one of his facts slightly scrambled. Dellerba was never Baltimore's starting halfback. He carried the ball just twice all season. Shurnas was released by the Colts in training camp. How the 49ers managed to defy Ingram's plea for the strong to assist the weak wasn't explained. But the "share the wealth" plan had officially been shelved by the commissioner.

"We don't want to penalize our good teams any more,"[6] Ingram said. The Browns emerged stronger without Blandin, Dellerba, Mayne and Shurnas than they'd been with them. Tittle and Leicht never wore a Cleveland uniform. The Yankees sorely missed Barwegan and Johnson. Spec Sanders and Buddy Young more than compensated for the loss of Prokop and Proctor.

After finishing his tirade against the league and the Browns, Flaherty went to work preparing the Yankees to host the Colts on September 16. Three days wasn't enough time to recover from the beating on the west coast and get ready for another encounter with Tittle. The Colts flattened the Yankees, 27–14, before just 18,959 fans on a Thursday night. Tittle completed ten of 17 passes for 241 yards. The Yankees had lost just two games in 1947. They'd already lost three in 1948, and the slow start cost Flaherty his job. He was asked to resign by Dan Topping the next day.

"It is felt that a change in leadership is necessary to put the club back on a winning stride,"[7] said the press release announcing the coaching change. Two of Flaherty's assistants, Jim Barber and Mike Pecarovich, also resigned. Backfield coach Norm (Red) Strader was appointed interim head coach for the rest of the season.

The AAFC desperately wanted a strong (read: winning) franchise in Chicago. The team of owner John Keeshin and coach Dick Hanley had parted ways after just two games in 1946. Keeshin sold the club at the end of the season. New ownership in 1947, led by a new coach in Jim Crowley, a proven winner as a college coach, had produced a 1–13 season. Another ownership, and another coach, were in place in 1948, and the Rockets were 1–2 as they prepared for a crucial home-and-home series with the Browns that would go a long way toward determining the team's future in Chicago.

"I thought we had the makings of a winner when we opened by losing to Los Angeles by one touchdown," said coach McKeever. "Then the next week, the roof caved in at Buffalo. But last week, I was pleased the way the team came back against Baltimore. I think we have a lot of possibilities." The Rockets would face the Browns twice and the 49ers in the next three weeks, with two of the games at home. The first game was against Cleveland at Soldier Field. McKeever knew how important that stretch would be. "This is the first of three tough games in a row we have to play, and I think we can win the city's support by making a good showing against the Browns. We expect at least 35,000 fans ... we've got a chance to sell 'em on our type of football. If we get our brains beaten out by the Browns tonight, the outlook won't be very promising, for from here we go to Cleveland next Sunday, then we come back to play the San Francisco 49ers. We can't expect to take three bad lickings and still expect the people to get excited about us."[8]

The Rockets fell short both in the stands and on the field in the first of those three games. A better than average, but not as good as anticipated, crowd of 30,608 watched the Browns defeat the home team, 28–7, on September 17. Harold Sauerbrei, who covered the Browns for the *Cleveland Plain Dealer*, described the Rockets as "a team that resembled the old Chicago Rockets in many respects" despite its infusion of talent. Cleveland pummeled the Rockets for 299 rushing yards. It was the final game of Angelo Bertelli's brief professional career. Hampered by injuries, Bertelli had been traded by the Dons to the Rockets and unable to establish himself as the starting quarterback on the league's worst team. He retired on September 22, saying he'd devote his time to running a sporting goods store in his hometown of Springfield, Massachusetts.

The NFL opened its season on the 17th of September. The Packers clobbered the Boston Yanks, 31–0, in Fenway Park. The crowd was estimated at 18,000, a good gathering for a Yanks game. Both leagues were now competing for the attention of the nation's football fans.

The first game of the season between the AAFC's west coast rivals took place in Kezar Stadium on Sunday, September 19. In a typical San Francisco fog, the 49ers thrashed the Dons, 36–14. Frankie Albert threw for three touchdowns and ran for another. San Francisco's defense held Los Angeles to seven first downs. A crowd of 45,420 squinted through the mist to make out what was happening on the field.

The final weekend of the first month of the season found six of the AAFC's eight teams in action. On Sunday, September 26, in Buffalo, a crowd of 31,103 watched the Bills lose to the 49ers, 38–28, despite the heroics of George Ratterman. Ratterman threw 35 passes and completed 23 for 299 yards, but couldn't keep pace with Albert and the visitors. In Baltimore, Tittle's hot hand helped the Colts top the Dodgers, 35–20, as 35,554 watched in the newly-christened Babe Ruth Stadium. And in Cleveland, the Browns had their hands full with the Rockets, who stunned 37,190 fans by taking a 10–0 lead into their dressing room at halftime. It was only the second time in their history the Browns had trailed at the intermission, and they corrected matters quickly, pulling away for a 21–10 victory.

A similar scenario played out in the last game of the month, on September 29. The Yankees, under the direction of interim head coach Red Strader, took a 10–0 lead over the Dons into the fourth quarter at Memorial Coliseum. Then Glenn Dobbs and the Los Angeles offense awoke and scored three times for a 20–10 triumph, spoiling Strader's debut. A gathering of 35,655 watched.

The AAFC standings after one month:

Eastern Division

Baltimore	3–1–0	121–83
Buffalo	1–3–0	97–122
New York	1–4–0	73–136
Brooklyn	0–4–0	50–109

Western Division

San Francisco	5–0–0	186–66
Cleveland	4–0–0	110–44
Los Angeles	3–2–0	72–72
Chicago	1–4–0	45–112

The new AAFC looked a lot like the old AAFC: four strong teams (with Baltimore a newcomer to that category), and four weak teams (with the Yankees a newcomer in that category.) The NFL would fare worse in the competitive balance department once the season was over.

October began with a familiar scenario, at least for Cleveland fans. Paul Brown's name was being linked to the head football coaching and athletic director's positions at UCLA. Neither position was open at the moment, but that didn't stop the rumor mill from grinding. "There have been rumors that I am leaving the Browns, and there have been rumors that the Browns are going to be sold," said an impatient Brown. "As far as I know, there isn't any foundation for any of them. I don't have time to be discussing every rumor that pops up."[9] And rumors about Brown deserting Cleveland to take a college coaching job popped up frequently during the autumn of 1948.

One of the reasons Brown's name was mentioned for every college job that became available, and some that were expected to but didn't, was because the future of the AAFC was murky as its third season progressed. It was assumed by most so-called "experts" that a coach of Brown's stature would grow weary of the constant speculation that the league would fold, and trade the uncertainty for the security of a college coaching position. One of Brown's closest friends in the coaching profession, Buck Shaw of the 49ers, complained that "if the two leagues don't get together, and soon, there won't be any more pro football, and the holiday for the players will come to an end."[10]

Shaw's boss, 49ers owner Tony Morabito, candidly assessed the state of the AAFC heading into October. "We have a definite problem in Chicago, another in Baltimore, and still a third in Brooklyn. Buffalo is beginning to show promise of paying its way, and interest is growing, but the only teams really making a go of it in our league are Cleveland, New York, and our own 49ers. But we can't go on supporting the rest of the league."[11] Morabito's words about supporting the league would prove prophetic, at least as far as the Chicago situation was concerned.

October opened with a familiar scenario: the Rockets lost again in front of a small crowd at Soldier Field on the first day of the month. This time Morabito's 49ers did the honors, 31–14. Only 14,553 fans were on hand. McKeever's worst nightmare had become reality. The Rockets had absorbed three "bad lickings" at the hands of the AAFC's two powerhouses. And things would only get worse for the AAFC's Chicago franchise.

Although Morabito had pointed to Buffalo as a franchise that was showing promise, the Bills weren't drawing the crowds to their home games in 1948 that they'd drawn in 1947. Only 17,694 ventured to Civic Stadium on Sunday, October 3, to watch the Bills top the Dodgers, 31–21. Buffalo's defense held Brooklyn to nine yards rushing. Brooklyn's defense held Buffalo to 222 yards on the ground. Hunchy Hoernschmeyer's two touchdown passes kept the winless Dodgers in the contest.

Morabito called Baltimore one of the AAFC's problem franchises, but the Colts, unlike the Bills, continued to attract sizable crowds to their home games. A Tuesday night contest against the Browns was expected to put 50,000 fans in Babe Ruth Stadium, but a rainy, windy night cut that figure by more than half. Rain fell for 12 hours before the game and didn't let up during the contest. The field was reduced to a muddy mess. Combined with gusty winds, the conditions weren't conducive to throwing the football, which both the Browns and Colts specialized in. The players slogged through mud up to their ankles and Cleveland prevailed, 14–10. A crowd of 22,239 braved the miserable weather.

On Friday, October 8, the Dons hosted the Rockets and out-scored their guests, 49–28. The crowd in Memorial Coliseum was 31,119.

Cleveland's Municipal Stadium was a busy place on Sunday, October 10. When, in late September, it appeared that the Indians were headed for the World Series, the fifth game of which would be played in the American League participant's ballpark on the 10th of October, the Browns considered switching their scheduled game with the Dodgers to Brooklyn. The Dodgers would then move their December 5 home game against the Browns to Municipal Stadium. That was quickly ruled out, as was the idea of playing the game on a weeknight. Instead, the Browns moved the kickoff from 2:00 to 8:30. After a record crowd of 86,288 watched the Indians lose to the Boston Braves in the afternoon, a clean-up crew had roughly three hours to get the huge stadium ready for the evening's football game. It was an impossible task.

For the second straight year, the Browns had more trouble on their home field with the Dodgers than they should have. The game was tied twice, at 10–10 and 17–17, before Cleveland pulled away for a 30–17 victory. The Browns remained undefeated. The Dodgers remained without a victory. The crowd of 31,187 meant a total of 117,475 people had witnessed two sporting events in Municipal Stadium on that October day.

In Buffalo, the Yankees rallied from a 13-0 third quarter deficit to edge the Bills, 14–13. Spec Sanders ran four yards for a score in the third period, then heaved a 53-yard scoring pass to Lowell Wagner with five seconds to play to complete the comeback. Harvey Johnson converted both extra points for New York, giving him 52 consecutive successful kicks in an era when extra points weren't automatic, as they would eventually become, until the distance was lengthened to 33 yards in 2015. In spite of the intra-state rivalry, the game drew only 18,825 fans to Civic Stadium.

In Baltimore, the weather had cleared and the fans returned to Babe Ruth Stadium. They didn't like what they saw. The 49ers humbled the Colts, 56–14. Frankie Albert set an AAFC record for passing efficiency by completing 13 of 15, two of them for touchdowns. The lone highlight for the 37,209 Colt fans was Lu Gambino's 40-yard gallop for his first professional touchdown.

The Rockets generally played their home games on Friday nights, to avoid competing with the Bears and Cardinals. Somehow, a Sunday afternoon home contest had been scheduled for October 31. Chicago's two NFL teams would both be playing at home that day, and Rockets management, alarmed by the small crowds the team was drawing when it was competing with high school games on Fridays, envisioned a potential disaster on Halloween afternoon. The game with the Yankees was transferred to New York, where the Giants would be on the road. Not that it mattered. The Yankees didn't mind going head-to-head with the NFL rival that played less than a mile away. The Yankees would visit Chicago on December 5, the final Sunday of the regular season. The game was changed a second time to December 4.

On October 15, the Dodgers beat the Rockets in Ebbets Field, 21–7. The battle between the two weakest clubs in the AAFC drew a crowd of 8,671, which cheered Carl Voyles' first victory as a professional coach. In Los Angeles, the Colts stopped the Dons, 29–14. The visitors broke a 14-all tie with 15 fourth quarter points on a touchdown, two field goals and a safety. A crowd of 40,019 watched. On Sunday the 17th, the Browns defeated the Bills in Cleveland, 31–14. The crowd of 28,054 was the smallest ever to watch the Browns at home. Even as the Browns continued to win, and continued to lead all of professional football in attendance, the crowds in Municipal Stadium got progressively smaller. In New York, the 49ers polished off the Yankees, 21–7. The game was viewed by 29,043 fans.

The National Football League's policy since Arch Ward announced the formation of the All-America Football Conference in 1944 was to ignore it. But it was impossible to ignore the money owners were spending to out-bid each other for talent, and Philadelphia Eagles owner Alex Thompson thought he could put a stop to the madness. Thompson, presumably without the blessing of commissioner Bert Bell or his fellow owners, proposed a "meet and greet" session in his New York office for late in October. "I just about had it fixed," Thompson lamented. "I felt that if they would get to know each other, they might settle their differences and end this silly business of throwing money away."

Thompson's olive branch toward the AAFC was snapped by Dan Topping on October 18, the day before the scheduled meeting. Topping told writers in New York that the Giants would lose $200,000 in 1948, a suggestion the Mara family immediately and vehemently denied. That was the end of the peace conference. "When my people heard what Dan had said, they backed out of the meeting," Thompson seethed. "Now it's impossible to do anything more about it, and from now on I'm in the fight against the All-America as strongly as our other owners. Any conciliation between the leagues is impossible. I've made my efforts, and now the hell with it. From now on, it's really going to be a battle."[12]

Topping was contrite about the statement that had ruined the first chance for a face-to-face dialogue between the owners of teams in the two leagues. "When I pointed out last week that football under the current set up was a losing proposition, I did not wish this to be construed as derogatory of any club or individuals. I hope we can all make money some day and that we can find the set up to do so."[13] Topping made the statement on October 27, the day he announced that Red Strader had been hired as the Yankees' head coach and general manager for 1949.

Thompson's bravado was short-lived. He was tired of losing money and would continue seeking ways to end the war between the two leagues. The remaining 14 months of the AAFC's existence would be filled with rumors of peace agreements with the NFL.

The Browns and Yankees had met six times in the brief history of the AAFC, twice for the league's championship. With Strader in charge of the Yankees, it was anticipated the Cleveland–New York match up in Municipal Stadium on October 24 would be just as bitterly contested as the first six had been. The 46,912 who attended the game were destined to be disappointed. With the once powerful visitors still in a state of disarray, the Browns waltzed to a 35–0 lead and controlled the game from the opening kickoff. The only bright spot for the Yankees was that they managed to break the shutout with a touchdown in the closing seconds. Otto Graham shredded the Yankee defense for 21 completions and 310 passing yards, plus four touchdowns. The fact the Browns and Yankees had drawn a crowd in excess of 80,000 the last time they'd clashed in Cleveland was seen by many observers of professional football as a cause for concern, and an indication that the AAFC was in serious trouble. Even the fans of its flagship franchise seemed to be getting bored with it.

Elsewhere in the AAFC on that Sunday, the 49ers overcame a 10–0 deficit and beat the Colts, 21–10, in Kezar Stadium before a surprisingly small crowd of 27,978. Four hundred miles down the coast in Los Angeles, the Bills beat the Dons, 35–21, in a game the home team led at one point, 14–0. The crowd in Memorial Coliseum was 26,818. In Soldier Field, the Dodgers finished a sweep of their home-and-home series with the Rockets, 35–14. Only 5,964 die-hard football fans showed up to watch. The Rockets would be the only team the Dodgers would defeat in 1948.

Through the games of October 24, the AAFC was averaging 29,029 per game, a minimal increase over attendance through the same number of contests (33) in 1947. The 49ers were averaging 41,000 fans per game. The Colts were drawing an average of 32,000. Compared to 1947, attendance was up by 8,000 in San Francisco, by 7,000 in Baltimore, by 6,000 in Chicago and by 1,000 in Brooklyn. The attendance boosts in Chicago and Brooklyn were negligible, and both franchises were sources of extreme concern for the AAFC.

The NFL had played 26 games through October 24, with an average attendance of 28,859.

Three AAFC games were played on Halloween. In Yankee Stadium, where the Rockets game versus the Yankees had been transferred to avoid competing directly with the Bears and Cardinals, New York walloped Chicago, 42–7. Yankees quarterback Pete Layden, filling in for Spec Sanders, accounted for 332 yards of offense. Layden completed nine passes for a whopping 216 yards (24 yards per completion) and ran for another 116 yards. Harvey Johnson was perfect on six extra point attempts, giving him 60 successful conversions in a row. The professional record was 72, held by Jack Manders of the Bears. Manders set the mark from 1933 to 1937. Only 13,329 attended the game. The short notice of the change of venue may have held the crowd down. Or the fact it was Halloween. Or maybe Yankee fans couldn't get excited about their team playing the wretched Rockets, even though it meant a sure victory.

Not far away, in Ebbets Field, the Dodgers lost to the Dons, 17–0. Glenn Dobbs played only three minutes due to bruised ribs, but in that short period he completed five of five passes, one for a touchdown. The Dons' defense held the Dodgers to 80 rushing yards. As bad as the Dodgers had been, it was the first time they'd failed to score in a game. The action was viewed by 12,825.

All the AAFC games took place in New York state on October 31. In Buffalo, a crowd of 23,694 was treated to an offensive explosion the likes of which the league had never seen. The Bills and Colts combined for 893 yards of offense. In a duel of the league's two premier young quarterbacks, Buffalo's George Ratterman, in his second year, threw for 295 yards. Baltimore's prize rookie, Y.A. Tittle, answered with 269 passing yards. The Bills won, 35–17.

The AAFC standings at the close of October:

Eastern Division

Buffalo	4–5–0	225–226
Baltimore	4–5–0	201–223
New York	3–6–0	143–212
Brooklyn	2–7–0	144–208

Western Division

San Francisco	9–0–0	315–111
Cleveland	8–0–0	220–92
Los Angeles	5–4–0	173–164
Chicago	1–9–0	115–289

Commissioner Ingram's effort to improve competitive balance had paid off in the east, where all four teams had a shot, admittedly, a long shot in Brooklyn's case, at winning the division. On the other hand, it isn't hard to understand why fans had a difficult time getting excited over the prospect of a team with a losing record claiming the eastern title, which was a distinct possibility.

It was a different story in the west, where arguably the two best teams in professional football resided. The Browns and 49ers would meet twice in November and produce the kind of epic struggles that were expected from two teams who'd combined to win all of their games through the season's first two months. The Dons remained good but not good enough. Their 5–4 record would have put them on top in the east. And the Rockets were still the Rockets, in spite of management's (and Ingram's) best efforts to strengthen them.

The first showdown between the undefeated Browns and undefeated 49ers would be Sunday, November 14, in Cleveland. The Browns prepared for it by defeating the Colts, 28–7, in Municipal Stadium on November 7, as a crowd of 32,314 watched. The 49ers warmed up by trouncing Chicago, 44–21, in Kezar Stadium. San Francisco jumped out to a 37–0 lead which allowed coach Buck Shaw to rest many of his regulars in the second half, in preparation for the visit to Cleveland the following week. The Rockets scored three cosmetic touchdowns against the 49ers' reserves. A crowd of 25,306 approved.

In the east, Buffalo took sole possession of first place by edging the

Dodgers in Brooklyn, 26–21. Rookie quarterback Bob Chappuis accounted for all but 12 of his team's 265-yard offensive output. Chappuis completed 26 of 51 passes for 211 yards, and ran for another 42. The 26 completions and 51 attempts were AAFC records for an individual. The Dodgers threw 53 passes and ran only 15 times. After his hot week against Baltimore, Ratterman cooled off considerably against Brooklyn, throwing just 13 passes and completing only three. But the Bills didn't have to throw. They bludgeoned Brooklyn's defense for 419 rushing yards. The crowd in Ebbets Field was just 7,805.

In Yankee Stadium, the Yankees ran over the Dons, 38–6, to tie Baltimore for second place. Only 17,386 fans were on hand. Buffalo was in first place with a record of 5–5, followed by Baltimore and New York at 4–6. Brooklyn, at 2–8, still had a mathematical shot at winning the division. Compared to the west, it's understandable that fans of the eastern teams weren't impressed. The Bills, Colts and Yankees were knocking themselves out for the chance to be steamrolled by either the Browns or 49ers in the championship game.

It was like the good old days in Cleveland the next Sunday, if a three-year-old sports league can have an era known as the good old days. For the first time in modern professional football history, two teams with a combined record of 19–0 met on the gridiron, and 82,769 fans descended on Municipal Stadium on a cold afternoon to watch the heavyweights duke it out. A 49er team loaded with rookies may have shown some early jitters when Forrest Hall fumbled the opening kickoff. Lou Saban recovered for Cleveland, and three plays later the Browns were on the board on a 14-yard scramble by Otto Graham.

The visitors answered with an 80-yard march that ended with a one-yard plunge by Joe (the Jet) Perry that tied the score at the end of the first quarter. It remained 7–7 until early in the second half. The Browns took the kickoff and navigated 84 yards for a touchdown, coming on a four-yard run by Edgar (Special Delivery) Jones followed by Lou Groza's extra point. That finished the day's scoring, and the Browns, at 10–0, had moved half a game ahead of the 49ers in the race for the western division title.

Cleveland's defense held San Francisco's potent passing attack to just 32 yards. Coach Shaw had an explanation. "They were knocking our ends down in scrimmage," he explained. "The only time we could get loose was when we spread our ends."

Shaw thought his team's inexperience, compared to the veteran-laden Browns, worked against it. "I think we were tightened up. About half our club consists of first-year men in pro ball. They were a bit in awe of the Browns. We gave away one touchdown—that first one—as a gift. But that other one was really earned by the Browns. They're a good, solid team. But we just couldn't get the ball often enough. When you consider that the Browns had the ball about 75 percent of the time, our boys must have played good ball to keep the score as close as it was."[14]

The Browns were 10–0, the 49ers were 10–1. Shaw and his team wouldn't have to wait long for another shot at the defending champions. It would come on November 28 in Kezar Stadium.

Contrast that with the free-for-all raging in the east. While the Browns and 49ers were battling, the Dons beat the Bills, 27–20, in Buffalo. Glenn Dobbs hit Joe Aguirre with a touchdown pass in the final half-minute for the victory. The loss dropped the Bills into a three-way tie for first with the Yankees and Colts. In keeping with the season-long trend in Buffalo, attendance was a good, but hardly overwhelming 23,725. The Bills were fighting for first place, but they weren't lighting a fire under their fans.

The Colts kept pace by scoring 28 second half points for a 38–24 victory over the Rockets in Baltimore. A crowd of 21,899 watched. In New York, the Yankees took down the Dodgers, 21–7. According to the Associated Press correspondent who covered the game, "until its dying seconds, it was the season's dullest in the huge ballpark, providing hardly enough action to keep the 15,555 paying customers awake." Harvey Johnson's three successful extra point conversions gave him 68 straight, five away from establishing a new professional record.

The Bills, Colts and Yankees were all 5–6. The Dodgers slipped to 2–9 with their loss to New York, but still weren't mathematically eliminated, being three games behind with three to play.

After personally viewing the Browns' victory over the 49ers, commissioner Ingram was expected in New York the next morning to meet with some of the NFL's club owners. Alex Thompson's initiative had accomplished one thing: the NFL was no longer refusing to acknowledge that the AAFC even existed. That was progress. Ingram said he thought the crowd of nearly 83,000 fans in Cleveland would get the older league's attention. "I think the crowd and high grade of football will have a tremendous effect on negotiations with the National League, and influence those gentlemen in the league having personal pet peeves,"[15] said Ingram.

Cleveland's victory over San Francisco was its final home game of the regular season. The Browns had four games remaining, all on the road. Three would be played within a span of eight days, starting in Yankee Stadium on Sunday, November 21. This was no quirk in the AAFC schedule. This was Branch Rickey's grand experiment, designed to prove a professional football team could play two games per week, every week, for three months.

"If Brown had come to me and kicked loud enough about the schedule, I'd have thrown it in the waste basket," said Ingram after Brown moaned about his team's upcoming trip to three cities on two coasts in eight days. "But he himself told me any schedule would be acceptable to him as long as he didn't have to make two trips to the coast. Then, when the tentative schedule came up for a vote, seven teams voted for it, and only Brown was against it."[16] Brown got his wish not to make two trips to the west coast. The Browns would start the trip in New York, then play the Dons in Los Angeles and the 49ers in San Francisco.

The Browns-Yankees game on November 21 may not have been the clash of powerhouses the fans of both teams had grown accustomed to, but it was still a critical game for both teams and a potential preview of the AAFC championship. The Browns were in first place in the west, the Yankees were tied for first place in the east. The largest crowd to witness a professional football game in New York City in 1948, 49,931, traveled to Yankee Stadium and watched the visitors take a fast 14–0 lead. The home team tied it. The Browns then scored 20 unanswered points and posted a relatively easy 34–21 victory. Two games remained in Rickey's odyssey.

Harvey Johnson converted all three extra points for New York, leaving him one shy of tying the professional record and two short of setting a new one.

While the Browns and Yankees were skirmishing in the Bronx, the wildest shootout in pro football's history was going on in Brooklyn. The 49ers and Dodgers combined for a staggering 103 points with San Francisco winning, 63–40. The combatants rolled up 1,030 yards of offense and established 16 AAFC records for ball movement. Unfortunately, only 9,336 fans saw the historic game.

Down the eastern seaboard in Baltimore, the Dons nosed out the Colts, 17–14. Ben Agajanian's 17-yard field goal with 35 seconds to play provided the winning points. The crowd was 25,228.

In the west, Cleveland was 11–0. San Francisco was 11–1. In the east, the idle Bills took first place by a half game over New York and Baltimore. Buffalo was 5–6, the Colts and Yankees were 5–7.

On Thanksgiving, 60,031 Los Angeles residents postponed their turkey dinners, or ate them early, so they could watch the Dons host the Browns in Memorial Coliseum. Cleveland did all of its scoring in the middle of the game, with 14 points in the second quarter and 17 more in the third. That was more than enough to dispatch the Dons, 31–14. Immediately after the game, the Browns boarded a plane for San Francisco, their perfect season intact at 12–0. They'd have two days to prepare for the game that would probably determine the western division's champion.

In Soldier Field, 6,305 people also postponed their turkey dinners, or ate them early, so they could watch the Rockets blow a winnable game to Buffalo, 39–35. The Bills scored a pair of touchdowns in the game's final four minutes on a 90-yard punt return by Rex Bumgardner and a 61-yard fumble return by Vic Kulbitski. The victory evened Buffalo's record at 6–6. The Bills had a one-game lead in the eastern division with two games left. Like the Browns, the Bills had little opportunity to enjoy their Thanksgiving victory.

They got on a plane for New York, where they had a date with the Yankees in just two days.

If the Browns were going to defeat the 49ers and clinch their third straight division title, it appeared they'd have to do it without Otto Graham. The league's premier quarterback suffered a knee injury in the victory over the Dons, and wasn't expected to even suit up for the San Francisco game. "I felt it snap and I was afraid it was broken,"[17] Graham said on the flight to San Francisco. But he said he felt better on the morning of the game and told Brown he wanted to try warming up with his teammates. Brown left the final decision up to his quarterback.

"I felt pretty sure I could pass, even if I couldn't run," said Graham. "When I told Brown I wanted to try it, he said it was up to me, that he didn't want to take the chance of ruining me for good. We agreed then that I would start the game, and let him know if I couldn't stay in there."[18]

San Francisco coach Buck Shaw was so impressed by Graham's grit that he gave his defensive players an extraordinary order: as badly as Shaw wanted to beat the Browns, he instructed his players not to intentionally target Graham's ailing knee in an effort to put him out of the game, and possibly jeopardize his career. Perhaps even more amazingly, Shaw's players heeded their coach's order. When told of the gesture after the game, Graham expressed his appreciation for Shaw's sportsmanship.

If Graham had known of a rumor floating around Kezar Stadium prior to the kickoff, wild horses couldn't have kept him off the field. In mid–November, a series of coin flips were conducted to determine where playoff games would be held in the event of ties for the division titles. The Browns won the flip with the 49ers, meaning if the two clubs had tied for the western title, the playoff would have been held in Municipal Stadium, where a crowd in excess of 80,000 would be virtually guaranteed, despite Cleveland's miserable December weather. With the Browns all but assured of winning their final game in Brooklyn, the rumor mill said they would take a dive against the 49ers to set up a playoff that would earn each player on both teams an extra game's pay. In Graham's case, that would amount to about $1,500.

"If I had known about it, I wouldn't have deliberated a second about playing!" raged Graham after the game. "I would have played on a broken leg. How can people be so stupid and narrow-minded?"[19]

In the loss to the Browns two weeks earlier, Forrest Hall had fumbled the opening kickoff and Cleveland recovered, leading to a quick touchdown. In the game in Kezar Stadium, 49ers running back Jim Cason fumbled on the game's first play from scrimmage. Cleveland linebacker Tony Adamle recovered at the San Francisco 41, and Graham wasted no time connecting with Dante Lavelli for a touchdown and a 7–0 lead. Only 63 seconds had elapsed. Lou Groza's field goal gave the Browns a 10–0 lead after the first period.

The 49ers scored twice in the second quarter for a 14–10 halftime lead, and expanded the lead to 21–10 in the third period. With six minutes gone in the second half and the 49ers up by 11, San Francisco took possession of the ball on Cleveland's 27 yard line. Another touchdown might have put the game out of reach, but the Browns' defense stiffened and kept the 49ers off the board. Then Graham, injured knee and all, went to work. He led the Browns to three touchdowns in an eight-minute span and the score was 31–21 as the fourth quarter began. With their season hanging in the balance, the 49ers started the fourth period by marching 79 yards for a score on a pass from Frankie Albert to Joe Perry, cutting their deficit to three points. The crowd of 59,875 was on its feet, begging for another score.

Three games in eight days in three different cities on both coasts had taken their toll on the Browns' defense. Graham watched his teammates stagger off the field after Perry's touchdown and knew what the offense had to do. Six minutes and 50 seconds remained when the Browns received the kickoff. The offense held the ball for six minutes, driving to the San Francisco 12 yard line before turning it over on downs. Paul Brown didn't want to risk a block of a Groza field goal attempt on fourth down. The defense sacked Albert on the game's final play, and the Browns were 31–28 winners. They were also 13–0 and champions of the AAFC's western division.

Graham had completed 11 of 23 passes for 234 yards and four touchdowns. "Under the circumstances, it was Otto's greatest performance,"[20] said Brown.

The eastern division title was still up for grabs, but the Bills secured a piece of it with a 35–14 thrashing of the Yankees on November 28. Harvey Johnson's two extra point conversions gave him 73 straight, a new professional record. A crowd of 18,376 watched the game in Yankee Stadium.

The Colts kept their hope of forging a tie and forcing a playoff (which would be played in Babe Ruth Stadium if it was necessary) by bouncing the Dodgers in Brooklyn, 38–20. Baltimore overcame a three-point third period deficit, helped by the passing of Tittle, who completed 20 of 26 for 249 yards and two scores. Only 7,625 watched the Dodgers' 11th loss against two victories.

The Bills were 7–6, the Colts 6–7. They'd clash the following week in Baltimore in the final game of the regular season.

The final weekend of the AAFC season featured two significant games. In Baltimore, the Colts could tie for the eastern division championship with a victory over the visiting Bills, who could clinch the title with a victory over the host Colts. In Brooklyn, the Browns would try to become only the third major league football team of the modern era to complete its season without a loss or a tie. The 1934 Bears were 13–0 before losing the championship game to the Giants. The 1942 Bears were 11–0 before losing the championship game to the Redskins.

The potentially history-making accomplishment was being greeted with a yawn everywhere, even in Cleveland. In his game preview of December 4, Harold Sauerbrei of the *Cleveland Plain Dealer* wrote, "With nothing of importance riding on the game itself, some interest will center on individual performances," such as Graham's attempt to lead the league in total offense. Later in the same column, Sauerbrei reiterated the fact that the game was "meaningless." As far as Cleveland's newspapers were concerned, an undefeated, untied season meant nothing. Not so to Paul Brown and the players, however.

Before the players got off the plane in Cleveland following the division title-clinching victory over the 49ers, Brown spoke to them and said, "We've come a long way, and I wish you fellows would continue to bear down for two more weeks. I'd like to finish without a defeat. That hasn't happened very often in professional football."[21] An undefeated season may not have been important to the men who covered the Browns for Cleveland's three daily papers, but it meant something to the men who'd been laying it on the line since late in August.

The AAFC's final weekend opened with the Yankees handing the Rockets their 11th straight loss, 28–7, in front of a crowd that could barely be detected without the aid of a magnifying glass in 100,000-seat Soldier Field. The real mystery was why 4,930 people couldn't find anything better to do that Saturday. An interception and two recovered fumbles helped the Yankees to a quick 21–0 lead, and they cruised from there. The depths of the mess that was the Chicago franchise would be revealed at a meeting of the AAFC's team owners in Cleveland the weekend of the league's championship game.

On December 5 in Los Angeles, the 49ers beat the Dons, 38–21. Frankie Albert threw 55 passes and completed 27 for 405 yards and three touchdowns. Albert ran for 26 yards, and his 431 yards of total offense broke Brooklyn's Bob Chappuis' record of 367, set earlier in the year. In a league as young as the AAFC, records tended not to stand for very long. Albert's 405 passing yards shattered his own single-game record of 356. The three touchdown tosses gave Albert 29 for the season, eclipsing Sid Luckman's professional record of 28 for the Bears. A crowd of 51,460 watched the intra-state rivalry. Despite the big gathering, the Dons' season attendance of 286,317 represented a decline of 14,000 from 1947. As for the 49ers, their record of 12–2, both defeats to the Browns by a total of ten points, earned them nothing more than a ticket home to begin their off-season jobs.

Meanwhile, in Baltimore, two teams with 13-victories between them squared off with the eastern title at stake. The Colts easily polished off the Bills, 35–15, to secure a tie and force a play-off the following week. A crowd of 33,090 roared its approval.

The Browns took their head coach's words to heart. They jumped to a

31–0 lead over the Dodgers in their quest to finish off an undefeated, untied regular season. When Brown called off the dogs, the Dodgers came to life, scoring three touchdowns against the Cleveland reserves. An alarmed Brown put his regulars back in the game to nail down the 31–21 victory, and achieve a slice of history. An Ebbets Field crowd of 9,821 watched what would prove to be the last game the Brooklyn football Dodgers would ever play.

At the conclusion of the AAFC's third regular season, the standings showed:

Eastern Division

Buffalo	7–7–0	.500	360–358
Baltimore	7–7–0	.500	333–327
New York	6–8–0	.429	265–301
Brooklyn	2–12–0	.143	253–387

Western Division

Cleveland	14–0–0	1.000	389–190
San Francisco	12–2–0	.857	495–248
Los Angeles	7–7–0	.500	258–305
Chicago	1–13–0	.071	202–439

As was the case in 1946 and 1947, the AAFC's strength was concentrated in the west in 1948. Ingram's "share the wealth" plan had helped build the Colts into a respectable team, but it had done nothing for the woebegone Rockets. The Browns were still a juggernaut despite the loss of some talent thanks to Ingram's re-distribution effort, and the 49ers, due in part to their refusal to cooperate with Ingram, had become one. When the league's owners met in Cleveland the weekend of December 18, the Brooklyn and Chicago situations would top their agenda. So what else was new?

Through three quarters of their divisional play-off with the Bills in Babe Ruth Stadium on Sunday, December 12, the Colts were in control and appeared to be on their way to Cleveland for the AAFC championship game. Then Bills quarterback George Ratterman got hot. Trailing 17–7 with 11 minutes to play, Ratterman connected with Bill Gompers on a 66-yard catch-and-run that sliced Baltimore's lead to 17–14. With five minutes to go and the Colts hanging on to their three-point lead came the play that completely changed the game's momentum.

Ratterman was moving the Buffalo offense when Colts tackle Johnny Mellus fell on a loose ball, apparently ending the Bills' threat and possibly saving the game for Baltimore. That was what 27,325 fans thought, but side judge Tommy Whelan disagreed. Whelan ruled the play an incomplete pass rather than a fumble, and Buffalo retained possession. It wasn't the first call Whelan had made on the afternoon that had angered the Baltimore fans, and they became even angrier when, six plays later, Ratterman put the Bills ahead with a 26-yard pass to Alton Baldwin. Bills linebacker Ed (Buckets) Hirsch quashed any chance of a Colts comeback when he intercepted a Y.A. Tittle pass and returned it for a score, making the final 28–17.

It wasn't known how many furious Colt fans stormed the field after the final gun, but they all made a beeline for Whelan, who needed police protection to get into the referees' dressing quarters. He arrived with torn clothing and a swollen eye, courtesy of some fans who'd managed to get a pop at him in spite of the presence of the police. Hundreds of fans gathered outside the stadium's administration wing, where the referees dressed, and tossed bottles at the structure. Others lingered inside and started fires to vent their anger. Whelan had to be smuggled out of the building and out of town on the Bills' team bus. Before departing, he defiantly told deputy commissioner Scrappy Kessing "that's the way I saw it, and I'd call it that way seven days of the week!"[22]

Bob Embry, the Colts' irate team president, angrily confronted commissioner Ingram and told him Whelan's officiating had cost his team the game and a shot at the league championship. Ingram declined to talk to reporters after the contest, but Embry had plenty to say. He said he probably wouldn't file a formal protest of Whelan's officiating, and he ultimately didn't. But he did formally ask Ingram never to assign Whelan to officiate another Colts game, either in Baltimore or on the road.

The melee resulted in just one arrest. A Colts rooter named Charles Ledvinka was charged with disorderly conduct, and fined $10 and court costs.

While the statisticians compiled the numbers the players had amassed on the field during the 1948 season, the accountants compiled the numbers that mattered most to the owners. Overall, according to the Associated Press, attendance in professional football was down by 11.9 percent from 1947. In the AAFC, attendance had plunged by 196,928, or a 10.8 percent decline from 1947. The league's games had averaged 28,888 patrons. The news wasn't all bad, as the 49ers had experienced an attendance increase of 45,394. The Colts saw a modest rise of 7,000 over the previous season. Back to the bad news: even though they'd led all of professional football in attendance for the third straight season, the undefeated Browns attracted almost 75,000 fewer fans to Municipal Stadium in 1948 than in 1947. The mammoth crowd of 82,769 that watched the game with the 49ers represented more than 25 percent of the full season's attendance. The Dodgers had drawn just 72,497 customers, or barely more than 10,000 per game. Although the Rockets managed to lure 104,481 fans to their seven home games, the attendance at their last three games had been a pitiful 17,199.

For the third straight season, the AAFC's per game average attendance exceeded the NFL's: 28,888 fans to 27,783.

It was little wonder that owners in both leagues were desperate for some sort of détente between the AAFC and NFL. Ignoring the AAFC hadn't made it magically disappear, so the NFL realized something had to be done to come to terms with its pesky competitor. The *Chicago Daily News* reported on December 15 that George Halas had met with Dan Topping and Ben Lindheimer, the Chicago resident who owned the Los Angeles Dons. The newspaper boldly proclaimed that an "armistice" was at hand.

First, there was the formality of crowning an AAFC champion for 1948. The odds makers didn't think much of Buffalo's chance of defeating the Browns, especially in Cleveland. The Browns were established as 17-point favorites.

The Associated Press announced its combined AAFC-NFL all-pro squad on December 17. Only an offensive team was selected, and of the 11 players chosen, four of them toiled in the AAFC. Quarterback Otto Graham, end Mac Speedie and fullback Marion Motley of Cleveland were picked, along with offensive lineman Dick Barwegan of Baltimore.

The struggle for supremacy of the AAFC would be staged only for the eyes of those who purchased tickets, and for the ears of those listening on the radio. Negotiations to beam the signal back to Buffalo's WBEN-TV, using the facilities and equipment of Cleveland's WNBK-TV, which had been on the air barely a month, fell through at the last moment. The league tried to make a deal with NBC to televise the game to its affiliates in the Midwest, but that effort, too, went nowhere. The network couldn't find one single sponsor for the game. Such was the AAFC's lack of prestige with the corporate world.

"We've worked hard for this game," said Paul Brown on December 18, the day before the title tilt. "We're in good physical shape, and the players have an intense desire to finish unbeaten. They will make a sincere effort to succeed where every other professional team has failed."[23]

And succeed the Browns did. As an embarrassingly small crowd of 22,981 watched in massive Municipal Stadium, the Browns walloped the Bills, 49–7. Slogging their way through 35-degree temperatures and two inches of snow, the two teams played on relatively even terms in the first half. All Cleveland's offense could manage in the first half was Edgar Jones' three-yard run in the first quarter for a 7–0 lead. The defense contributed the second score, when George Young returned a fumble 18 yards for a touchdown. The Bills went to their dressing room trailing 14–0 at halftime and harboring legitimate aspirations of pulling off a huge upset. Then the roof caved in on them in the second half.

Jones caught a nine-yard scoring pass from Graham, Motley ran for three touchdowns, and Lou Saban picked off a pass by Buffalo's reserve quarterback, Jim Still, and returned it 39 yards for the game's final touchdown. The Bills dented the scoreboard on a ten-yard pass from Still to Alton Baldwin

Running back Edgar Jones (left), quarterback Otto Graham, fullback Marion Motley (76) and linebacker Lou Saban (front) celebrate the Browns' 49-7 trouncing of the Buffalo Bills in the 1948 AAFC title game. The victory capped a 15-0 season, the first of only two undefeated, untied seasons in modern professional football history. The Browns' accomplishment is not recognized by the NFL (Michael Schwartz Library, Cleveland State University).

in the third quarter. That denied the Browns a shutout, about the only accomplishment they failed to achieve in 1948. The Browns became the first team in modern major league football history to put together an undefeated, untied (15-0) championship season. The NFL, to this day, refuses to acknowledge the accomplishment. In the opinion of the NFL, the only undefeated, untied league champion in professional football history was the 1972 Miami Dolphins.

"Undoubtedly the greatest team in football history,"[24] said Jimmy Phelan, whose Dons had fallen to the Browns twice in 1948.

"It's the best team I've ever coached," said Paul Brown, stating the obvious. "I've thought that all season long, of course, but I didn't want to mention it until I had a chance to watch them play it out."[25]

The Browns wanted a chance to play one more game, against the NFL champion Philadelphia Eagles. While the Browns were buffaloing the Bills, the Eagles squeezed out a 7-0 victory over the Chicago Cardinals in a blizzard in Philadelphia. The conditions were so miserable that commissioner Bert Bell ruled before the game there would be no measurements to determine the position of the ball. The decision of the referee would be final. The game's only points were scored on a five-yard run by Hall of Fame halfback Steve Van Buren early in the fourth quarter.

"We're ready to meet them any place and any time,"[26] said Brown when asked about a play-off with the Eagles. Alex Thompson felt the same way. Thompson lost money even though his team had won its first NFL championship, and he knew he could recoup some of that money, or maybe even turn a small profit, with his share of the proceeds of an AAFC-NFL championship game.

Thompson's fellow owners, whose permission he needed to stage such a game, wouldn't hear of it.

9

Wounded, but Still Alive

It was a phrase that would be heard often during the final year of the All-America Football Conference's existence.

A sensible solution.

Owners on both sides insisted that was all they asked for. But they couldn't decide what constituted that sensible solution. In the opinion of each and every AAFC owner, that sensible solution included a common draft of college players to eliminate the bidding wars that were driving up every team's payroll. George Halas, whose Chicago Bears were among the handful of teams that turned a profit in 1948, disagreed.

"I don't believe there is any chance of a common draft between the two leagues," said Halas on December 19, the day the Browns played the Bills for the AAFC championship and the Cardinals took on the Eagles for the NFL crown. "But certainly we can sit down and work out *a sensible solution*."[1]

The Associated Press polled the ten NFL owners in late December and asked their opinions regarding some sort of working agreement with the AAFC. Without revealing any individual votes, the wire service said four NFL owners were opposed to any kind of agreement with the AAFC, two favored an agreement, and four were non-committal.

Said Ted Collins, the owner of the Boston Yanks, "I'm only interested in the National Football League."[2] Collins wanted to move his Yanks to New York, which, under the current conditions, would have given the Big Apple four professional football teams.

Said George Preston Marshall, the irascible owner of the Washington Redskins, "I'm not interested in the All-America Conference. The National League can get along without them."[3]

Tim Mara, co-owner of the New York Giants, answered "absolutely no! What could we gain?"[4]

Ray Benningsen of the Cardinals chipped in, "I don't see any practical purpose in getting together with the AAC. The AAC has only proved that it is a failure. I don't think the Chicago Rockets have taken one customer from my ball club."[5] The Rockets would've been hard-pressed to steal a single customer from a Pop Warner team.

Art Rooney of the Pittsburgh Steelers and Curly Lambeau of the Green Bay Packers were among the more moderate voices. Said Rooney, "I'm in favor of any *sensible solution* to the pro football problem."[6] Added Lambeau, "I'm in favor of any *sensible solution*, but definitely not a merger. I am not in favor of a common draft."[7] If a merger and a common draft were off the table, what else was left but a continuation of the status quo?

While hardliners such as Marshall and Mara insisted they wanted no part of the AAFC, in truth there were two franchises the NFL coveted: the Browns and the 49ers. Some NFL owners had opposed Dan Reeves' request to move the Rams from Cleveland to Los Angeles in January of 1946, and shortly after the transfer became official, those owners made an offer to Mickey McBride to abandon the AAFC and move his Browns into the NFL. McBride wasn't interested. There's reason to believe the "sensible solution" most NFL owners wanted consisted of the Browns and 49ers joining the old league, and the rest of the AAFC's teams disbanding. And Cleveland and San Francisco would be welcomed into the fold only on the NFL's terms.

On the morning of the two league championship games, the news on the field competed with the news off the field for space in the nation's newspapers. Rumor had it that a confab had been arranged between the NFL's owners and a committee representing the AAFC for the following day in Philadelphia. Halas confirmed reports that he'd met with Dan Topping and Ben Lindheimer. "As individuals, we had a meeting of minds on the subject. But nothing can be done until the league takes up a discussion of the matter."[8]

The AAFC's publicity office released a response to Halas' statement. "The All-America Conference is happy to learn that a member of the National Football League is of the opinion that the time for peace has arrived. We sincerely hope something will develop along that line."[9] And not just any member of the NFL was expressing hope for peace, but George Halas, the league's founding father, whose Bears had survived three different challenges from rival leagues prior to the AAFC. Despite its problems, the AAFC wasn't going to collapse like those other leagues, and Halas recognized that.

And the AAFC did have some serious problems, which were addressed at its pre-championship game meeting in Cleveland on December 17 and 18. The most pressing problem, as it had been at the pre-championship game owners meetings in 1946 and 1947, was again what to do about the Rockets? The group that purchased the Rockets in the spring of 1948 apparently wasn't the same group that had expressed an interest in the team after the 1947 season, a group of businessmen commissioner Jonas Ingram had claimed were worth a collective $33,000,000. The group that bought the Rockets had some impressive credentials, two elected public officials being among them, but, apparently, no cash. It was revealed at the owners meeting that McBride, Topping and 49ers owner Tony Morabito had grudgingly advanced the Rockets $100,000 between them in October to keep the team from folding. Although all three men may have been personally inclined to let the Rockets disband and be done with them, it would've wreaked havoc with the league's schedule, so each anted up $33,333 to let the team meet its payroll and finish out the season.

Nonetheless, Ingram told reporters before the two-day session that the AAFC was planning to proceed into 1949 with the same eight franchises that finished 1948. "Our only problem will be Chicago, and we expect to make that our main topic the next two days. A year ago, we had three problems: Chicago, Brooklyn and Baltimore. Brooklyn had a bad year from the attendance and victory standpoints (what other standpoints were there?), but Branch Rickey has assured me his baseball operations will carry football and he expects to continue. He is making plans for next year, and says he hopes to bring Brooklyn a winner."[10] Until he got a look at the final ledger sheet.

Lindheimer said all eight teams, including Chicago, would participate in the draft of eligible college players scheduled for the day after the championship game. He claimed the Rockets were still a member in good standing of the AAFC and the present ownership would remain in control if the team stayed in Chicago. He said the Rockets had until the league's next scheduled meeting in late January to come up with $200,000 to guarantee they could operate in 1949.

Then, sounding much like Ingram had sounded in 1947 when he talked about the future of AAFC football in Chicago, Lindheimer added. "if they fail to do so, or decide to quit, we have another extremely substantial financial group, in another city, waiting to take over the franchise."[11] The AAFC always seemed to have "extremely substantial financial groups" waiting to assume control of ailing franchises. Especially Chicago's.

Ingram said when the Rockets were on the verge of bankruptcy in mid–October, he was in favor of letting the franchise fold. But he'd changed his mind since then. He called Chicago the hub of American football, and said it was important for the AAFC to be represented there by a strong franchise. Ingram suggested that Lindheimer might sell the Dons and buy the Rockets, or he might buy the NFL's Cardinals and move them into the AAFC.

As for the possibility of peace with the NFL, Ingram said, "I'm confident seven of the owners in the National League are in favor of some kind of working agreement now. I'm confident some kind of settlement will be made within the next month. It really shouldn't be very difficult to put a plan in operation. The main thing is to work out the make up of the leagues, arrange a schedule that will have no conflicts, and plan a common draft. I'm in favor of two eight-team leagues, with a team from Chicago in each."[12] Disbanding the Rockets and having Lindheimer buy the Cardinals and move them into the AAFC would fit that scenario.

The problem, or one of the problems, was the common draft. The AAFC insisted any peace agreement had to include one. The NFL swore it would never agree to one, even though its owners were as weary of paying untested rookies huge salaries as the AAFC owners were. How the NFL owners expected to control player salaries without a common draft isn't known. The NFL owners didn't say how they wanted to do it, only that they wanted to do it. And they'd do it if the sensible solution called for the Browns and 49ers to defect and the rest of the AAFC to quietly go away.

Eagles owner Alex Thompson was one of the few NFL moguls not opposed to a common player draft. Despite winning the league championship, Thompson had lost $32,000 running the Eagles in 1948. "I'd be a fool if I didn't try and resolve a situation in which most of us are losing money," he said. "If the two leagues form a pool from which they draft players, it will cut out competitive bidding and keep down player salaries."[13]

Marshall scoffed at Thompson's idea. Marshall said he spent only a third of his team's operating budget on player salaries and saw no need for a common draft. Marshall, of course, was on record as seeing no need for the AAFC. "The real trouble is simple," he said of the financial losses suffered by both leagues. "Not enough people will pay enough money to see pro football games."[14]

At the conclusion of the AAFC's pre-championship game meeting, Ingram dropped a bombshell. First, he said that "we are proceeding with our plans for next year, and will hold our draft meeting as planned. Co-operative relations continues to be the desire of our conference." Ingram had been hired as commissioner two years earlier and charged with achieving an end to the pro football war. He'd failed to that point, and he was growing increasingly frustrated. "Unless there is peace between the two leagues within the next 30 days, I am through with professional football. I took this job two years ago, after my retirement from the Navy, with the intention of staying only one year. I thought I could bring about a settlement between the two leagues. It's still my hope to see them get together, and if that doesn't happen soon, I'll step out."[15]

The AAFC owners professed to be blind-sided by Ingram's announcement, but rumor had it that he was being forced out by those same owners. Word was that Lindheimer, who recommended Ingram for the job, was disappointed by his performance and wanted him replaced. For public consumption, Lindheimer said Ingram had done an outstanding job, and the AAFC hoped to retain him as its commissioner for many years to come.

After clobbering the Bills to put an exclamation point on their undefeated championship season, the Browns had to share the headlines the following morning with stories about McBride's departure for Philadelphia the night before. Ingram led the AAFC's delegation, accompanied by McBride, Morabito, Topping, Lindheimer, and Bills owner Jim Breuil. "Since they are coming here, I assume they have something to offer,"[16] said Mara tersely.

Speculation flew about possible scenarios that would be discussed at the peace conference. A hot rumor had Ted Collins' New York Yanks merging with Topping's New York Yankees and playing in Yankee Stadium. The New York Yanks had been the Boston Yanks before Collins announced he was transferring the team to New York on December 18. An equally sizzling rumor claimed the Cardinals and Rockets would merge. The one-day gathering of the warring factions produced nothing.

A joint statement summarizing the day's events was released to the press. "Representatives of the National Football League and the All-America Conference concluded a meeting tonight in Philadelphia. Efforts by both sides to formulate a mutually satisfactory agreement were not consummated. The committees terminated the meeting with the expectation that future meetings might provide some formula for a common understanding between the two leagues."[17]

The NFL's terms were essentially these: the Browns and 49ers would be welcomed into the NFL for 1949. The rest of the AAFC would fold. The stumbling block was the refusal of the Baltimore Colts to surrender their franchise. The Colts insisted on joining the NFL, and Marshall wanted no part of a franchise so close to his Redskins.

NFL boss Bert Bell said he hoped negotiations would continue in the future, and said Marshall hadn't been an impediment to a peace agreement. He reiterated that peace would be reached on the NFL's terms, or not at all.

"I don't see any solution to this problem, because they are the type of men who go down with the thing," Marshall said of the fruitless negotiations. "They are all nice fellows, but they don't know how to run a football business." Then Marshall added an observation that would prove to be prescient. "They didn't know a seven-team league wouldn't work."[18]

If the AAFC did proceed as a seven-team league in 1949, the team to be jettisoned wouldn't be the Bills. Owner Breuil spoke to reporters before departing Buffalo's harsh December climate for Florida two days before Christmas. "Professional football will stay in Buffalo," he promised. "Although our meeting in Philadelphia wasn't successful, it pointed to a lot of sense coming out of the meeting. I have no positive statements to make at this moment, because I don't want to say anything that might hurt professional football, but I can say the pro game will stay in Buffalo."[19] The only way pro football would stay in Buffalo was if the AAFC stayed in business. The NFL wasn't interested in absorbing the Bills.

The *New York Daily News* reported on December 21 that Carl Voyles had been fired as head coach of the Dodgers, who won just two games and lost 12 in 1948. The newspaper said Voyles would earn the $12,500 he was due on his contract by serving as Brooklyn's business manager in 1949. To make room for him in that capacity, business manager Gerry O'Brien had been dismissed. A team spokesman, who asked not to be identified, denied the report. There was ample reason to believe there wouldn't be a Dodger team for Voyles, or someone else, to coach in 1949.

Bob Cooke, sports editor of the *New York Herald-Tribune*, predicted a "new order" in professional football in his column of January 11, 1949. Cooke said he'd learned from "authoritative sources" that Topping would be willing to liquidate the Yankees and rent Yankee Stadium to Collins, if that would facilitate a peace agreement between the AAFC and NFL. Cooke wrote that Topping was fed up with losing money on his football team. According to Cooke, if Topping dissolved the Yankees, "it is the considered opinion among professional football people that the two leagues can amalgamate in a happy manner if the case of the Baltimore Colts can be settled."

"We are willing, but please don't say we are anxious, to become a landlord, if it means peace in pro football," admitted Topping. "I would like to stay in the game, and if peace doesn't come, I will operate a team." Topping said the vote to accept the merger proposal offered at the December meeting in Philadelphia had been 9–1, with Marshall voting against it. The NFL constitution required a unanimous vote.

"Pressure will have to be brought to bear on Marshall,"[20] Topping said of the next scheduled peace conference. He also said that since the NFL wouldn't include his Yankees in a merger agreement, he expected his players and coaches to be taken care of.

The results of the next scheduled peace conference, according to the United Press, were expected to be a 14-team NFL with two divisions. The Yankees, Dodgers and Rockets would fold. The Dons and Rams would merge. The Browns, 49ers, Colts and Bills would join the NFL. The Yanks would rent Yankee Stadium from Topping. The U.P. claimed Reeves and Lindheimer had met twice to work out the details of a merger of their teams, and that Bob Embry hoped to meet with Marshall to assuage his concern about having the Colts in the same league with his Redskins.

Prior to the AAFC owners meeting scheduled for January 18, McBride mounted a one-man crusade to keep the league alive. McBride tried to convince Branch Rickey to give the Dodgers one more year; to keep the Rockets in Chicago; and to talk Morabito into operating the 49ers in a six-team AAFC, should the worst-case scenario (that the Rockets and Dodgers would both fold) come to pass. Morabito said he believed it would be financial folly to run a league with only a half dozen teams. If the AAFC didn't field eight clubs in 1949, Morabito was out.

Conventional wisdom said the owners of the Rockets, finding themselves unable to post the $200,000 guarantee for the coming season required by the league, would turn the team over to the AAFC, which would terminate it. If a buyer could be found at the last minute, McBride said he and his fellow owners would make sure the team had the funds to navigate through a full season, even if it sustained significant losses. "This time, all owners will have to guarantee in writing that they'll be able to meet their obligations,"[21] he said, remembering the money he'd squandered to help keep the Rockets alive in 1948.

Before the league meeting began, Lindheimer said he'd be interested in a swap of the Rockets for his Los Angeles Dons. He'd be willing to move the Dons to Chicago, if a buyer could be found who'd move the Rockets to Los Angeles. He found no takers for that proposition.

When a professional football team draws just 72,000 fans in a season, as the Dodgers did in 1948, a huge financial loss had to be anticipated. In Brooklyn's case, it was a staggering $319,000. Rickey personally covered $80,000 of the loss. The baseball Dodgers, who owned the football Dodgers, were on the hook for the rest. Rickey, who was once described as a man who tossed around nickels like they were manhole covers by a baseball player he'd negotiated a contract with, had no intention of subjecting himself, or his profitable baseball operation, to another financial bath in 1949. If Brooklyn was to return to the AAFC, substantial financial concessions would have to be made. Rickey's fellow owners agreed to waive the league minimum $15,000 guarantee paid to the visiting team when the Browns, Yankees, Dons and 49ers played in Ebbets Field. Those four teams agreed to play in Brooklyn for free. That would save Rickey $60,000. But that wouldn't be enough. The Dodgers threw in the towel. They had won just eight games in three futile seasons in the AAFC. There was no "extremely substantial financial group" waiting in the wings to bail them out. There was no mention of a merger with the Dodgers' next door neighbors, Topping's Yankees, but that would be their eventual fate.

In the flurry of activity between late December and late January, it can be difficult to separate fiction from fact. Rumors about the AAFC's future, or lack of a future, flew faster than cars around the Indianapolis Motor Speedway on Memorial Day. Between January 16 and 19, it was first reported that Lindheimer and Reeves had agreed to merge the Dons and the Rams, with Lindheimer owning controlling interest in the amalgamated team. That story was false. Then it was reported that Lindheimer had purchased the Rockets. That story was full of holes as well. It was then reported that Lindheimer, who lived in Chicago and had many business connections, had arranged for $300,000 in financing to keep the team afloat and in Chicago. That story had legs. The men putting up the cash would be introduced in February.

9. Wounded, but Still Alive

As he'd promised to do if peace between the AAFC and NFL hadn't been achieved by the next league meeting, commissioner Ingram submitted his resignation on the 21st of January. "I'm definitely through with professional football," he said in stepping aside. "Now that we have set this thing up to operate another year, I think they should get a new and younger man to carry on from here. There are no weak links in the chain as it stands today."[22]

The owners chose neither a new nor a younger man to guide them. Well, not much younger. They elevated deputy commissioner Oliver Owen Kessing to replace his old boss. Kessing was hired for one year at a salary of $30,000. "I am deeply appreciative of the honor and will do all in my power to preserve the strength and integrity of the All-America Conference,"[23] the new commissioner said. The position of deputy commissioner, created by Ingram to accommodate Kessing, wouldn't be filled.

On January 21, McBride met with eight NFL owners and proposed a pair of seven-team leagues, a plan Marshall and Mara rejected out of hand. Some of their fellow owners, tired of battling the AAFC and losing money, were getting weary of the intransigence of the owners of the Redskins and Giants. Alex Thompson had already had enough and sold the Eagles in mid-January. The owners who favored McBride's plan urged him to ask for an audience with commissioner Bell, although there were some observers in the nation's sporting press who wondered whether Bell or Marshall was actually running the NFL. McBride said talking to Bell would be a waste of time.

"I gave it a lot of thought, and decided to recommend [to his fellow AAFC owners] going along by ourselves under the seven-team set-up. I don't think we would have gotten very far by sending someone to see Bell,"[24] a weary McBride said.

Said Bell smugly, "My door has been open right along. I'd be glad to talk with them any time."[25] One unidentified NFL owner said Bell had been talking with Tony Morabito and his attorney, Marshall Leahy, in an effort to convince the 49ers to defect from the seven-team AAFC and join the NFL. Morabito didn't like the thought of losing revenue by playing just six games in Kezar Stadium rather than seven, now that the Dodgers had bowed out. Ultimately, however, the AAFC owners had been bonded into a close-knit fraternity by their shared experience of butting heads with the NFL, and Morabito chose not to leave his comrades high and dry. Losing the 49ers probably would've meant the end of the AAFC.

McBride was tired of ceaseless speculation that his coach, Paul Brown, was reaching for the doorknob. So was Brown. On January 31, McBride extended Brown's contract by five years, through the 1955 season. The financial terms remained almost identical to the contract he'd signed in 1945, and which still had two years remaining. Brown would be paid $25,000 per season and receive 15 percent of the club's profits.

In the happy Municipal Stadium dressing room following his team's victory over Buffalo in the 1948 title game, Brown had said simply, "I do not intend to leave Cleveland. I never have."[26] And while he spent 1948 denying rampant rumors that he was a candidate for every college football head coaching vacancy that opened up, he admitted on the day he signed his new contract that he'd received numerous feelers from colleges about his availability. And he considered some of them.

"I had to make up my mind because several schools were pushing me for a decision,"[27] he confessed. He told McBride about the offers, and McBride responded with a five-year contract extension which Brown accepted. In spite of the shaky status of the AAFC, Brown decided to stick with the professionals. It truly wasn't much of a gamble, because there was no doubt the Browns would wind up in the NFL. The only question was when.

Brown's 15 percent of the team's profits amounted to a big, fat zero in 1948. Due to declining attendance, McBride said his football business lost $35,000. McBride estimated that Baltimore had lost $43,000; New York $50,000; Buffalo $100,000; Chicago $100,000; and Los Angeles $250,000. San Francisco eked out a minuscule profit of three thousand dollars. McBride didn't like losing money, but $35,000 was hardly going to break him. Topping could easily withstand the Yankees' loss, as could Breuil in Buffalo. Losing a quarter of a million dollars wasn't going to bankrupt Lindheimer in Los Angeles, and the Colts numbered among their shareholders Jerry Hoffberger, reported to be the wealthiest man in Maryland. Chicago's loss, of course, had forced its owners out of the sport, as had the Dodgers' loss of almost $320,000. Branch Rickey could have stuck it out another year, but saw no reason to throw good money after bad. Brooklyn had never supported professional football, dating back to the arrival of the NFL in 1931, and there was no reason to believe that would suddenly change in 1949.

As Whitey Lewis wrote in the *Cleveland Press*, "Don't get the idea the AAC or its individual club owners are short of cash. The AAC is probably sounder than the National League. The latter has all the heritage, but it lacks fast men with a free buck." Those fast men, however, hadn't acquired those free bucks by investing in losing propositions. Another financial bath like the one the AAFC endured in 1948 would be disastrous.

On Groundhog Day, football fans in Chicago were introduced to the men Lindheimer had recruited to put up $300,000 to keep the Rockets in town and try to revive them. The principal financial backer was 52-year-old banker James Thompson. Thompson's partners were attorney Lee Freeman and public utilities executive Irwin Rooks. On the surface, it appeared that the Rockets would again be operated by men with more prestige than money, although McBride had made it clear that any prospective owners would have their finances thoroughly investigated before their bid was accepted. If

Lindheimer said the new owners of the Rockets had $300,000 to operate the team, they must have had it.

"Let's have a helluva good team in Chicago, and then worry about peace with the National League,"[28] Thompson said to the assembled writers. He admitted that as late as the day before the introductory news conference, he had no idea where the team's office was. But he intended to learn about the Rockets' operation quickly.

The first order of business in re-building the team was to change its nickname. Chicago's AAFC representative would henceforth be known as the Hornets. Twenty-six members of the defunct Brooklyn Dodgers would have their contracts transferred to Chicago, including quarterback Bob Chappuis, halfback Hunchy Hoernschmeyer (formerly a Rocket), ends Hank Foldberg, Dan Edwards and Max Morris, and center George Strohmayer. Halfback Bob Schweiger would be sent from the Yankees to the Hornets.

The second order of business was finding a coach. Ed McKeever had already been fired after a miserable 1–13 season. Thompson's group hired the best available man: former Yankees head coach Ray Flaherty. Flaherty's track record gave the Hornets instant credibility. He'd coached the Washington Redskins to three NFL championship games, winning twice, and he'd won a pair of AAFC eastern division titles with the Yankees. Flaherty wasn't desperate to return to coaching and studied the Hornets' roster before accepting the job.

"I looked over the possible material for five days before I took the job," he said. "The club had to guarantee me some more players before I agreed to be the coach. I would say the team we have is at least equal to the men we had in New York when we won the divisional championship."[29] That assessment would prove to be overly optimistic, but Flaherty's Hornets would be significantly improved over Jim Crowley's dismal 1947 team and McKeever's equally wretched 1948 squad.

On the topic of coaches, the first coach of the Rockets, Dick Hanley, was still fighting with the team's first owner, John Keeshin, over his contract. Three years after the fact, Hanley continued to insist Keeshin had fired him, and hadn't paid off his contract. Keeshin claimed Hanley quit, and was sticking to his story. Hanley filed a lawsuit against the AAFC, seeking payment of the $38,750 Keeshin owed him. Commissioner Kessing said it wasn't the league's problem and told Hanley to take it up with Keeshin.

On February 6, the Associated Press reported that Bell would hold a press conference the following day to set the record straight, at least as he saw it, regarding the failure of the Philadelphia meeting in December to result in peace between the AAFC and the NFL. The press conference took place as scheduled, and the AAFC quickly responded. It was, of course, illogical at best and asinine at worst to expect the differences between the two leagues to have been overcome in one day, but that was the expectation of the fans (and the owners) on both sides, and both sides had spent the month of January explaining what went wrong.

In a nutshell, Bell claimed that the failure of the Philadelphia conference had not been the fault of the NFL, and specifically, it had not been the fault of George Preston Marshall and Tim Mara.

The AAFC's response, also in a nutshell, was that the failure of the Philadelphia conference was entirely the fault of the NFL, and the two owners most to blame for the failure were George Preston Marshall and Tim Mara.

Specifically, Bell made the bizarre accusation that the AAFC owners arrived in Philadelphia with several peace proposals, then rejected each one before the NFL had a chance to consider them. Bell said the owners of the AAFC's strongest teams tried to force a merger with the NFL, with as many as five AAFC teams being absorbed into the older league. Realizing that idea was doomed, Bell said the AAFC owners then tried to ram a merger involving two or three teams down the NFL's throat. Failing that, Bell said the AAFC owners wanted to invest in existing NFL teams.

"Obstacles to a merger were insurmountable," Bell summarized. "Under present conditions, there was no hope for a common draft or inter-league play."[30]

Lindheimer and McBride wasted no time responding to Bell's claims. It's significant that the AAFC didn't issue its rebuttal to Bell through newly-elected commissioner Scrappy Kessing, but rather through Lindheimer, who was described by the International News Service as the AAFC's executive chairman. Lindheimer insisted the AAFC had put forth no proposals to merge with the NFL.

"We have never believed that a one-league operation is practical," he said. As to Bell's claim that owners of the strong teams, such as Lindheimer's Dons, were willing to sacrifice the weaker teams in order to achieve a merger, he responded that "never at any time have we considered any plan that did not first deal fairly and honorably with all members of our conference. We were always assured that a majority of the members of the National Football League were in favor of working out a mutually agreeable plan in the best interests of major league football. The entire membership of the All-America Conference have always been in favor of such a plan."[31]

But who was going to define "the best interests of major league football?" Obviously, the AAFC and NFL had vastly different definitions of that term. In the opinion of the AAFC owners, the best interests of major league football would be served by two separate but equal leagues who operated under a common draft, and whose champions met at the end of each season in a championship game. In the opinion of the NFL owners, the best interests of major league football would be served by the Browns and 49ers joining their league and the rest of the AAFC fading into oblivion.

9. Wounded, but Still Alive 177

One day in Philadelphia wasn't going to change the perception of either side.

McBride, in an interview with the *Cleveland Press*, provided some details of the proposals the AAFC took to Philadelphia. And he laid the blame for the failure of the meeting squarely at the feet of Marshall and Mara. McBride said the only concession the two NFL hardliners were willing to make was to accept a merger of the Dons and Rams into a single Los Angeles team. They wanted Cleveland and San Francisco in the NFL, but not Buffalo, the Yankees (especially Mara) and Baltimore (especially Marshall). Mara couldn't be blamed for resisting a third NFL team in New York (the Boston Yanks had moved to New York and would share the Polo Grounds with the Giants), and Marshall couldn't be blamed for not wanting an NFL team 25 miles to the north of his Redskins. Still, McBride blasted both men for their refusal to cooperate. "Marshall and Mara blocked the deal. They didn't want peace—all they wanted was the Browns and the San Francisco 49ers to join the National League. We held out for recognition of the [AAFC]." In truth, Marshall and Mara did want peace—but, as Bell pointed out repeatedly, *only on the NFL's terms*. Those terms had been made clear to the AAFC, and they were exactly as McBride said—the Browns and 49ers would join the NFL, and the rest of the AAFC would disintegrate and blow away.

McBride elaborated on some rather interesting proposals the AAFC placed on the negotiating table in Philadelphia. Proposals that, according to Bell, the same owners who suggested them immediately rejected. "We proposed that they put the Philadelphia Eagles and the Chicago Cardinals in our league to replace the Brooklyn Dodgers and the Chicago Rockets," he told the *Press*. Since the Eagles had defeated the Cardinals in the NFL championship game, it's little wonder the NFL wasn't interested in that proposal, allowing two of its strongest teams to defect to the AAFC to replace its two weakest clubs. "Several National League owners seemed willing to compromise by transferring the Cardinals and the Detroit Lions to our league and giving us the merged Los Angeles teams, but Marshall and Mara wouldn't budge."

He went on, "I insisted at the meeting, and later in informal chats with National Leaguers, that two seven-team leagues was the healthiest solution, but nothing will happen as long as Marshall and Mara hold out for one league which includes only the Browns and the 49ers."[32] That explains Marshall's comment that the AAFC owners didn't seem to understand that a seven-team league wouldn't work.

Minus Brooklyn, or a replacement for it, a seven-team league was what the AAFC was stuck with, and it was the arrangement the league was prepared to move forward with in 1949. "The All-America Conference will continue to operate through the years, independent of any other league," Lindheimer said confidently. "Its members are sufficiently stable financially to insure a sound business operation. We know that the football fans of America are whole-heartedly interested in knowing who are the champions in major league football. We have always been ready and willing to determine this all-important question by offering to play our championship team against the National League's championship team on any terms and under any circumstances. The working out of such an agreement is solely within the province of the National Football League."[33] Public pressure for an AAFC-NFL championship game hadn't influenced the NFL so far, and it wouldn't influence the NFL in February of 1949.

There had been a significant difference between the haves and have-nots in both the AAFC and NFL in 1948. In the AAFC, the top two teams, Cleveland and San Francisco, were a combined 26–2, with both of the 49ers' losses coming courtesy of the Browns. The Bills, Colts and Dons finished at .500. The Yankees were 6–8. The Dodgers and Rockets were a combined 3–25. Both of Brooklyn's victories were at Chicago's expense. The Dodgers were 0–12 against the rest of the AAFC.

In the NFL, the Eagles, Cardinals and Bears were a combined 30–5–1. The Redskins and Rams were a combined 13–10–1. The rest of the league (Giants, Steelers, Yanks, Packers, Lions) combined for a record of 16–44. The Cardinals' two-year reign as champions of the NFL's western division was about to end. There were unverified rumors that George Halas, despite being the coach of the Cardinals' arch-rivals, had surreptitiously funneled talented players to them in order to strengthen them for the crucial battle against the Rockets for fan support. During the 1946–48 seasons, the Cardinals won two division titles, one NFL championship, and posted an overall record of 27–10 (including post-season games.) From 1943–45, the Cardinals had won but one game and lost 29. Halas figured he'd deal with the Cardinals once the AAFC threat was eliminated. The Rockets helped enormously by constantly tripping over their own feet. They'd be under their fourth ownership and their eighth head coach when the 1949 season opened.

The merger of the Yankees and Dodgers was completed on February 23. The front offices of the two clubs were combined in a corporation called the Brooklyn–New York Football Club, Incorporated. Dan Topping was the team's president. Branch Rickey was chairman of the board. The team would play its home games in Yankee Stadium and continue to be called the Yankees. Red Strader was the club's head coach and general manager. Carl Voyles' contract had been assigned to the baseball Dodgers. The Associated Press said Voyles would report to Brooklyn's spring training camp to perform unspecified duties. Most of the football Dodgers' former players had already been re-assigned to the Chicago Hornets. The Yankees didn't need or want them.

Thanks to three consecutive AAFC championships, including the unprecedented undefeated season of 1948, the cost of doing business was increasing for the Browns. Paul Brown, whose job it was to sign the players to contracts before coaching them to championships, wasn't happy about it. The players who'd lost just three games in three seasons, and none since October of 1947, thought they deserved to be compensated for that accomplishment. Brown didn't necessarily disagree, but he thought many of the 17 players who hadn't signed by early in April had overvalued their services. And he made it clear he wouldn't hesitate to break up the team if keeping it together became too expensive. The rest of the AAFC could only hope.

"I'm not making any secret of the fact that we are having some difficulty coming to terms in some of our salary negotiations," he said. "If things get too far out of line with some of the boys, I'm just going to make some sales. I have some definite plans for a few of them. It will apparently be necessary in order to keep some semblance of order in the salary talks. I don't intend to pull a Connie Mack and break up my team completely, but the public will be in for some surprises unless the attitude of some of the fellows changes."[34] Mack was the legendary manager of the Philadelphia Athletics who'd broken up both of his team's dynasties (1910–1914 and 1927–1932) by selling off his players. In both cases, the Athletics plunged into the American League's cellar for extended periods.

In order to enhance their chances of winning the battle for fans and ticket money in Los Angeles, the Rams announced in April that they would reduce the price of some 60,000 seats in the 100,000-seat Memorial Coliseum for their six home games in 1949. Tickets on the 50 yard line would sell for $2.50, and 40,000 other tickets would go for just $1.50. Dan Reeves was willing to make a smaller profit on each ticket in the hope of selling a lot more tickets. More, he hoped, than the Dons would sell.

Branch Rickey was determined to prove a professional football team could handle playing twice a week, thus doubling the number of games it could play, and, theoretically, doubling the amount of money his organization could make. Though Rickey no longer owned a team in the AAFC, he was chairman of the board of the Yankees, and volunteered his team for the same grueling eight-day stretch the Browns had somehow survived in 1948. The one difference was that the Browns played all three of their games on the road. The Yankees would open their stretch of three games in eight days at home, hosting Cleveland on Sunday, November 20. They'd then fly to the west coast to meet the Dons in the Coliseum on Thanksgiving, November 24, and finish the meat grinder with a game against the 49ers in Kezar Stadium on Sunday, November 27. If the Browns could do it, Rickey was convinced the Yankees could do it. And if the Yankees were up to the task, Rickey would have his proof that any professional football team could play twice a week. Rickey had suggested the AAFC play a 29-game schedule in 1949. That was before the Dodgers merged with the Yankees, and the league's schedule was cut to 12-games. If the AAFC survived into 1950, he would likely have proposed a 24-game season. Each team playing its six opponents four times would've gotten tiresome quickly.

In late April, the Browns announced they'd host their bitter rivals, the 49ers, in an exhibition game with the proceeds benefiting the Cleveland Zoo. Brown said if the match was well-attended, a benefit for the zoo might become an annual pre-season event, and might even attract an NFL team as an opponent in the summer of 1950. Of the on-going war between the leagues, Brown responded, reportedly with a smile on his face, that "the situation has reached a point where one doesn't make a move without the other. That should be significant of something."[35] Whether it meant secret negotiations were taking place to bring about the *sensible solution* both leagues were seeking wasn't mentioned. Nothing transpired in the coming months to indicate that any such talks were going on.

Spec Sanders confirmed on June 9 what had been reported back in December: injuries forced him to retire at the age of 31, following two highly productive and one mildly productive season in the backfield of the Yankees. Like just about everyone in the AAFC, Sanders' career got a late start due to his military commitment. He didn't play his first professional game until he was 28. In three seasons with the Yankees, Sanders gained exactly 2,900 yards rushing. He led the league with 709 yards in 1946 and a professional record 1,432 in 1947. His 169 rushes paced the league in 1948, but his yardage gained plunged to 759. As a passer, Sanders completed 48.9 percent of his 421 passes, good for 2,829 yards, 23 touchdowns and 37 interceptions. Sanders would come out of retirement in 1950, when the Yankees merged with the New York Bulldogs of the NFL. He'd see action in 12 games, mostly as a punter and safety. He averaged 42.3 yards on 71 kicks and returned six punts for an average of 15.5 yards. He wouldn't carry the ball from scrimmage but threw three passes and completed two. His punting earned him a spot on the Pro Bowl team.

The AAFC announced its 1948 MVP on July 2. It wasn't explained why the league waited until just a few weeks remained before training camps opened to select the previous season's most valuable player. San Francisco's Frankie Albert and Cleveland's Otto Graham shared the award, each receiving four votes from the AAFC's head coaches. Albert's coach, Buck Shaw, couldn't vote for his own quarterback. Nor could Graham's coach, Paul Brown.

Bidding wars for college talent, which could've been eliminated had the NFL (read: Marshall and Mara) not steadfastly refused to even consider a common draft, still raged in the summer of 1949. On July 13, Southern Methodist University quarterback Gil Johnson told the Associated Press he'd probably sign with the Yankees. Johnson left the door open a crack for the

NFL, however, saying he'd give the new owners of the Eagles a chance to increase their offer. But he fully expected to cast his lot with the AAFC, and he did.

The Eagles drafted Johnson in the 11th round. In 1948, Johnson completed 59.4 percent of his passes for ten touchdowns. Philadelphia wasn't inclined to raise its offer to Johnson, and it was probably glad it stood its ground. Johnson's professional career lasted one year. He saw action in nine games for the Yankees in 1949, starting none. He completed 12 of 36 passes with no touchdowns and five interceptions. He carried the ball three times and gained 21 yards. It was never revealed how much the Yankees paid Johnson, but it's little wonder owners in both leagues were growing weary of bidding against each other for what often turned out to be, as in Johnson's case, meager production.

The most highly-publicized bidding war following the 1948 season involved quarterback Stan Heath of the University of Nevada. Despite the insistence of both Bert Bell and Scrappy Kessing that Heath's college class wouldn't graduate until the spring of 1950 and he was ineligible to be drafted, Heath was selected by the Yankees in the AAFC and the Packers in the NFL. Heath made it clear he was forgoing his final year of college eligibility to cash in on the war for talent between the two leagues. Heath turned heads when he fired six touchdown passes and threw for 327 yards in just 18 minutes of action in a 79–13 victory over Oklahoma City University. He finished fifth in the Heisman Trophy balloting, and was the fifth player chosen in the NFL draft. The Yankees reportedly offered Heath a contract calling for $20,000 per season. Curly Lambeau broke the bank to out-bid Topping and sign Heath, and nearly broke the Packers at the same time. Heath was a bust in the NFL, playing just one season and completing a pathetic 24.5 percent of his passes, good for one touchdown and 14 interceptions. He was out of football by 1950, and the Packers were nearly out of business. Then as now the only publicly-owned pro football franchise, the Packers almost went bankrupt after the AAFC folded, thanks in part to disastrous expenditures like Heath's contract. Topping could afford a draft bust like Gil Johnson. Lambeau couldn't afford to misfire on the fifth player chosen in the draft. Yet Lambeau was among the hard-liners who opposed a common draft with the AAFC.

The blatant stubbornness on the part of both sides is difficult to understand. Marshall had criticized the AAFC owners for being willing to go down with the ship by plunging ahead with just seven teams in 1949, instead of agreeing to the NFL's draconian terms for peace. But the NFL owners were just as pig-headed. Lambeau was willing to risk bankrupting the team he'd founded almost 30 years earlier rather than admit his Packers couldn't survive without a common draft.

The Bills opened their training camp on July 18 without star quarterback

George Ratterman who, in the words of the Associated Press, "wants much more money than the Bills want to pay." Ratterman was back at his alma mater, Notre Dame, studying for a law degree when Bills head coach Red Dawson started camp in his team's effort to return to the AAFC playoffs.

On July 22, yet another effort was made to match the AAFC's champion against the NFL's champion to determine the best team in professional football. This time, the offer came from Glen McCarthy, whose oil wells in Texas had made him a millionaire several times over. McCarthy wanted a franchise in either the NFL or the AAFC for his hometown of Houston, but in the meantime he'd settle for promoting an AAFC-NFL title game. Oddly, he didn't offer Houston as a site for such a game, suggesting instead that it be played in either Chicago, New York or Los Angeles, each of which had much larger stadiums to accommodate much larger crowds than any venue in Houston could accommodate. As others before him had done, McCarthy played the charity card. The game's proceeds would go to charity, but McCarthy was willing to put up $125,000 of his own money to guarantee that the winning team would receive $75,000 and the losing team would get $50,000. As always, the NFL played the villain. Kessing accepted the offer. Bell rejected it, but countered with an offer of his own. Bell said the NFL would be happy to play a post-season all-star game for charity. The post-season Pro Bowl wouldn't come into being until after the 1950 season. McCarthy wasn't interested in sponsoring such a contest.

After the riot that ended the Buffalo-Baltimore playoff game in December, with side judge Tommy Whelan having to be whisked out of town on the Bills' team bus to escape irate fans who blamed him for the Colts' loss, Baltimore would seem to be an odd place for the AAFC to conduct a pre-season seminar for officials. Then again, the circumstances may have made Baltimore the perfect place for the seminar. All 16 of the AAFC's officials, including Whelan, whose presence wasn't welcomed by the Colts' front office or their fans, were scheduled to attend. All 16 officials would participate in the exhibition game between the Colts and Yankees in Babe Ruth Stadium on August 16. Each four-man officiating crew would work one quarter of the game.

Four Colts players wouldn't be participating in that game, much to the surprise of coach Cecil Isbell. On July 23, guards Earl Cook and Don Zangara, end Frank Kosikowski, and tackle Len Simonetti marched into Isbell's office and unexpectedly turned in their uniforms. No reason was given for the mass exodus, but Kosikowski and Simonetti had played for the Browns in 1948 and may have decided that toiling for an also-ran like the Colts was beneath them.

Also on July 23, commissioner Kessing announced the AAFC wouldn't drop or amend its archaic rule barring unlimited substitutions. The NFL allowed unlimited substituting, and college football allowed coaches to substitute without limitation when the ball changed hands. The AAFC chose to remain behind the times in 1949. Kessing also said the league would begin using a brown ball with two white stripes around each end for night games. Previously, for games played under the lights, the league had used a yellow football. Or, as the Associated Press described it, "lemon colored."

Elroy (Crazylegs) Hirsch never really wanted to be a Chicago Rocket, and one of the reasons the Rockets never soared was because Hirsch failed to live up to expectations, largely because of injuries, including a fractured skull sustained in a loss to the Browns early in the 1948 season. Hirsch played in just five games in both 1947 and '48. He caught only 44 passes for 730 yards and seven touchdowns in three seasons in Chicago. When his contract expired, he dealt a blow to the newly re-named Hornets, and the AAFC as a whole, by jumping to the Los Angeles Rams on July 26. Surrounded in Los Angeles by talent such as quarterbacks Bob Waterfield and Norm Van Brocklin, former college star Glenn Davis (who joined the Rams in 1950), and wide receiver Tom Fears, Hirsch's career took off. He'd help the Rams to the 1950, 1951 and 1955 NFL championship games and contribute to one of the most powerful offenses in NFL history. Hirsch wound up in the Pro Football Hall of Fame. Losing him to the NFL was a bitter pill for the AAFC to swallow. Especially for the Hornets, who could ill afford to lose anyone.

As had been the case each season of its existence, the AAFC would start its regular season almost a month before the NFL. So, in preparation, all seven AAFC clubs had opened their training camps by July 30. Only the Eagles and Rams in the NFL had begun preparing for their campaigns by that time. In Bowling Green, Ohio, the defending champion Browns had congregated for the fourth consecutive year, and coach Paul Brown warned his players, and Cleveland's sportswriters, that winning another league title would be no cakewalk.

"I honestly believe we're going into our toughest season," Brown said. "In the first place, we are facing the pressure of preserving our perfect record. Furthermore, everybody will be gunning for us with strengthened teams. Not only have the Chicago Hornets and New York Yankees been bolstered by players who were with Brooklyn, but the Los Angeles Dons, San Francisco 49ers and Buffalo Bills have made improvements where they needed them."[36] Whether or not Brown intentionally neglected to mention Baltimore, when all was said and done, the Colts weren't improved and would slip to the back of the pack in 1949.

Brown said his primary goal was to improve his team's depth, and proceeded to demean some of the players who'd helped him win three straight AAFC titles by bemoaning the fact that the Browns' performance, in his opinion, declined dramatically each time over the past three seasons that he'd rested his regulars and given the second-stringers a chance to play. Not to the point that games were lost, but enough that Brown decided a significant roster make-over was in order. Improving the team's depth would be a daunting task considering the AAFC owners had chosen to cut their payrolls by reducing rosters from 35 players to 32.

At Cleveland's training camp, newly-acquired tackle Darrell Palmer confided to Bob Yonkers of the *Press* that his former team, the Yankees, under the guidance of Ray Flaherty, had intentionally tried to injure fullback Marion Motley when the two clubs played in 1946 and 1947. "We didn't resort to any dirty tactics, but we tried to hit Motley as hard as we could, and with as much concentrated power from our big men as we could muster," Palmer confessed. "But we got the worst of it. Several of our players had to leave the game after pouring it to him while Marion just kept going as strong as before."[37] It sounded as if the Yankees tried to harm Motley strictly to sideline him and increase their chance of winning. Other AAFC teams tried their best to incapacitate Motley and his teammate, Bill Willis, for reasons that had nothing to do with competitiveness on the field. Many Caucasian players simply didn't want to be on the same field as two African Americans and did their best to render Motley and Willis physically unable to play. No one succeeded.

The Buffalo Bills opened the 1949 exhibition season with a resounding 79–0 triumph over the Jersey City Giants of the minor American Football League. The Giants were a farm club for the NFL team of the same name. That was as close as an AAFC team would ever come to playing an NFL club. Illustrative of the vast difference between football's major and minor leagues, Jersey City managed just two first downs and a dozen yards of total offense against Buffalo's defense. Astonishingly, a crowd of 31,089 attended the mismatch in Civic Stadium. A few weeks later, the Bills would pick on another AFL team, the Bethlehem (Pennsylvania) Bulldogs, and clobber them, 48–0. Buffalo led, 42–0, at halftime and went through the motions in the second half strictly for exercise. How much the two blow-outs helped prepare the Bills for AAFC competition is questionable.

In the Los Angeles Memorial Coliseum, the 49ers beat the Dons in an exhibition game, 28–7. In a market (and a stadium) it shared with the AAFC, the NFL surely must have noticed the attendance for the meaningless game: 81,272. Late in August, the other occupants of the Coliseum, the Rams, would host the Redskins in an exhibition game. The crowd for that encounter would be 64,227.

The NFL and the *Chicago Tribune*, represented by Arch Ward, the man who founded the AAFC, signed a ten-year agreement to continue the annual college all-star game on August 16. After Marshall had criticized the game in the summer of 1948 and urged the NFL to pull out of its contract with the *Tribune*, AAFC commissioner Jonas Ingram said the AAFC's champion would gladly replace the NFL's champion in the charity game if Marshall got his way. He didn't.

Two NFL players jumped to the AAFC on August 17. Guards Bob Dobelstein of the Giants and John Mastrangelo of the Steelers signed with the Yankees. The terms weren't disclosed. The signings hardly represented a major, or even a minor, coup for the junior league. The Steelers, seeking to reduce their payroll, had given Mastrangelo permission to negotiate with other teams, and he chose the Yankees. The Giants insisted losing Dobelstein to their AAFC rival which played less than a mile away was no big deal.

"Dobelstein did not fit into our plans for 1949. He goes with our blessing," said a press release issued by the Giants' PR department. Still, the AAFC wasn't about to ignore an opportunity to tweak its bitter rival. For the record, Dobelstein quickly wound up with the Dons, playing in eight games in what would be the last season of his four-year career. Mastrangelo would see action in a dozen games for the Yankees in 1949.

The Browns tied the 49ers, 21–21, in an exhibition game in Municipal Stadium on August 19. Paul Brown wasn't pleased with his team's effort, and Mickey McBride couldn't have been happy with the size of the crowd, even though he received none of the receipts from the game. The 49ers took home $25,000 for their trouble, and the rest of the gate was given to the Cleveland Zoo. The attendance was a disappointing 31,157. A week later, for their final exhibition, the Browns drew just 19,441 to the Akron Rubber Bowl for a meeting with the Yankees. The Browns' first exhibition, against Brooklyn in August of 1946, had attracted more than 35,000 people to the Rubber Bowl.

As for the numbers compiled by his team on the field, Brown minced no words. "We don't look good yet," he wailed. "We have to get better. I wasn't at all satisfied with several performances."[38] He added for emphasis, "If we don't do any better than that when the real thing starts, we'll have a helluva time beating anybody."[39]

And the real thing was at hand.

10

1949

Shortly after his defending AAFC champions opened their 1949 training camp, Browns owner Mickey McBride expressed optimism about the future of the struggling league. "The die-hards in [the NFL] are sitting around waiting for us to fold up. But the truth of the matter is we're in better condition than they are. We've got more money. We've got the bigger stadiums. We have eliminated a weak spot in Brooklyn while they have brought about an impossible situation by putting the Bulldogs [formerly the Boston Yanks] into the Polo Grounds with the Giants. We've got a much better balanced league than the National League. All of our teams will be improved over last year."[1]

The AAFC did seem to hold the stronger hand in its battle with the NFL. But when the 1949 season was in the books, it would be the AAFC's owners signing the surrender papers that ended the four-year old professional football war.

The final season of the All-America Football Conference kicked off at Soldier Field on Friday evening, August 26. Strengthened by the addition of a number former members of the defunct Brooklyn Dodgers, and coached by a proven winner in Ray Flaherty, the re-named Hornets started the season with an exciting 17–14 victory over the Bills. Bob (Hunchy) Hoernschmeyer, back with Chicago after two seasons in exile in Ebbets Field, tossed a pair of second quarter touchdown passes to Jimmy Clement. Buffalo's offense, struggling in the absence of hold-out quarterback George Ratterman, managed to tie the score. A 21-yard field goal by Jim McCarthy, kicked from "a fairly difficult angle" according to the Associated Press' game story, decided the issue in the game's final minutes. The attendance was an encouraging, but hardly overwhelming, 23,800. After just one game, Chicago had matched its victory totals for 1947 (1) and 1948 (1).

Only two games were played on the AAFC's opening weekend. With just seven teams in the league, no more than three games could be played on any given day. In San Francisco on Sunday, August 28, the 49ers started the Colts on a downward spiral from which they wouldn't recover. Led by Frankie

Albert, the AAFC's co-MVP for 1948, San Francisco took a 17–0 lead at halftime. Baltimore, paced by the AAFC's top rookie of 1948, quarterback Y.A. Tittle, rallied for 17 points in the third quarter. Touchdown runs by Norm Standlee and Verl Lilywhite in the final period gave the 49ers a 31–17 victory before what the United Press described as a "surprisingly small" crowd of 29,095 in Kezar Stadium.

The Bills realized the quarterback tandem of Jim Still and Jesse Frietas couldn't get the job done and met Ratterman's demands on August 29.

The 32-player roster claimed an illustrious victim at the end of August. With three fewer players available than in 1948, it was imperative that those kept on a team's roster be versatile. Veteran Ben Agajanian's toe had won games for the Los Angeles Dons in 1947 and '48. His 54-yard field goal was the longest in AAFC history. Overall, however, the 29-year old Agajanian had connected on only 20 of 39 field goal attempts in two seasons, including a miserable five of 15 tries in 1948. He'd missed two of 72 extra point conversion attempts. But Agajanian was strictly a kicker, and that cost him his job. The Dons' coach Jimmy Phelan released him and replaced him with center Bob Nelson. Agajanian would change leagues, signing with the Giants. He kicked eight of 13 field goals and 35 of 36 extra points in 1949. Pulling double duty as a center and placekicker, Nelson would try only six field goals and make three. He missed one of 35 extra point attempts.

The Colts finished their season-opening west coast trip by visiting the Dons in Los Angeles on Saturday, September 3. Ben Lindheimer was disappointed by the opening day crowd of just 20,211 in Memorial Coliseum, but he wasn't disappointed by the developments on the field. The Dons rolled up 528 yards of offense and steamrolled the suddenly hapless Colts, 49–17. As had been the case in their first game in San Francisco, Baltimore was competitive in the contest briefly, holding a 17–14 lead at one point before the Dons pulled away for the rout. Los Angeles had experienced a massive roster overhaul during the off-season. Twenty-one of its 32 players were rookies. The early result was promising, although the caliber of the opposition had to be considered.

On September 4, the 49ers mauled the Hornets, 42–7, as 28,311 watched in Kezar Stadium. San Francisco jumped on Chicago for four first period touchdowns and cruised to the lopsided victory. The loss was a painful one for the visitors in more ways than on the scoreboard. Chicago quarterback Walt MacDonald suffered a dislocated throwing shoulder, tackle Ted Hazelwood broke his nose, and guard Marty Wendell sustained a concussion.

The Browns opened their defense of their AAFC championship with a re-match of the 1948 title game against the Bills on September 5. Buffalo broke a 7–7 halftime tie by staggering the visitors with three touchdowns in the third quarter, sending the crowd of 31,389 at Civic Stadium nearly into delirium. Cleveland answered with three fourth quarter touchdowns. Otto Graham torched the Bills' secondary for 14 completions in 16 attempts in the game's final 15 minutes, including touchdown strikes to Mac Speedie and Horace Gillom. The game ended in a 28–28 tie, and Cleveland's unbeaten streak remained intact. Barely.

A report out of Houston on September 9 speculated that the AAFC would once again be an eight-team league in 1950, with Houston joining the fraternity. Having failed in his effort to arrange an AAFC-NFL championship game after the 1948 season, "fabulously wealthy" oil man Glenn McCarthy had made a deal with the AAFC for a post-season game to be played in Houston on December 17. The game would either pit the AAFC's newly-crowned champion against a team of AAFC all-stars or, if the champion decided it had had enough football for one year, two teams of all-stars would go at it. The proceeds would be donated to charity. The game was considered a litmus test for Houston's readiness to enter major league sports. A large crowd would probably mean McCarthy would be granted a franchise for the 1950 season.

"I'd like to see Houston come into our league," said Paul Brown. "It would be the leg the All-America Conference needs on those long trips to California every year, an ideal stopping off place."[2] Brown later revealed that McCarthy made a bid to add Houston to the AAFC in 1949, at the expense of Cleveland. Brown confirmed that McCarthy, whose business holdings included the $20,000,000 Shamrock Hotel in Houston, tried to buy the Browns from Mickey McBride and re-locate them to Texas. McBride rejected the offer. Brown made it clear that Clevelanders needn't fear losing their team to Houston or any other city. The Browns, despite their declining attendance, weren't for sale.

As to why McCarthy didn't purchase the Brooklyn Dodgers, who were very much available, and transplant them to Houston, he was a proud Texan who demanded the best and only the best for his hometown. The Dodgers were pathetic. The Browns were the best the AAFC had to offer, and that's why he wanted them in Houston.

The AAFC's third weekend of competition began on Friday, September 9, with the Hornets recovering nicely from their misadventure in San Francisco and edging the Dons, 23–21, in Los Angeles. After his team had blown a 20–0 lead, Jim McCarthy saved the day with his second game-winning field goal of the young season. McCarthy's 31-yard boot with 90 seconds to play gave the Hornets their second victory of the year, or twice as many games as they'd won in either of the two previous seasons. The crowd in Memorial Coliseum was 30,193.

Harvey Johnson duplicated Jim McCarthy's heroics for the New York Yankees in Buffalo on September 11. The Bills, perhaps suffering from the after-effects of their near-miss versus Cleveland, couldn't hold a 14–0 lead.

Johnson's 21-yard field goal with 70 seconds left in the game gave the Yankees a 17–14 victory as 30,140 disappointed fans watched.

About 120 miles to the southwest in Cleveland, the Browns opened their home season with a lackluster 21–0 victory over the reeling Colts. The smallest crowd ever to witness a Browns game in Municipal Stadium, just 21,621, was on hand. "It was a disappointing crowd, but no one is complaining," admitted McBride. "We're in the show business and you're up one week and down the next. People had been reading about the Colts losing a couple of games and having 80 points scored against them. They figured it wouldn't be a contest and didn't come out." The game marked the first time in four years the Browns had failed to draw 60,000 or more to their home opener. Did it signal a third straight season of declining attendance for the AAFC champs? McBride sounded discouraged.

"All we can do is give the fans a winner," he said. "We've done that. We can't do any more."[3] McBride noted that ticket sales for the visit by the archrival 49ers later in the season were brisk. In fact, he said he could sellout Municipal Stadium twice over for that game. Unfortunately for McBride, the enthusiasm for the Browns' four other home games was lacking.

If Clevelanders were going to watch professional football in 1949, they'd have to see it in person in Municipal Stadium. The American Broadcasting Company would televise NFL games into every AAFC city except Cleveland, by order of commissioner Bert Bell. Network executives said they had no idea why Bell wouldn't permit the NFL's "Game of the Week" to be shown on Cleveland's ABC affiliate. Bell said he made the decision to black out Cleveland in the best interest of the NFL. He refused to address speculation that he was trying to curry favor with McBride by removing televised competition to Browns games from the Cleveland market.

The surprising Hornets hammered the Colts, 35–7, in Soldier Field on Friday, September 16. It was Chicago's third victory in four games. New ownership, the infusion of talent from Brooklyn, and the hiring of Ray Flaherty as head coach appeared to be paying off. Still, Chicagoans weren't convinced that things had changed with their AAFC team. Only 18,843 fans attended the game.

On Sunday the 18th, the 49ers mangled the Dons, 42–14, in Kezar Stadium. San Francisco scored 21 points in the second quarter and 21 more in the third. Two teams who'd attracted better than 80,000 fans to an exhibition game in Los Angeles in August drew a crowd of 31,960 to a game that counted in September. In Cleveland, two teams that had drawn a mob of better than 80,000 to Municipal Stadium two years earlier lured just 26,312 to the same venue on a rainy afternoon. The Browns, bearing little resemblance to the team that had run off 15 victories without a defeat in 1948, managed to hold off the Yankees, 14–3. Cleveland's offense registered just five first downs, and the task of beating the Yankees was left to the defense.

Watching the contest from the press box in Municipal Stadium was Colts coach Cecil Isbell, who was reported to be taking copious notes, particularly when the Browns' offense was at work. The Colts had already played their game for the weekend, and Cleveland would be their next opponent at Babe Ruth Stadium on September 25. Isbell wouldn't be on the sideline, however. His tenure as Baltimore's coach ended on September 20.

The parting of ways between Isbell and the Colts was announced as a resignation, and Isbell went along with it. "Quitting is the nice way to put it,"[4] he said, and the press release said he'd be paid for the remainder of his contract, which expired after the 1949 season. But the deposed coach couldn't maintain the charade for long and told the United Press a few days later that he'd been fired. Making matters worse, he read about his dismissal in the newspapers before being informed by the club.

Isbell was replaced by the Colts' team president and general manager, Walt Driskill, for the rest of the season. Driskill didn't want the job. "The majority of the directors felt a change was in order," he said. Four straight defeats by a composite score of 136–41 was more than the directors could stomach. "I protested strenuously. I was in favor of keeping Isbell. I felt there was nothing wrong with the football team a victory wouldn't cure. But I didn't have a chance. The board suggested that I take over the coaching job and I objected strongly. I don't want to do any more coaching."[5] Driskill had never been a head coach, his experience being obtained as an assistant at four colleges including the University of Maryland. He said Isbell's assistants, Red Conkright and Mike Michalske, were welcome to stay if they wanted.

The AAFC's schedule was always meticulously crafted at a pre-season meeting, so it was no coincidence that the Yankees were scheduled to play at home on the Thursday night the NFL opened its season less than a mile away at the Polo Grounds. The Yankees wanted to go head-to-head with their new rivals for fan interest in the Big Apple, the New York Bulldogs (formerly the Boston Yanks.) As a steady rain fell, the Yankees managed to beat the Dons in the slop at Yankee Stadium, 10–7, on yet another last minute field goal. Harvey Johnson's 30-yard kick with 21 seconds to play proved to be the game-winner. Playing on a weeknight in New York wasn't a particularly good idea, and only 14,437 fans turned out. It was a bigger crowd than the Bulldogs drew, however.

Given an attractive opponent in the defending NFL champion Philadelphia Eagles, the transplanted Boston club drew a miserable gathering of 8,426 to the NFL's first regular season game of 1949. Ted Collins had been convinced moving his team to New York would solve all of his financial problems, and he'd gotten his wish. The Bulldogs lost a boring contest to the Eagles, 7–0.

The Browns spoiled Walt Driskill's debut as Colts coach on Sunday, September 25. Baltimore played inspired football in the first half and took a 13–0 lead into the Babe Ruth Stadium dressing room at halftime. The Browns played inspired football in the second half and left town with a 28–20 victory, witnessed by 34,879 spectators, the largest crowd in the AAFC so far in 1949. In Buffalo, the Bills defeated the 49ers, 28–17. Buffalo racked up 445 yards of offense to San Francisco's 230. It was the first win of the season for the Bills, and it was witnessed by a robust throng of 32,097 in Civic Stadium.

Brown could smile after his team had pulled out a close victory in Babe Ruth Stadium. He was cheered by the size of the crowds drawn by the games in Baltimore and Buffalo. "Those National Leaguers who thought Baltimore and Buffalo were weak spots in our league have a surprise in store for them,"[6] he said.

The AAFC wrapped up September with San Francisco's 42–24 thumping of the Hornets in Chicago on the 30th day of the month. 49ers quarterback Frankie Albert tossed three touchdown passes, then let his rugged running game take it from there. San Francisco gouged Chicago's defense for 357 yards on the ground while allowing the Hornets just 91. The Hornets blew a golden opportunity to impress a solid gathering of 31,561 in Soldier Field. But the bottom line was, despite being significantly improved, the Hornets still weren't in the 49ers' class.

The standings as of September 30:

Cleveland	3–0–1	91–51
San Francisco	4–1–0	174–90
Chicago	3–2–0	106–126
New York	2–1–0	30–35
Buffalo	1–2–1	84–79
Los Angeles	1–3–0	91–92
Baltimore	0–5–0	61–164

The top four clubs would qualify for the playoffs. Using criteria it would take the NFL another 34 years to adopt, the team with the best record would earn the number one seed and home field advantage throughout the post-season. The team with the second-best record would host a semi-final playoff game against the team with the third-best record. The top seed would host the team with the worst record in the tournament in the semi-finals.

The Browns weren't having any trouble selling tickets to their match-up with the 49ers in late October, and the 49ers weren't having any difficulty selling tickets for their game against the Browns in early October. When the game sold out, the 49ers asked the AAFC to drop its ban on televising home games so the fans who couldn't purchase tickets could watch from the comfort of their homes, or wherever a television was available. This was 1949, and not many homes had television. The new-fangled gadget was largely confined to public places such as bars, restaurants, and the front windows of department stores.

October began with the Browns flashing the form their fans and their coach had become accustomed to. Unfortunately, not many of those fans turned out at Municipal Stadium to watch. The Browns trashed the Dons, 42–7, to the cheers of just 30,465 spectators on Sunday, October 2. The romp stretched Cleveland's unbeaten streak, which was approaching two years in chronological length, to 29 games. In Buffalo, the Colts gave Walt Driskill his first victory as a head coach, out-scoring the Bills, 35–28. It would be Driskill's only victory as a head coach, and Baltimore's only victory of the season. The crowd in Civic Stadium was 25,692. The suddenly inept Colts weren't much of a draw on the road.

On Friday night, October 7, the Yankees sent the Hornets to their second straight defeat, 38–24, in Soldier Field. The crowd of 17,098 was slightly more than half the size of the crowd that had seen Chicago's previous game against San Francisco.

The eyes of the AAFC were on San Francisco on October 9 as the 49ers hosted the Browns. More importantly to Tony Morabito, the eyes of 59,770 paying customers in Kezar Stadium were on his team, and they screamed themselves hoarse as the 49ers took out three seasons' worth of frustration on the visitors. Cleveland's unbeaten streak, which had seen it win 27 games and tie two, came to a screeching halt, 56–28. The eight touchdowns were the most the Browns had ever allowed in a single game.

Sounding almost relieved, Paul Brown said, "It had to come some time. Now the pressure is off and maybe we can start playing football again."[7] The Browns had been performing like a team carrying the burden of keeping a record-breaking streak alive each week. But Brown wasn't so charitable after he'd had time to look at the game film and assess the embarrassing loss as only a coach can. He accused his team of being old, over the hill, and suggested strongly that if the Browns didn't bounce back convincingly against the Dons in Los Angeles the next Sunday, he wouldn't hesitate to do what a lot of fans of other AAFC teams had been praying for, he'd break up his champions and re-build them from scratch, beginning immediately.

Understandably, the Browns didn't take kindly to their coach's tirade. It was, after all, their first defeat in 30 games and almost two calendar years. Many players said that they wouldn't have minded the stinging criticism if Brown had administered it in the privacy of the team's dressing room instead of through the newspapers. Players who'd won three AAFC titles for Brown didn't appreciate being labeled suddenly "too old." If ever there'd been an opportunity for a bunch of angry athletes to quit on an overly demanding coach, this was it. Brown couldn't have carried through on his threat to break up the team in the middle of a season, so his words were most likely nothing more than a motivational ploy. But that ploy had the potential to backfire disastrously.

Four hundred miles down the California coast in Los Angeles, the Bills entered their game with the Dons as favorites. They exited the Memorial Coliseum losers by a score of 42–28. The game was a showcase for two of the AAFC's star quarterbacks, George Ratterman of Buffalo and Glenn Dobbs of Los Angeles. Ratterman passed for 305 yards and two touchdowns. Dobbs threw for 283 yards and gained 48 more rushing. The victory was a tonic for the Dons' owner Ben Lindheimer, who was in a Chicago hospital. The loss was the end of the line for Red Dawson as Buffalo's head coach.

After playing for the AAFC championship in 1948, the Bills staggered from the starting gate in 1949. The loss to the Dons dropped Buffalo's record to 1–4–1. Owner Jim Breuil met Dawson in the team's dressing room in the Memorial Coliseum and asked for his resignation. Dawson refused. The two men argued for a while. "We just could not agree,"[8] Dawson said. Breuil fired Dawson and elevated line coach Clem Crowe to head coach for the rest of the season. Crowe said he was "surprised and shocked by the unexpectedness"[9] of the change. Crowe's first assignment was preparing the Bills to face the rampaging 49ers in San Francisco the following Sunday.

While the victory may have been good for what ailed Lindheimer, the size of the crowd wasn't. The game was witnessed by just 16,757 fans.

Paul Brown rolled the dice and won. He knew his team could explode with righteous indignation and quit on him after he threatened to break it up following the 28-point loss to San Francisco. He also knew his players could respond to his cutting criticism by playing the game of their lives to prove him wrong. He bet on the latter, and he was right. On Friday night, October 14, the Browns wrapped up their west coast road swing by ripping the young Dons, 61–14. It was the second highest point total in the club's brief history, achieved largely through the efforts of Otto Graham, who launched six touchdown passes. Graham's back-up, Cliff Lewis, added a seventh. Cleveland steamrolled the Los Angeles defense for 607 yards of offense. Even a perfectionist like Brown couldn't find anything to criticize after the performance. But the 27,437 fans in Memorial Coliseum could, and the spent the evening showering their team with jeers.

Clem Crowe's indoctrination to head coaching in the professional ranks was a rough one. Any hope on the Bills' part that the 49ers might suffer a letdown after their emotional pounding of the Browns the week before vanished quickly before a crowd of 35,476 in Kezar Stadium on October 16. San Francisco scored two first quarter touchdowns and tacked on three more plus a safety in the second quarter. The final score was 51–7. It proved to be the low point of Crowe's brief head coaching career. The Bills wouldn't lose again during the regular season.

Across the continent that afternoon, the Yankees squeezed past the Colts, 24–21. Bob Kennedy's three-yard run in the fourth quarter provided the winning points. The Colts weren't winning, but that didn't stop fans from paying their way in to Babe Ruth Stadium. The game was witnessed by 32,645 patrons. If the AAFC and NFL were going to merge at season's end, as they had almost done at the end of the 1948 season, Baltimore fans wanted to make sure their Colts were part of the deal. Whether George Preston Marshall liked it or not.

Jim Breuil continued his housecleaning in Buffalo. Less than two weeks after dismissing his head coach, Breuil fired assistant coach and chief scout Hank Reese. Reese cried foul and took his case to commissioner Scrappy Kessing. Reese claimed he had a contract with Breuil running through the end of the 1949 season, but rather than paying him off, Breuil gave Reese just two weeks severance pay. Breuil's assistant, Jim Wells, told a different story. According to Wells, both Red Dawson and Reese were working without contracts.

Yankees owner Dan Topping saw the weekend of October 23 as football's version of Armageddon. Both the Yankees and Giants were playing at home that Sunday afternoon, their games taking place roughly a mile apart geographically. Each had an attractive opponent: the Yankees were hosting the powerful and star-studded 49ers, the Giants were taking on the Monsters of the Midway, George Halas' Chicago Bears. Topping viewed the weekend as a showdown to determine which league would survive the four-year old professional football war. He said that the league whose team drew the smaller of the two crowds would have to approach the other league with "hat in hand" and accept that league's surrender terms.

"The basis for the solution of this war is definitely here in New York," Topping said. "There is no reason why it can't be terminated, and next weekend may do it. There is no reason why a solution can't be worked out." He said that if each game drew at least 30,000 fans, it would prove New York could support two teams. He said nothing about the NFL's other team in New York, the Bulldogs. Topping said each game should draw more than 60,000.

"That is the way it would be if they were being played on separate Sundays. There is no sense to continue to schedule these competing attractions. And I don't think we will much longer."[10] Topping wouldn't be the only AAFC owner to suggest that the war between the leagues needed to end, and soon.

Topping's Yankees brought the high-flying 49ers back to Earth on October 23. After scoring 149 points in their previous three games, the 49ers were held to a field goal by New York's stingy defense. Frankie Albert and company failed to register so much as a first down in the game's second half and fumbled an embarrassing six times. The Yankees waltzed to a 24–3 victory. The crowd at Yankee Stadium was 36,197.

Across the Harlem River in the Polo Grounds, the Giants defeated the Bears, 35–28. The attendance was 30,587. Bert Bell did not show up at Scrappy

Kessing's office the next morning, his hat in one hand and a white flag of surrender in the other. Topping's moment of triumph would be short-lived.

In Buffalo on October 23, the Bills gave Crowe his first victory as a head coach, 17–14, over Los Angeles. The Bills managed to hold off Glenn Dobbs in the second half after taking a 17–0 lead at the intermission. The victory, watched by 21,310 in Civic Stadium, started the Bills on their march to the AAFC's fourth playoff seed. In Babe Ruth Stadium, the Colts suffered from the same problem that plagued the 49ers: an inability to hang on to the football. Baltimore fumbled six times and handed the visiting Hornets a 17–7 triumph before 23,107.

In Los Angeles, the Dons, despite being among the AAFC's best-run franchises, were falling apart. Owner Ben Lindheimer was having health problems. Crowds at Memorial Coliseum were dwindling. The influx of youth was taking its toll, and the team was out of contention for the post-season, even though more than half of the AAFC's seven teams would make the playoffs. On October 24, general manager Harry Thayer jumped ship. Lindheimer replaced him with Gil Haynes and Jack Drees. Head coach Jimmy Phelan couldn't have been encouraged by that decision. Haynes was the Dons' traveling secretary, and Drees was their public relations director. They were now in charge of making player personnel decisions.

The situation in Chicago was deteriorating as well. Ray Flaherty's Hornets were in the hunt for the AAFC's fourth playoff spot, but the fans weren't responding. After the Hornets laid an egg against the 49ers in front of a crowd of better than 31,000 in late September, the fans seemed to give up. In a match-up of two floundering franchises on Friday, October 28, the Dons beat the Hornets, 24–14. Only 11,249 (11 percent of Soldier Field's capacity) showed up to watch.

Browns minority owner Dan Sherby painted a grim picture of the AAFC's future in late October. Possibly discouraged by Cleveland's sudden indifference toward its champion Browns, Sherby declared that the owners of teams in both leagues would lose a combined $2,000,000 in 1949. He said he knew of no peace talks scheduled between the AAFC and NFL.

"Although there have been no new developments, it does not mean that something couldn't happen very suddenly. After all, the two leagues stand to lose two million dollars this year." Then Sherby got to the heart of the matter, perhaps knowingly, perhaps not. "No businessmen, no matter how wealthy they are, have any desire sinking that much money into an enterprise every football season. Something has to give, and soon."[11] It can be reasonably assumed that Sherby was speaking not only for himself, but his friend and business partner, Mickey McBride. Owners with deep pockets such as Topping, Morabito, Lindheimer, Breuil and McBride could continue losing money indefinitely and not feel the pinch. But why would they want to? The novelty of owning a major league football team had long since worn off for all those men. Particularly McBride, who would quickly have even more reason to be discouraged.

As October came to a close, rumor had it that the Bulldogs and even the legendary Packers were so financially strapped they wouldn't be able to finish their 1949 schedules. Commissioners Kessing and Bell repeatedly denied that the two leagues would consolidate into a 12-club NFL in 1950. But, as Sherby said, something had to give, and soon.

The Browns didn't have to wait long for their re-match with the 49ers. Two weeks after taking a licking in San Francisco, the Browns hosted their arch-rivals in Municipal Stadium. For one day, it resembled the franchise's good old days, which hadn't been all that long ago. A crowd of 72,189 filed into the stadium on Cleveland's lakefront and watched the AAFC's two heavyweights do battle on October 30. The Browns struggled but prevailed, 30–28, on a Lou Groza 38-yard field goal with 9:45 remaining in the game. Cleveland's defense managed to hold Frankie Albert at bay the rest of the way. The tight victory moved the Browns into second place, a half game behind New York. Still, McBride wasn't happy. The owner interrupted a vacation in Florida to return to Cleveland and attend the game, and the near-sellout didn't impress him. He'd claimed in September that he could've sold 160,000 tickets for the game. Instead, he had several thousand tickets left over.

"I thought we'd turn 'em away on a nice day like this,"[12] he said dejectedly.

McBride's discouragement paled in comparison to Topping's. A week after defeating the Giants in the (attendance) battle for New York, Topping's Yankees drew just 10,692 fans for a game against an admittedly inferior opponent, the Colts. Still, the tiny crowd had to come as a shock to Topping and the entire organization. On the Yankee Stadium turf, New York jumped to a 21–0 halftime lead and then held off a second half Baltimore rally for a 21–14 victory.

The story was drastically different in Los Angeles, where the Rams had started their season with six straight victories and hosted the Bears in a key western division game on October 30. The showdown drew 86,080 fans to Memorial Coliseum, and the Rams won, 27–24. The Rams were putting on a better show than the Dons, and the fans were responding. In one afternoon, the Rams had attracted only 8,000 fewer fans to Memorial Coliseum than the Dons had drawn all season.

The standings as November arrived:

New York	6–1–0	137–97
Cleveland	6–1–1	252–156
San Francisco	6–3–0	312–182

Lou Groza watches his game-winning field goal sail through the uprights as the Browns beat the 49ers, 30–28, at Municipal Stadium in October of 1949. The two teams would meet in Cleveland again in December in the AAFC championship game, the final AAFC game ever played. Number 93 is San Francisco's Jim Cason (Michael Schwartz Library, Cleveland State University).

Chicago	4-4-0	161-185
Los Angeles	3-6-0	202-254
Buffalo	2-5-1	168-221
Baltimore	1-8-0	138-254

Technically, every team was still in the race for the post-season tournament, although the next loss by Baltimore, or the next victory by the Hornets, would eliminate the Colts. Realistically, only the fourth playoff spot was still up for grabs, and three clubs had a shot at it, with the inside track belonging to, of all teams, Chicago. Playoff seeding was very much in doubt, however. Any ties for playoff positioning would be broken by flips of a coin.

November kicked off with the Browns clobbering the Hornets in Cleveland, 35-2, on November 6. The visitors couldn't have been blamed if they felt like they were playing in a nearly empty Soldier Field as the game was attended by just 16,506 fans. The Hornets ventured into Cleveland territory only three times. They were turned back by a lost fumble, an interception, and the gun that ended the contest. In Baltimore, the 49ers had no trouble sending 23,704 fans home unhappy by trouncing the Colts, 28-10. And in New York, Chet Adams' 12-yard field goal with 2½ minutes remaining lifted the Bills to a 17-14 upset of the Yankees. Yankee Stadium was nearly as deserted as Cleveland's Municipal Stadium on an afternoon when AAFC owners took a hit to their wallets. Only 16,758 watched the game, in spite of its playoff implications. With a record of 2-5-1 entering the fray, Yankee fans could be excused if they found it hard to consider the Bills a legitimate threat for the post-season.

The first weekend of November was a tough one for both leagues at the box office. The Browns found themselves in the strange position of having played before the smallest crowd in all of professional football, followed closely by the Yankees. The Bears drew 47,218 for their game against their ancient rivals, the Packers. The Eagles enjoyed an attendance of 38,209 for their battle with the western division-leading Rams. The other six games played that afternoon drew 26,000 customers or fewer.

The following weekend, the Browns and Bills tied for the second time in 1949, their game in Municipal Stadium ending in a 7-7 deadlock. Cleveland's Lou Groza's attempt at a 51-yard game-winning field goal with 15 seconds left came up short. The crowd was just 22,511. The tie kept Buffalo's faint playoff hopes alive. It sliced the Browns' lead over the Yankees to a half game in the race for the top seed in the playoffs, thanks to New York's 14-10 win over the pesky Hornets in Yankee Stadium. Buddy Young returned the game's opening kickoff 91 yards for a score, and New York held off the visitors from there. The attendance for the important game, with the Hornets battling for the fourth playoff berth, was a pathetic 9,091. That was exactly 19 more fans than the Bulldogs drew to their game across the river in the Polo Grounds which was contested at the same time. The Cardinals steamrolled their hosts, 65–20. The two professional football games played in New York on November 13 were witnessed by a total of 18,163 spectators. That was roughly 300 more people than watched the 49ers and Dons in the Los Angeles Memorial Coliseum later that afternoon. The same two teams had played an August exhibition in the same stadium before a throng of better than 80,000. Only 17,880 showed up for the game that counted in the standings, and San Francisco won, 41–24. The small crowds his Dons were attracting weren't helping Ben Lindheimer's health problems.

On November 16, it was revealed that Bills star quarterback George Ratterman had played the season essentially "on loan" from his future employer, Ted Collins' New York Bulldogs. He assured stunned Bills fans that "I'll continue with the Bills the rest of this season, and I'll give them the very best I've got in our battle to win the playoffs." Ratterman said that after reaching a contract impasse with Breuil in the summer, he met with Collins and agreed to a four-year deal worth $10,000 per season, but the contract didn't take effect until the 1950 season. Ratterman then enrolled in Notre Dame's law school and had every intention of sitting out the 1949 season.

"But after I watched the Bills in the opening game of the year against the Chicago Hornets in Chicago, Mr. Breuil flew to South Bend to see me," Ratterman explained. "I signed a contract to play with the Bills this year. Mr. Collins gave me permission to do so. I sure hate to leave Buffalo, especially after the fans have treated me so nicely this year."[13]

The AAFC had no grounds on which to contest Ratterman's contract with the Bulldogs. "When his contract expired, he had a right to sign with anyone he pleased,"[14] said a league spokesperson. Ratterman was also up front when he met with Breuil after the Bills lost their season opener. He told Breuil of his contract with the Bulldogs, so the Bills knew they were essentially "renting" their star quarterback for one more season. It was another reason for Breuil to be determined that the AAFC would fight the NFL to the bitter end.

"I have not enjoyed one minute of contact I have had with the National League," a angry Breuil told the Buffalo Touchdown Club on November 17. "I do not like the National League." While his fellow owners were complaining about the salaries they were dishing out to their players, Breuil made it sound like the AAFC had been created for purely philanthropic reasons.

He told the football fans of Buffalo that the purpose of the AAFC had been to "permit boys to make a decent and honorable profession out of football and receive a decent and honorable wage for their efforts. What did the National League ever do for football players? The average boy did well if he made $2,000 a year." Most players, and certainly the stars, were making much more than that in 1949, thanks to the AAFC, and most of Breuil's fellow owners in both leagues were getting sick and tired of it. Breuil said he'd continue to promote professional football, but only if the status quo was maintained. A return to an NFL monopoly wasn't acceptable.

"Unless there is survival of two competing leagues, and no monopoly, it's got to go,"[15] Breuil insisted.

The day after Breuil made those comments, he was sued by his former head coach and his former chief scout. Red Dawson and Hank Reese were asking for a combined $13,900. Dawson claimed he and Breuil had reached a "verbal agreement" on the first day of June for him to coach the Bills in 1949. Dawson's salary was to be $10,000. He wanted to be paid what he believed he was owed for the remaining seven months of the agreement, and said he had been fired "without just cause." Reese asked for the $3,900 he claimed Breuil owed him for his verbal agreement to serve as assistant coach and chief scout.

The AAFC's owners had scheduled their post-season meeting for December 15 and 16 in Houston, to coincide with Glenn McCarthy's all-star game. They wanted a chance to check out the city in the event they'd invite McCarthy to join them in 1950. Despite the Browns' problems at the box office, Mickey McBride spoke confidently of the league's future.

"I can't speak for the other owners, but as far as I'm concerned, I'm going down to Houston determined to keep the All-America Conference intact," he told Bob Yonkers of the *Cleveland Press*. "I've always been in favor of two leagues. I think it is the healthiest thing for pro football. And, as I've said before, I firmly believe that our league is as strong as the National League. Look at Baltimore. The Colts have won only one game, yet their average attendance this year is over 28,000. There are several teams in the National League that can't match that number."[16] McBride said the AAFC would be considering bids from Houston and Dallas for its eighth franchise.

McBride said something else in the middle of November, and he said it to both the *Plain Dealer* and the *Press*. He said he'd sell the Browns before he'd merge them into the NFL. The reason was purely personal. He accused the NFL of being run by "a couple of people who would treat me as a small fry, and I don't intend to be pushed around by anybody."[17] Without mentioning names, McBride undoubtedly meant George Preston Marshall and Tim Mara. McBride and the other AAFC owners who'd accompanied him to the "peace talks" in Philadelphia in December of 1948 felt they'd been treated as second-class citizens by their NFL brethren, notably Marshall and Mara, and the wounds hadn't healed almost a year later.

Both sides were undeniably stubborn. "It's a matter of pride and principle at any cost," McBride admitted. "We [the AAFC owners] all consider ourselves good businessmen, and realize we aren't proving it by sinking a lot of money into a losing venture. But we're determined to keep fighting until the National League recognizes us."[18] But for how much longer?

In spite of all the bravado coming from both sides, teams in both leagues were gushing red ink, and the war between the two leagues couldn't continue. Said an AAFC official who spoke on condition of anonymity in the same article in which the *Press* quoted McBride, "Something is going to happen in a hurry, probably before our league meeting in Houston next month. The situation is not good."[19] That official knew what he was talking about.

With two weekends left in the AAFC season, the top seed in the league's "Shaughnessy playoff," named for famed college football coach Clark Shaughnessy, who devised the system, was still up for grabs. The Browns were 7-1-2, the Yankees 7-2, the 49ers 7-3. Cleveland and New York would meet in Yankee Stadium on Sunday, November 20, with the winner having the inside track to the percentage championship and the number one overall postseason seed. Yankees head coach Red Strader was asked by the New York press corps about Paul Brown's offense, which hadn't been clicking on all cylinders for much of the season.

"They're stereotyped," Strader said. "Paul Brown hasn't changed 'em in three years." Then he added confidently, "We will win!"[20]

Why change a system that had worked almost flawlessly for four seasons? Using the system Strader criticized as "stereotyped," the Browns scored 31 first half points, then rested. They flattened the Yankees, 31-0, to clinch the number one seed in the playoffs. The Browns weren't drawing at home, but they were still the AAFC's top attraction on the road. Their presence, plus the game's playoff implications, enticed 50,711 football fans to Yankee Stadium. The Yankees slipped to 7-3 and would finish the season with a two-game trip to the west coast.

In Buffalo, the surging Bills overcame a Civic Stadium field described as a "quagmire," and beat the visiting Hornets, 10-0. Halfback Bobby Livingstone, who'd been waived by Chicago in October and claimed by Buffalo, scampered 80 yards for the game's only touchdown. A crowd of 18,494 watched their team's final home game. The Bills improved to 4-5-2 and controlled their playoff destiny. The Hornets, after their fast start, had lost six of their last seven games. With a record of 4-7, a Chicago loss to Cleveland on Thanksgiving day would eliminate the Hornets from the playoffs. If the Bills beat the Colts the following Sunday, they were in no matter what Chicago did.

Had the Hornets not harbored slim playoff hopes, their holiday game against the Browns might have been canceled due to snow, and a lack of interest. The crew hired by Hornets management to clear Soldier Field of a heavy snowfall didn't show up on time, and the task of removing several inches of snow fell to the players on both teams. Only 5,031 Chicagoans interrupted their celebration to venture to Soldier Field, and they were treated to a dull exhibition as the Browns put forth just enough effort to win, and the disheartened Hornets put forth even less. The final score was 14–6. After a promising start, the Hornets had fizzled, finishing a dreary 4–8. As evidenced by the Thanksgiving day crowd, the fans had given up long before.

Otto Graham didn't throw many passes in the cold and snow. He gained just 88 yards through the air, but those 88 yards gave him 2,735 passing yards for the season, establishing an AAFC record that would stand forever.

Snow wasn't a problem in Memorial Coliseum, where the Yankees held off the Dons, 17–16, to keep alive their chance of capturing the second playoff seed, and a home game in the semi-finals. Los Angeles led, 7–0, after three periods before the Yankees' offense woke up and put 17 points on the scoreboard. The Dons threatened to tie the game with half a minute left when George Taliaferro returned a punt 52 yards for a touchdown, but Bob Nelson's extra point attempt was blocked as a crowd of 20,096 groaned. Two days later, the Yankees would meet the 49ers in Kezar Stadium with second place on the line.

A pair of games on Sunday, November 27, brought down the curtain on the AAFC regular season. In San Francisco, the 49ers spanked the weary Yankees, who were enduring the same torturous three-games-in-eight-days grind the Browns navigated in 1948. The Browns won all three games. The Yankees lost two of three. The 35–14 drubbing gave the 49ers second place and set up a re-match with New York in a playoff semi-final game the following week. A hearty gathering of 44,828 enjoyed the proceedings. Some of them stopped at the Kezar Stadium box office to buy tickets for the following Sunday's game on their way out.

With nothing to play for but pride, and a .500 season (no one wanted to go to the playoffs with a losing record), the Bills roped and tied the Colts in Baltimore, 38–14. Ratterman threw 31 passes and completed 22, three for touchdowns. A Babe Ruth Stadium crowd of 16,323 watched their Colts conclude a dreadful season on a six-game losing streak.

The final standings of the AAFC's final season:

Cleveland	9–1–2	.900	339–171
San Francisco	9–3–0	.750	416–227
New York	8–4–0	.667	196–206
Buffalo	5–5–2	.500	236–256
Chicago	4–8–0	.333	179–268
Los Angeles	4–8–0	.333	253–322
Baltimore	1–11–0	.083	179–341

The Shaughnessy system had worked, at least to an extent. The playoff seedings hadn't been determined until the last game of the year. Only the pathetic Colts had been eliminated quickly. The Hornets entered their last game of the season with a (slim) chance at making the playoffs. The Yankees bounced back after a mediocre 1948 season, but even though they won eight games, they were out-scored by their opponents. So were the Bills, who overcame a 1–5–1 start to claw their way into the fourth playoff seed. They got a date with the Browns in Cleveland for their effort.

Still, the Browns and 49ers were the cream of the crop, and by a substantial margin. Again.

11

The Final Gun

With the 1949 season in the books, the AAFC faced a familiar problem. The Baltimore Colts were in financial trouble.

In spite of respectable attendance, the Colts had lost between $70,000 and $100,000. In the words of general manager and head coach Walt Driskill, they were broke. Even though one of their stockholders was reported to be Jerry Hoffberger, the wealthiest person in the state of Maryland, the responsibility of reaching into their own pockets to pay the club's bills fell to board chairman Charles McCormick and vice chairman Bob Embry. And neither man believed that to be fair.

Driskill said the Colts had an excellent chance of improving their miserable 1–11 record in 1950, if they could stay afloat financially. "We have some of the finest players in the country on our draft list," he said. "But it takes money to get them. If this money is raised, the 1950 Colts can be a team any city can be proud of."[1] And if that money was to be raised, it would be up to the residents of Baltimore to raise it, just as it had been after the 1947 season. Colts fans had anted up $200,000 to keep the team functioning after its first season in Baltimore, and they'd be asked to pony up a quarter of a million to enable the team to operate in 1950.

The Colts would be required to post a $250,000 guarantee for the 1950 season when the AAFC's owners held their winter meeting, and Baltimore mayor Thomas D'Alesandro had a novel way of raising the money. He asked the city's football fans (and non-football fans) to purchase 50,000 tickets, at five dollars per ticket, for an as yet unscheduled exhibition game in Babe Ruth Stadium the following summer. As only a politician can, D'Alesandro tried to rally the city in support of its beleaguered football team.

"I urge Baltimoreans to lend a hand in helping the Baltimore Colts through this severe crisis," the mayor exhorted. "This may well represent Baltimore's epoch life or death battle for major league representation, not only in football, but in baseball and other sports as well. I appeal to all public-spirited individuals to rally to the support of the Colts by joining the Fifty

Thousand Club."[2] The Colts were reported to have lost less money in 1949 than some other AAFC teams, but none of the others would make an appeal to the public to bail them out.

The Associated Press reported on November 30 that Texas oil multimillionaire Glenn McCarthy had obtained the necessary paperwork to apply for an AAFC franchise for Houston in 1950. No action was expected to be taken by McCarthy, or by the league, until its meeting on December 15 and 16. That meeting would take place in Houston in the days before the charity all-star game McCarthy had arranged. The wire service also reported that Houston would have competition for the AAFC's eighth franchise, and it wouldn't come from Dallas. It came from Richmond, Virginia, home of the Rebels, regular season champions of the American Football League. The same minor league whose members had been treated rudely by the AAFC in a pair of exhibition games in August. The AAFC had won those games by a composite score of 127–0.

"I have taken it under consideration," said commissioner Scrappy Kessing of Richmond's bid for an AAFC team. "I have told Mr. H.C. Siebold, owner of the Richmond club, that I will bring the matter up before the owners at our annual meeting."[3] It seemed unlikely that the AAFC would choose Richmond over Houston, particularly since Houston's bid was backed by McCarthy, one of the richest men in the United States. Still, in spite of Kessing's cautious (and seemingly dismissive) response to Richmond's request, Siebold claimed that his group had been "tentatively offered"[4] the AAFC's eighth franchise.

In the wake of Baltimore's financial woes, there was brave bluster from other AAFC outposts regarding the league's future. A spokesperson for the Dons, who reportedly lost a substantial amount of Ben Lindheimer's money in 1949, said "the Dons positively intend to play ball in 1950."[5]

Said James Thompson, majority owner of the Hornets, "We are in better shape today than at any time. We'll operate in 1950." But Thompson added, perhaps ominously, "if there is a next year."[6]

Buffalo's Jim Breuil said the Bills had lost money in 1949, but claimed the loss wasn't "excessive." In Baltimore, meanwhile, the good residents responded to their mayor's impassioned plea. Commissioner Kessing said on December 4 that the city had already raised $150,000. That left it $100,000 short of its goal with 11 days to go before the deadline.

The players on the four teams that had qualified for the AAFC playoffs wouldn't get a cut of the receipts from the semi-final games, and that didn't please the San Francisco 49ers. The AAFC's second seed practiced on November 29 in preparation for their game with the New York Yankees. Before the practice scheduled for November 30, the players requested a meeting with co-owners Tony and Vic Morabito. The players were represented by team captain Norm Standlee and Len Eshmont. They told the Morabito brothers that unless each player received a $500 bonus for the playoff game, they would strike. The demand was immediately rejected. The players left the team's practice facility. The Morabitos had earned their fortune in the lumber business. Labor problems were nothing new to them. They had a blunt answer for Standlee and Eshmont. "We've given them until 9:30 tomorrow morning [December 1] to show up for practice in uniform at Menlo Park. If they do not do it, they are to turn in their suits, the season is over, we will forfeit our game to the Yankees. This is not a bluff. We are not kidding."[7] Standlee and Eshmont declined to answer most reporters' questions, but they did say the players would report to Menlo Park on December 1 as ordered. Whether or not they'd practice remained to be seen.

Kessing said he'd back the Morabitos in whatever action they took, including a forfeit. "Contracts call for a full season, including playoff games," he explained. "All of the players were notified to that effect on June 1st."[8]

San Francisco coach Buck Shaw tried to act as peacemaker, without success. "I feel terrible about this. A lot of people are going to get hurt,"[9] he said.

Browns co-owner Dan Sherby didn't doubt the resolve of the Morabitos. "Tony was flabbergasted, to say the least, when he heard of this," Sherby said. "Those of us who have operated in the league meetings know he won't change his mind. Tony can be a stubborn man, and if the players fail to play Sunday, this could be the end of the 49ers."[10]

An angry bunch of football players reported to Menlo Park on December 1. They put on their uniforms and practiced. There would be no strike, and there would be no forfeit. The players hadn't acted on impulse. When the 49ers arrived in Cleveland for their October 30 game with the Browns, several of them approached Cleveland's players, told them of their plan to demand to be paid for the semi-final playoff game, and asked for their support. The Browns weren't inclined to help their arch-rivals, even though players on all the playoff teams stood to benefit if the 49ers forced the Morabito brothers to give them the bonuses they wanted. If the Morabitos caved in, what was to stop the Browns, Bills and Yankees from making the same threat to strike?

The Browns, facing a dismal turnout for their game against Buffalo, noted in their ticket advertisements that they'd be trying to beat Buffalo for the first time in 1949. That didn't arouse the passion of a fan base that had become blasé about their championship football team, and just 17,270 (including an estimated 3,000 who made the trip from Buffalo) watched what turned out to be a highly competitive and entertaining game. With less than five minutes remaining and Cleveland clinging to a 24–21 advantage, the Bills were driving toward a game-tying field goal or game-winning touchdown when Browns rookie defensive back Warren Lahr intercepted a George Ratterman pass and returned it 52 yards for the game-clinching score. Cleveland escaped with a 31–21 victory. The home team's players noticed the sparse gathering in Municipal Stadium.

"Buffalo has a fine team and it played a great game," said Browns linebacker Lou Saban. "Too bad so many people stayed away."[11]

Forty-niners fans didn't stay away from Kezar Stadium on that December 4, and their 49ers rewarded them with a 17–7 win over the Yankees. The crowd was 41,393, well over twice the size of the crowd in Cleveland. That gave Tony Morabito an idea. He presented his case to Kessing to play the championship game the following Sunday in San Francisco, even though the Browns were the tournament's top seed and had earned home field advantage.

Noting the small crowd that had attended Cleveland's semi-final win over Buffalo, Morabito said, "They'll be lucky to draw 20,000 if its ... cold. All we'll be playing for is peanuts, and who likes peanuts?" Morabito was right, but Kessing refused to change the rules at that late date. When he arrived with his team in Cleveland on December 9, a grumpy Morabito told reporters what Kessing told him about transferring the game to San Francisco, where, in all probability, it would've sold out Kezar Stadium.

"I was told the fairest arrangement was to play the finals on the home field of the team with the highest percentage. It was claimed we'd be destroying good will in Cleveland if we took the game out to the coast." Morabito wasn't concerned about Cleveland's feelings. He was concerned about his share of a probable 60,000 gate as the host team as opposed to his share of a probable 20,000 gate as the visitor. He claimed, however, that he was only thinking of his poor players, whose welfare hadn't concerned him much a few days earlier, when they asked to be paid for playing in the semi-finals.

"Hell, the main thing is to build up the biggest gate possible for the players. It's their game. And we'd have packed the stadium in San Francisco,"[12] he said. Secretly, Mickey McBride and his players may have agreed with Morabito. The Browns weren't intimidated by big crowds in foreign stadiums and were supremely confident they could beat any team, anytime, anywhere. They'd spent four years proving it. They probably would've preferred to benefit from the bigger gate generated by a sellout crowd in San Francisco. But they couldn't say so. The game would be played in Cleveland. And it would be an anti-climax.

Unbeknownst to everyone except the participants, peace talks were taking place in Philadelphia on December 8. The only people involved were NFL commissioner Bert Bell, Browns minority owner Dan Sherby, and Arthur Friedlund, the team attorney for the Yankees. On December 9, Bell announced that a merger agreement had been hammered out, and the result would be a 13-team football league to be known in 1950 as the National-American Football League. It would consist of the ten existing teams in the NFL, plus the

Browns, 49ers, and, surprisingly, the Colts, the AAFC's weakest franchise. Or, at best, the league's second weakest, possibly behind the Hornets.

The AAFC was officially dead. The Bills would merge with the Browns, and Breuil would purchase a piece of the Cleveland club. The Yankees would merge with the NFL's Bulldogs. Lindheimer's Dons would merge with Dan Reeves' Rams. The Chicago Hornets would disband.

"I believe this is a constructive move," said Sherby. "There will be honest scheduling, as the season goes on, the fans will see the best there is in football, and for once we will be crowning a real champion."[13]

"The peace which came today and which we have worked on for so long is the most progressive step ever taken in professional football,"[14] said Reeves.

"Look at it from this standpoint," said Redskins owner George Preston Marshall, who had to personally agree to the deal. "Baltimore is only an hour away by train. The crowds could be tremendous. I'm very pleased to see that Baltimore is in the major leagues."[15] After blocking a merger a year earlier over the Baltimore question, Marshall was suddenly embracing the thought of having a team just 25 miles north of his Redskins. He'd decided the Redskins and the Colts would enjoy a lucrative rivalry. He also accepted what he termed a "nominal" payment to surrender his territorial right to the Baltimore area. It wasn't specified whether that payment came from the owners of the cash-strapped Colts, or from the AAFC, or, maybe, from Marshall's fellow owners in the NFL, who were grateful to have the war over with. A war some of those owners had privately been accusing Marshall of prolonging for the past year.

Said Eagles majority owner James Clark, "This is a great step for the benefit of the fans and pro football. It should ensure well-balanced teams and great competition. Commissioner Bell is to be congratulated for his patience and intelligence in working out this solution."[16] Clark said he'd be willing to have his Eagles, should they repeat as NFL champions, play the AAFC champions later in December. Bell immediately vetoed that idea. The two league champions would clash, and soon, but under circumstances dictated by the NFL.

Even though his team would be liquidated, Hornets owner James Thompson said, "I heartily approve of the action, but we decided not to join any other team and will dispose of our player contracts in the near future."[17] Thompson probably didn't have a choice. It's doubtful that either the Bears or the Cardinals were interested in merging with his Hornets.

As Bell would be the commissioner of the new National-American Football League, Kessing, whose contract with the AAFC was to expire in January of 1950, said he'd retire to his home in California. He said he would've preferred to keep the two leagues as separate but equal entities with a common draft, but since that proved to be impossible, "if this new set-up is good for football, then I'm for it."[18]

What of McBride, the majority owner of the AAFC's powerhouse Browns, the team the NFL had coveted since 1946? "I can't make any comments on the new league because I really don't know what happened in Philadelphia," he said. Even though his friend and co-owner, Sherby, had been one of the AAFC's two representatives, McBride knew nothing about the peace talks. That's how secret the meeting was. "Until I get a full report on the new set-up, and how the league is going to operate, I can't say whether I will stay in football."[19] If he did stay, he said he'd be happy to have Breuil as a partner. Even that part of the deal had been negotiated without McBride's knowledge or consent.

Said Bell, "This merger has not been a victory for the National League, nor for pro football. It has been a victory for the public. The fans demanded peace in pro football. They will also demand a fair schedule for every team. And I'll see that they get it."[20] That was the main concern of the league's three new members. How would they be treated by Bell and the old guard upon their entry into the NFL? Particularly the Colts. The Browns and 49ers would join the old league with some leverage. The Colts? Not so much.

George Halas, one of the NFL's founders, was said to have been pleased by the agreement. He called it "a sensible solution."[21] Essentially, it had been nearly total capitulation by the AAFC. And that had been the NFL's definition of "a sensible solution" all along.

The AAFC's founder, Arch Ward, was happy about the end of the war he'd started. After setting the wheels in motion, Ward abandoned his creation, leaving it to the owners he'd recruited, and the owners who replaced some of them, to run it. He reiterated that the AAFC's owners were much wealthier men than the NFL owners. "The [AAFC] gave the National League a terrific whipping," he claimed. "But in so doing, it took a terrific whipping itself. Professional football was facing oblivion unless the two leagues got together, because no business could be run at a loss year after year."

Ward, sounding much like Breuil had when he spoke to Buffalo's Touchdown Club, claimed his motive for starting a new football league was to improve the lives of professional football players. "My hope is the new league will recognize this fact: that professional football players must be paid salaries commensurate with their abilities, if the best of college players are to become professionals. My interest in promoting and organizing the [AAFC] was to prevent the exploitation of young college football players who were throwing away six or seven of the best years of their lives for salaries that did not exceed $1,000 a year."[22] The days of such meager wages in professional football may have disappeared, thanks to the AAFC, but salaries would soon return to what the owners considered to be more reasonable levels.

As Browns quarterback Otto Graham, one of the game's highest-paid players, noted when the merger was announced, Leon Hart wasn't likely to get the $25,000 annual salary he'd been asking for now that there'd be no competition for his services. Hart was Notre Dame's star end and winner of the 1949 Heisman Trophy. As several hotshot collegians did during the bidding war between the AAFC and NFL, Hart chose to be cagey after finishing his career with the Fighting Irish, saying he may bypass pro football altogether. He suggested that $25,000 a year sounded about right to lure him away from private business into the professional ranks. When there were two teams competing for his services, Hart was calling the shots. With the merger, the Detroit Lions could, and did, tell Hart to take their offer or leave it. He took it.

The AAFC ended where it started. A crowd of 60,135 in Cleveland's Municipal Stadium watched the league's first game between the Browns and Miami Seahawks on September 6, 1946. A crowd barely one-third that size watched the Browns defeat the 49ers, 21–7, in the league's final championship game on December 11. Cleveland took control early and was never seriously threatened as it won its fourth straight AAFC title. *Cleveland Press* sports columnist Whitey Lewis called the crowd of 22,550 "a disgrace to the city."

A few days after the championship game, the Associated Press announced its last combined AAFC-NFL All-Pro team. As always, only an offensive team was named. It included five players from the defunct AAFC: Graham; Browns end Mac Speedie; Bills halfback Chet Mutryn; Yankees tackle Arnie Weinmeister; and Colts tackle Dick Barwegan.

Technically, the final AAFC game was played in Houston on December 17. The champion Browns had agreed to meet an AAFC all-star squad in the Shamrock Bowl, arranged by the "fabulously wealthy" Glenn McCarthy. There was no need for Houston to put its best foot forward since there was no AAFC for it to join in 1950. With the NFL having just absorbed three former AAFC clubs, it was in no mood for further expansion. The contest was played in a driving rainstorm, and all the scoring was done in the first half. The All-Stars polished off the disinterested Browns, 12–7. Only 10,000 people sat through the monsoon to watch. McCarthy said the game raised $45,000 for charity. For the record, the prevailing opinion among the writers in attendance was that Houston wasn't ready for the major leagues. And the major leagues weren't ready for Houston.

As the sun set over southeastern Texas on that December Saturday, Arch Ward's creation faded into history. But one group wasn't quite ready to let it go.

The football fans of Buffalo felt they'd gotten shafted by the merger, and rightfully so. Buffalo had supported the Bills well. Their average attendance of better than 26,000 per game in Civic Stadium in 1949 was well above the NFL's average crowd of roughly 23,000. The Bills weren't bankrupt as the Colts were, yet the Colts would be welcomed into the National-American

11. The Final Gun   211

Football League. All the Bills got was a semi-merger with the Browns, consisting of the sale of tackle John Kissell, guard Abe Gibron, and halfback Rex Bumgardner to Cleveland. All three would make valuable contributions to the Browns as they dominated the NFL from 1950 to 1955 almost as thoroughly as they'd dominated the AAFC. In exchange for the three players, Breuil got a 25 percent stake in the Browns. The city of Buffalo was assured the Browns would play an exhibition game in Civic Stadium in the summer of 1950.

That wasn't enough for a group of die-hard Bills fans who raised $175,000 and asked for an audience with Bert Bell at the first meeting of the combined National-American Football League in January of 1950. They logically argued that a 13-team league was awkward and wouldn't fare any better than the seven-team AAFC had in 1949. They volunteered Buffalo to be the 14th team the National-American Football League needed. They had the cash for a guarantee. They might have succeeded with the support of Breuil, the owner of the liquidated Buffalo team. But after claiming he wouldn't have any involvement with a football "monopoly," Breuil embraced the peace agreement and was happy to own a piece of the Browns. Within days after the peace accord was announced, he expressed concern that Buffalo might somehow wind up part of the equation, and he wanted nothing to do with that. Breuil claimed to have lost $700,000 running the Bills for four years. No individual stepped forward to own an NFL team in Buffalo, and that helped doom the city's effort to obtain one.

After a conference with the Buffalo contingent prior to the league meeting, Bell opened the door a crack, saying they'd made an impressive presentation. The commissioner said there was no organized opposition to Buffalo becoming the NFL's 14th franchise, and said he'd draw up a 1950 schedule for a 14-team league that he'd bring to the NFL meeting. But he didn't. He brought, instead, a schedule for a 13-team league. Bell did allow the Buffalo group to state its case, then put the matter to a vote.

The first six franchises to vote on the Buffalo question voted "yes." Then Rams owner Dan Reeves said no, and Buffalo's bid was dead. The rest of the balloting was a mere formality. As required by the league constitution, the vote to admit a new franchise had to be unanimous. The final tally was 9–4 in Buffalo's favor.

Reeves said he wasn't against Buffalo per se. He didn't think the NFL needed a 14th franchise, regardless of where that franchise was located. He, and some other owners, were dubious about a 13-team NFL, and they were justified. By the end of the 1950 season, the Colts would go out of business. The Bulldogs, re-named the Yanks after the merger, would go belly-up after the 1951 season. But not before proving the mettle of the AAFC by posting a 7–5 record in 1950, a vast improvement from the miserable 1–10–1 mark the

Bulldogs had logged in 1949. As a result of the merger, the 1949 New York Yankees of the AAFC moved virtually intact to the NFL as the Yanks of 1950.

Buffalo had to wait ten years, until the formation of the American Football League in 1960, to return to the big leagues.

Epilogue

Bert Bell had resorted to a technicality to deny the Browns and Eagles the chance to meet on the gridiron at the end of the 1949 season. While it was true the NFL's constitution prohibited post-season games following the league's championship game, Eagles owner James Clark wanted his team to challenge the Browns. And the Browns had been waiting since 1946 to prove their mettle against the NFL's champion, whoever it may have been. It would have been simple enough to waive the constitutional prohibition against post-season games in order to play the game fans of both leagues wanted to see. But Bell was wise to stick to his guns. He knew the confrontation between the NFL's champion and the AAFC's champion would be the most eagerly-anticipated game in the history of professional football, and he wasn't about to have it organized haphazardly and thrown together hastily at the end of December 1949. Bell had an entire off-season to arrange and promote the first "Super Bowl," and he took advantage of every minute of it.

In order to enable as many fans as possible to watch the historic contest, Bell scheduled the game for Philadelphia's Municipal Stadium rather than Shibe Park, the Eagles' normal home field. Municipal Stadium's seating capacity was more than twice that of Shibe Park, the baseball stadium the Eagles shared with the Philadelphia Athletics and Phillies. Bell also scheduled the game on the Saturday night before the rest of the teams would open their seasons, to be certain the champions of the two leagues who'd spent four years at each other's throats would have the spotlight all to themselves. Now that the Browns were part of the family, Bell couldn't admit to stacking the deck in the Eagles' favor. He had vowed to be fair to everyone, including the Browns, 49ers, and Colts. But he wanted to put the upstart Browns in their place, as did everyone else in the NFL. Particularly George Preston Marshall, who said on many occasions that the worst NFL team could easily handle the best AAFC team, meaning Cleveland. Bell had been part owner and head coach of the Eagles in the 1930s. He wanted them to prove the NFL's claims of superiority over the AAFC hadn't been mere false bravado.

Paul Brown had been preparing for the moment since 1946. He was convinced that someday his team would meet the champions of the older league, and when they did, he wanted them to be ready. They were.

"For four years, coach Brown never said a word," revealed Otto Graham. "He just kept putting that stuff on the bulletin board. We were so fired up, we would have played them anywhere anytime, for a keg of beer or a chocolate milkshake. It didn't matter."

On Saturday evening, September 16, some 71,237 fans settled in to watch the carnage. The Eagles were favorites. The Browns were the lambs to be led to the slaughter.

Final score: Cleveland 35, Philadelphia 10. The score should've been 42–10, but a Cleveland touchdown was nullified by a penalty. Brown studied the game film and swore the call was wrong, that he spotted no infraction on the play in question. Not that it mattered.

Eagles coach Earle (Greasy) Neale wasn't impressed. He called the Browns' offense "basketball in cleats." A real football team won by running the ball in Neale's opinion, not by throwing it. The Browns unleashed a sophisticated passing attack the likes of which no NFL team had ever encountered, and Graham carved up the Eagles' secondary for 346 yards through the air. Brown didn't care for Neale's dismissive attitude toward his team. So, for possibly the only time in his coaching career, he did something impetuous and, by his own admission, silly. In the re-match with the Eagles in Cleveland, Brown ordered Graham not to throw a pass. The Browns ran the football on every offensive play. They beat the Eagles again, 13–7.

The rest of the Browns' storybook 1950 season is well known to football fans. They tied the New York Giants for the American (eastern) Division title with a 10–2 record, then beat them in a playoff by the unlikely score of 8–3. The next week, the Browns edged the western champion Rams, 30–28, on the frozen turf of Municipal Stadium. Lou Groza's 16-yard field goal in the game's waning seconds provided the winning margin. And nothing less than the NFL championship would've satisfied Brown and his players. Not after all the taunts they'd endured from the haughty NFL between 1946 and 1949. And all the cheap shots they'd endured on the playing field during the 1950 season, as the NFL's players tried, if they couldn't beat the Browns, to at least beat them up.

For the record, the Browns beat Marshall's Redskins twice, 20–14 and 45–21.

The other AAFC transplants found the going much tougher. San Francisco was just 3–9 in its first NFL season, and Baltimore was the league's doormat, winning only one of its 12 games. With an odd number of teams in the NFL, a swing team was needed, and Baltimore was that team. Rather than playing each team in its division twice, home-and-away, Baltimore played

Lou Groza shows Browns owner Arthur (Mickey) McBride the shoe he used to kick a pair of field goals in Cleveland's 8–3 victory over the New York Giants in the 1950 NFL American (Eastern) Conference playoff game in Municipal Stadium. Groza wouldn't wear his famous number 76 for a few more years (Michael Schwartz Library, Cleveland State University).

every team in the league once. It doomed the Colts to failure, and they folded after the season. The transfusion of talent from the AAFC's New York Yankees helped the New York Bulldogs (re-named the Yanks) improve their record from 1–10–1 in 1949 to a respectable 7–5 in 1950.

It has long been assumed that the overwhelming dominance of the

Browns was directly responsible for the AAFC's demise. Including playoffs, Cleveland's AAFC record was a mind-boggling 52 wins, four defeats, and three ties. By 1949, it was conceded that the Browns would win the championship, and everyone else was playing for second place. Attendance figures at Municipal Stadium would indicate that even Clevelanders had grown bored with the Browns' mastery over their competition. It will never be known what the AAFC's fate would have been had Brown returned to Ohio State as he'd been expected to after his release from the Navy. The league may have survived and even thrived. As was pointed out continuously, Arch Ward had recruited owners with deep pockets, deeper than those of most NFL owners, even if there were three failed ownerships in Chicago, two in Brooklyn, and one in Miami. And even if the Colts went bankrupt after both the 1947 and 1949 seasons.

Although most of the AAFC's owners were, in Mickey McBride's words, "good businessmen," they were also, apparently, surprisingly naïve. Never in the history of professional sports in the United States have the owners of teams in a new league been greeted warmly by the owners of teams in an established league, but all the evidence points to this being the type of greeting the AAFC expected from the NFL in 1945. The AAFC owners were genuinely baffled at the NFL's attitude toward them. All they wanted to do was start a new league and get along with everybody. According to Ward and Jim Breuil, the AAFC's owners were a bunch of generous, big-hearted guys who only wanted to raise the standard of living of the average football player. They couldn't understand why the NFL owners wouldn't join them in that undertaking. They couldn't understand why the NFL resented the competition. They couldn't understand why the NFL didn't embrace the AAFC as a full and equal partner in the business of professional football. They couldn't understand why NFL commissioner Elmer Layden didn't shake the hands of Brown and John Keeshin in the summer of 1945, invite them into his office, and amiably discuss ways the two leagues could peacefully co-exist for the benefit of everyone. Instead, Layden said until the AAFC actually had teams and played some games, there was nothing to talk about. Monopolies don't welcome competition. Not in the real world, and not in sports.

In analyzing the failure of the AAFC, it's difficult, if not impossible, not to compare it to the American Football League of the 1960s. In its almost century-long existence, the NFL has faced seven challengers. That doesn't include the United States Football League and the Trans-America Football League mentioned elsewhere in this book. Those leagues never advanced beyond the planning stage. The list does include the World Football League, which mounted its challenge to the NFL in 1974–75, and the United States Football League, which tried spring football from 1983–85. Only the fourth incarnation of the AFL (1960–69) wasn't driven out of business by the establishment. The only other challenger to survive for more than three seasons was the AAFC.

The AFL was proud of the fact that each of its original eight franchises survived through to the merger. Two clubs came perilously close to folding: the New York Titans and Oakland Raiders. The Chargers conceded Los Angeles to the NFL after the 1960 season and moved to San Diego. League founder Lamar Hunt reluctantly, but wisely, moved the Texans out of his hometown of Dallas to Kansas City in 1963. Despite being AFL champions, Hunt came to the accurate conclusion that the Texans couldn't compete with the NFL's Cowboys. The AAFC's disastrous experiment with football in Miami ended with the bankrupt Seahawks being moved to Baltimore, where the re-named Colts, despite strong fan support, flirted with bankruptcy twice. The Chicago Rockets could have, and possibly should have, folded midway through the 1948 season. McBride, Dan Topping, and Tony Morabito propped up the Rockets only to avoid the scheduling chaos that would've resulted from them going out of business in the middle of a season. Rather than cut its losses, the AAFC stubbornly insisted that it needed a presence in Chicago and found a fourth new ownership for the team for 1949. The AAFC wasn't reluctant to part with Brooklyn after the Dodgers lost more than $300,000 in 1948 and allowed the team to merge with the cross-town Yankees.

No one associated with the AFL denies that, in spite of the determination of its owners, one of whom, Wayne Valley of the Raiders, dubbed them "the Foolish Club," the league may well have met the same fate as all of the NFL's other challengers had it not signed a five-year contract with NBC to broadcast its games beginning with the 1965 season. The pact guaranteed each team a million dollars per year from NBC, and gave the AFL the prestige of having its games telecast by a major network. The AFL's games had been televised by ABC from 1960–64. The American Broadcasting Company could have been called the AFL of broadcasters at that time. A major network, but a rung below CBS, which televised the NFL's games, and NBC. The infusion of money served another purpose: it convinced the NFL that its rival wasn't going anywhere. The AFL would have to be dealt with.

No such life preserver was tossed to the AAFC. Television was in its infancy during the AAFC years, and big money contracts to broadcast sports didn't yet exist. Televising professional football was a gamble since its popularity trailed that of major league baseball, college football, college basketball, and even boxing. The American Broadcasting Company reached a deal to televise NFL games in 1949, but no network was interested in the AAFC. The league had failed to entice a network to broadcast its 1948 championship game, even though it featured the undefeated Cleveland Browns. Had such a lifeline as a network TV contract been tossed to the AAFC, its money would have lessened the blow of mounting financial losses. It may have allowed some clubs to turn a modest profit. A TV contract also would have given the AAFC much-needed national exposure. The public would have discovered, as it did with the AFL, that the AAFC's product was just as entertaining as the NFL, which had no team to compare with the excellence of the Browns. Had those circumstances existed, the AAFC may have been able to continue its fight with the NFL and achieve its goal of two separate but equal leagues with a common draft and a playoff between the champions at the end of each season. Or it may have forced a full merger, as the AFL would. In either case, the AFL most likely wouldn't have been born. If it had been, its chances of success would've been greatly diminished against two established leagues, or an 18-team National Football League.

It seems in the opinion of this author that the AAFC was trying to fill a need that didn't yet exist. At least, it didn't exist for long. The post-war sports boom fizzled out quickly, and there was no overwhelming demand for professional football. Baseball was still king. Based on the amount of coverage given to them in the newspapers researched for this book, college football and boxing were close behind in popularity. Professional football was more popular than it had been before the war, but was still finding its way. There's a reason the 1958 NFL championship game between the Giants and Colts is considered to be the game that put professional football on the nation's sports map. Professional football was gaining ground, but was still a second-tier attraction, until the first ever sudden death overtime game electrified the nation and began the fascination with the sport that continues unabated today.

Attendance nose-dived in the AAFC in 1949. The decline in Cleveland was particularly mystifying. It certainly left McBride scratching his head. He was continuing to give his city the best show in all of football, but Clevelanders found other things to do on game days. The Browns' attendance, record-breaking in 1946 and 1947, dropped significantly in 1948 and 1949. The theory was that the city's discriminating football fans knew their team was headed for the NFL eventually and weren't sold on the quality of competition in the AAFC. Neither were the city's newspaper columnists, who intimated the AAFC was inferior and couldn't wait for the Browns to be re-admitted to the "big time." But the crowds of 70,000 and 80,000 didn't return when the Browns joined the NFL. Cleveland's largest home crowd of the 1950 season was just 40,714 for a game against Pittsburgh. The divisional play-off against the Giants drew only 33,054 fans. The championship game versus the Rams, with its compelling storyline of the team that had jilted Cleveland six years earlier returning, attracted just 29,751 fans. The Browns drew a crowd of almost 60,000 for their home game against the Giants in 1951, but the crowds for their five other games were in the 30,000–40,000 range. They had three crowds (out of seven, including the championship game) in excess of

50,000 in 1952. After a whirlwind courtship by the AAFC, Cleveland's passion for pro football leveled off. If fans in Cleveland stopped flocking to Municipal Stadium to watch their team win, what incentive did fans of the AAFC's other teams have?

If the AAFC had had a firebrand like Al Davis to rally it (as the AFL did), it might have achieved its goal of peaceful co-existence with the NFL. As the 1950s dawned, all of the cities that had proven they could support a major league football team had one, with the exception of Buffalo. Baltimore was given a raw deal by the NFL and lost its team after the 1950 season. It would return in 1953, after Dallas, which had been under consideration by the AAFC, showed itself not to be ready for the big time, and its team became the new and (eventually) improved Colts. With the demise of the Hornets, Chicago still had one team too many. The Cardinals would move to St. Louis in 1960. New York was only big enough for one team, and the Yanks folded after the 1951 season. The pro football boom that began with the epic Giants-Colts overtime championship game in December of 1958 was still nearly a decade away when the AAFC's owners surrendered to the NFL. Ward's vision of two successful professional football leagues was 15 years ahead of its time. The AAFC was trying to fill a demand for pro football that just wasn't strong enough to support two leagues.

During the 2010 season, the original eight AFL teams wore throwback uniforms on designated occasions to celebrate the 50th anniversary of the renegade league's founding. The NFL embraces the history of the league that became its equal and forced a merger. No such commemorative events were held in 1996 to celebrate, or even acknowledge, the 50th anniversary of the AAFC. In fact, 1996 was the year the AAFC's flagship franchise and only champion, the Browns, became the transplanted Baltimore Ravens. Likewise, there wasn't even a mention, let alone a celebration, of the AAFC's 60th anniversary in 2006. Nor was anything done to commemorate its 70th anniversary in 2016. There's no reason to believe the sport will honor the AAFC's landmark 75th anniversary in 2021.

Not as long as the NFL continues to regard the AAFC as The League That Didn't Exist.

Chapter Notes

Chapter 1
1. *Cleveland Plain Dealer*, August 16, 1926.
2. Associated Press, October 9, 1926.
3. *Cleveland Plain Dealer*, November 1, 1926.
4. *Ibid.*
5. Associated Press, April 3, 1944.
6. Associated Press, November 28, 1944.
7. Associated Press, January 6, 1945.
8. United Press, June 2, 1945.
9. United Press, June 5, 1945.

Chapter 2
1. *Cleveland Plain Dealer*, September 3, 1944.
2. *Ibid.*
3. Associated Press, December 26, 1944.
4. Associated Press, January 10, 1945.
5. Associated Press, January 9, 1945.
6. Associated Press, January 11, 1945.
7. Associated Press, January 14, 1945.
8. *Ibid.*
9. *Cleveland Plain Dealer*, February 9, 1945.
10. *Cleveland Plain Dealer*, February 10, 1945.
11. *Ibid.*
12. *Ibid.*
13. *Cleveland Press*, February 10, 1945.
14. *Cleveland Plain Dealer*, February 11, 1945.
15. United Press, February 25, 1945.
16. *Cleveland Plain Dealer*, March 13, 1945.
17. *Cleveland Plain Dealer*, March 25, 1945.
18. *Cleveland Plain Dealer*, March 31, 1945.
19. *Cleveland Plain Dealer*, April 1, 1945.
20. Associated Press, April 21, 1945.
21. *Ibid.*
22. *Ibid.*
23. United Press, April 20, 1945.
24. *Cleveland Plain Dealer*, May 4, 1945.
25. *Cleveland Plain Dealer*, May 5, 1945.
26. *Cleveland Press*, May 4, 1945.
27. *Cleveland Press*, May 5, 1945.
28. *Cleveland Plain Dealer*, May 4, 1945.
29. *Ibid.*
30. Associated Press, June 3, 1945.
31. United Press, June 8, 1945.
32. Associated Press, August 31, 1945.

Chapter 3
1. United Press, October 18, 1945.
2. *Ibid.*
3. Associated Press, October 18, 1945.
4. United Press, October 18, 1945.
5. *Cleveland Plain Dealer*, October 24, 1945.
6. Associated Press, October 28, 1945.
7. *Ibid.*
8. *Ibid.*
9. Associated Press, November 8, 1945.
10. *Cleveland Plain Dealer*, November 13, 1945.
11. International News Service, November 26, 1945.
12. International News Service, December 5, 1945.
13. International News Service, December 20, 1945.
14. *Cleveland Plain Dealer*, December 22, 1945.
15. *Cleveland Press*, December 4, 1945.
16. *Cleveland Press*, December 30, 1945.

17. *Cleveland Press*, December 31, 1945.
18. International News Service, January 1, 1946.
19. Associated Press, January 4, 1946.
20. *Cleveland Press*, January 7, 1946.
21. *Ibid*.
22. *Cleveland Press*, January 9, 1946.
23. *Cleveland Plain Dealer*, January 13, 1946.
24. *Cleveland Press*, January 14, 1946.
25. Associated Press, February 2, 1946.
26. *Cleveland Press*, February 12, 1946.
27. Associated Press, March 3, 1946.
28. *Cleveland Plain Dealer*, March 20, 1946.
29. International News Service, March 31, 1946.
30. *Cleveland Plain Dealer*, May 4, 1946.
31. Associated Press, May 29, 1946.
32. United Press, May 8, 1946.
33. Associated Press, June 5, 1946.
34. Associated Press, July 3, 1946.
35. Associated Press, July 6, 1946.
36. *Cleveland Plain Dealer*, July 25, 1946.
37. United Press, July 24, 1946.
38. *Cleveland Plain Dealer*, August 10, 1946.
39. *Cleveland Plain Dealer*, August 11, 1946.
40. *Ibid*.
41. *Ibid*.
42. *Ibid*.

Chapter 4

1. *Cleveland Press*, August 27, 1946.
2. United Press, September 17, 1946.
3. *Cleveland Press*, September 20, 1946.
4. Associated Press, September 25, 1946.
5. *Ibid*.
6. United Press, September 27, 1946.
7. United Press, September 30, 1946.
8. United Press, October 1, 1946.
9. *Ibid*.
10. *Ibid*.
11. *Ibid*.
12. *Ibid*.
13. *Cleveland Plain Dealer*, September 29, 1946.
14. *Cleveland Press*, October 4, 1946.
15. *Cleveland Press*, October 22, 1946.
16. *Ibid*.
17. United Press, October 29, 1946.
18. *Cleveland Plain Dealer*, November 8, 1946.
19. *Cleveland Plain Dealer*, December 10, 1946.
20. *Cleveland Plain Dealer*, December 20, 1946.
21. *Ibid*.
22. *Ibid*.
23. *Cleveland Plain Dealer*, December 23, 1946.
24. *Ibid*.

Chapter 5

1. *Cleveland Plain Dealer*, December 24, 1946.
2. *Cleveland Plain Dealer*, December 20, 1946.
3. United Press, December 24, 1946.
4. Associated Press, December 24, 1946.
5. United Press, December 25, 1946.
6. United Press, December 29, 1946.
7. Associated Press, December 31, 1946.
8. *Cleveland Plain Dealer*, January 1, 1947.
9. Associated Press, January 3, 1947.
10. Associated Press, January 8, 1947.
11. United Press, January 16, 1947.
12. Associated Press, January 17, 1947.
13. United Press, January 16, 1947.
14. Associated Press, January 24, 1947.
15. United Press, January 22, 1947.
16. United Press, January 25, 1947.
17. United Press, January 29, 1947.
18. *Cleveland Press*, February 11, 1947.
19. United Press, February 10, 1947.
20. *Cleveland Press*, February 25, 1947.
21. United Press, February 27, 1947.
22. *Cleveland Plain Dealer*, March 11, 1947.
23. Associated Press, March 20, 1947.
24. Associated Press, March 25, 1947.
25. Associated Press, April 1, 1947.
26. Associated Press, April 2, 1947.
27. United Press, May 17, 1947.
28. Associated Press, July 13, 1947.
29. *Ibid*.
30. *Ibid*.
31. Associated Press, August 26, 1947.
32. *Cleveland Press*, August 21, 1947.

Chapter 6

1. *Cleveland Plain Dealer*, July 30, 1947.
2. *Cleveland Plain Dealer*, September 6, 1947.
3. *Ibid*.
4. *Cleveland Plain Dealer*, September 8, 1947.
5. *Cleveland Press*, September 10, 1947.

6. *Cleveland Plain Dealer*, September 9, 1947.
7. *Brooklyn Daily Eagle*, September 11, 1947.
8. *New York Daily Mirror*, September 11, 1947.
9. *Cleveland Press*, September 29, 1946.
10. *Cleveland Press*, September 26, 1947.
11. *Cleveland Plain Dealer*, October 5, 1947.
12. *Cleveland Plain Dealer*, October 6, 1947.
13. United Press, October 8, 1947.
14. *Cleveland Plain Dealer*, October 12, 1947.
15. *Cleveland Press*, October 10, 1947.
16. *Cleveland Plain Dealer*, October 13, 1947.
17. *Cleveland Press*, October 15, 1947.
18. United Press, October 18, 1947.
19. Associated Press, October 18, 1947.
20. Associated Press, October 22, 1947.
21. Associated Press, October 23, 1947.
22. *Cleveland Press*, November 17, 1947.
23. *Cleveland Plain Dealer*, November 17, 1947.
24. Associated Press, November 18, 1947.
25. Associated Press, November 24, 1947.
26. *Cleveland Press*, November 28, 1947.
27. *Ibid.*
28. *Cleveland Press*, December 3, 1947.
29. *Cleveland Plain Dealer*, December 14, 1947.
30. *Ibid.*
31. *Cleveland Plain Dealer*, December 15, 1947.
32. *Ibid.*

Chapter 7

1. *Cleveland Plain Dealer*, December 16, 1947.
2. United Press, December 30, 1947.
3. Associated Press, January 4, 1948.
4. *Ibid.*
5. Associated Press, January 7, 1948.
6. United Press, January 7, 1948.
7. *Cleveland Press*, February 5, 1948.
8. United Press, January 22, 1948.
9. *Cleveland Press*, January 26, 1948.
10. *Ibid.*
11. Associated Press, February 18, 1948.
12. *Ibid.*
13. *Ibid.*
14. Associated Press, March 14, 1948.
15. Associated Press, March 17, 1948.
16. Associated Press, April 16, 1948.
17. *Cleveland Press*, May 1, 1948.
18. *Ibid.*
19. *Ibid.*
20. *Ibid.*
21. United Press, May 20, 1948.
22. *Cleveland Press*, May 26, 1948.
23. Associated Press, June 16, 1948.
24. *Cleveland Press*, July 26, 1948.

Chapter 8

1. *Cleveland Press*, September 4, 1948.
2. *Ibid.*
3. *Cleveland Plain Dealer*, September 12, 1948.
4. *Cleveland Press*, September 13, 1948.
5. *Ibid.*
6. *Cleveland Press*, September 11, 1948.
7. Associated Press, September 18, 1948.
8. *Cleveland Press*, September 17, 1948.
9. *Cleveland Press*, September 29, 1948.
10. *Cleveland Press*, September 30, 1948.
11. *Ibid.*
12. Associated Press, October 23, 1948.
13. Associated Press, October 28, 1948.
14. *Cleveland Press*, November 15, 1948.
15. *Cleveland Press*, November 16, 1948.
16. *Ibid.*
17. *Cleveland Plain Dealer*, November 27, 1948.
18. *Cleveland Press*, December 2, 1948.
19. *Ibid.*
20. *Cleveland Plain Dealer*, November 29, 1948.
21. *Cleveland Plain Dealer*, November 30, 1948.
22. Associated Press, December 13, 1948.
23. *Cleveland News*, December 18, 1948.
24. *Cleveland Plain Dealer*, December 21, 1948.
25. *Cleveland Plain Dealer*, December 20, 1948.
26. *Ibid.*

Chapter 9

1. *Cleveland Plain Dealer*, December 19, 1948.
2. *Ibid.*
3. *Ibid.*
4. *Ibid.*
5. *Ibid.*
6. *Ibid.*
7. *Ibid.*

8. *Ibid.*
9. *Ibid.*
10. *Cleveland Plain Dealer*, December 17, 1948.
11. *Cleveland Plain Dealer*, December 19, 1948.
12. *Cleveland Plain Dealer*, December 17, 1948.
13. *Ibid.*
14. *Ibid.*
15. *Cleveland Plain Dealer*, December 18, 1948.
16. *Cleveland Plain Dealer*, December 20, 1948.
17. Associated Press, December 21, 1948.
18. *Cleveland Plain Dealer*, December 22, 1948.
19. *Cleveland Plain Dealer*, December 23, 1948.
20. United Press, January 12, 1949.
21. *Cleveland Press*, January 19, 1949.
22. *Cleveland Plain Dealer*, January 22, 1949.
23. *Ibid.*
24. *Ibid.*
25. *Ibid.*
26. *Cleveland Plain Dealer*, December 20, 1948.
27. *Cleveland Press*, February 3, 1949.
28. Associated Press, February 2, 1949.
29. United Press, February 2, 1949.
30. *Cleveland Press*, February 8, 1949.
31. International News Service, February 8, 1949.
32. *Cleveland Press*, February 8, 1949.
33. International News Service, February 8, 1949.
34. *Cleveland Plain Dealer*, April 8, 1949.
35. *Cleveland Plain Dealer*, April 29, 1949.
36. *Cleveland Press*, July 23, 1949.
37. *Cleveland Press*, August 2, 1949.
38. *Cleveland Plain Dealer*, August 20, 1949.
39. *Cleveland Press*, August 25, 1949.

Chapter 10

1. *Cleveland Press*, August 4, 1949.
2. *Cleveland Plain Dealer*, September 9, 1949.
3. *Cleveland Plain Dealer*, September 12, 1949.
4. United Press, September 21, 1949.
5. *Cleveland Press*, September 23, 1949.
6. *Cleveland Press*, September 26, 1949.
7. *Cleveland Plain Dealer*, October 10, 1949.
8. Associated Press, October 11, 1949.
9. *Ibid.*
10. United Press, October 20, 1949.
11. *Cleveland Press*, October 25, 1949.
12. *Cleveland Press*, October 31, 1949.
13. United Press, November 16, 1949.
14. *Ibid.*
15. Associated Press, November 17, 1949.
16. *Cleveland Press*, November 11, 1949.
17. *Cleveland Press*, November 15, 1949.
18. *Cleveland Press*, November 19, 1949.
19. *Cleveland Press*, November 16, 1949.
20. *Cleveland Plain Dealer*, November 19, 1949.

Chapter 11

1. United Press, November 28, 1949.
2. *Cleveland Plain Dealer*, November 29, 1949.
3. Associated Press, November 30, 1949.
4. *Ibid.*
5. *Cleveland Press*, November 30, 1949.
6. *Ibid.*
7. Associated Press, December 1, 1949.
8. *Ibid.*
9. *Ibid.*
10. *Cleveland Plain Dealer*, December 1, 1949.
11. *Cleveland Plain Dealer*, December 5, 1949.
12. *Cleveland Press*, December 9, 1949.
13. *Cleveland Plain Dealer*, December 10, 1949.
14. Associated Press, December 10, 1949.
15. *Ibid.*
16. *Ibid.*
17. *Cleveland Press*, December 10, 1949.
18. *Cleveland Plain Dealer*, December 10, 1949.
19. *Ibid.*
20. *Cleveland Press*, December 13, 1949.
21. *Cleveland Plain Dealer*, December 10, 1949.
22. Associated Press, December 11, 1949.

Bibliography

Newspapers

Akron Beacon Journal, January 1944–December 1950
Cleveland News, September 1926–November 1926; September 1936–October 1936; January 1944–December 1950
Cleveland Plain Dealer, September 1926–November 1926; September 1936–October 1936; January 1944–December 1950
Cleveland Press, September 1926–November 1926; September 1936–October 1936; January 1944–December 1950
New York Times, January 1946
Pittsburgh Post-Gazette, March–April 1944
Willoughby (OH) *News-Herald*, January 1944–December 1950

Wire Services

Associated Press, January 1944–December 1950
International News Service, January 1944–December 1950
United Press, January 1944–December 1950

Books

Brown, Paul, with Jack Clary. *PB: The Paul Brown Story*. New York: Atheneum, 1979.
Knight, Jonathan. *The Cleveland Browns Bible*. Kent, OH: Black Squirrel, 2013.
Piascik, Andy. *The Cleveland Browns: The Best Show in Football, 1946–1955*. Lanham, MD: Taylor Trade, 2007.
Schultz, Brad. *The NFL: Year One*. Dulles, VA: Potomac, 2014.

Index

Adamle, Tony 158
Adams, Chet 53, 54, 56, 58, 81, 91, 198
Agajanian, Ben 111, 114, 117, 120, 157, 187
Aguirre, Joe 71
Akins, Al 75
Albert, Frankie 70, 72, 110, 117, 119, 145, 148, 151, 159–160, 180, 186, 191, 194, 196
Alexander, W.A. 99
Alford, Bruce 117, 119, 125
Ameche, Don 16, 29, 111, 119
American Association (baseball) 86
American Broadcasting Company 217
American Football League (1960s) 99, 216–218
American Football League I 1, 6, 8, 12, 143
American Football League II 1, 8–9, 143
American Football League III 1, 9–10, 34, 143
American League (baseball) 179
American Professional Football Association 5, 126
Army (football) 17
Artoe, Lee 39
Auburn University 19, 59, 131

Babe Ruth Stadium 37, 145, 149–151, 159, 161, 182, 190–191, 194–195, 202, 204
Baker, Johnny 52
Baldwin, Alton 162–163
Ballati, Eddie 87
Baltimore Colts 92, 96, 98, 100–101, 106–110, 112–117, 119–120, 122, 127, 135–138, 141–142, 144–148, 150, 153–155, 157, 159–162, 168, 170–171, 178, 182–183, 186–187, 189–190, 192, 194–196, 198, 200, 202, 204–205, 208–209, 211, 213–216, 219
Baltimore Ravens 219
Banducci, Bruno 77, 86, 128
Bangert, Wilfred 54
Banonis, Vince 55, 57, 62, 91
Barber, Jim 147
Barwegan, Dick 137, 141, 146, 210
Battles, Cliff 70, 92, 106, 129, 133
Baugh, Sammy 113
Beals, Alyn 77, 86, 110

Bechtol, Hubert 97, 105
Bell, Bert 44, 46, 48–49, 51, 53, 56, 69, 86, 91, 93, 95–96, 100–101, 121–122, 128, 152, 164, 170, 173, 175–176, 181–182, 189, 194, 196, 207–209, 211, 213
Bennett, William 16
Benningsen, Ray 138, 166
Benton, Jim 45–46, 51
Berezney, Pete 137
Bertelli, Angelo 50–51, 53–54, 62, 73, 91, 100–101, 106, 140, 143, 146, 148
Bethlehem Bulldogs 184
Bidwill, Bill 88
Bierman, Bernie 73, 85
Bixler, Paul 30
"Black Sox" 96
Blackinger, John 92
Blanchard, Felix (Doc) 79, 90, 92–93, 127, 133
Blandin, Ernie 141, 147
Boedeker, Bill 57, 62, 120, 144
Boland, Pat 63, 70
Boston College 18
Boston Red Sox 88
Boston Shamrocks 8–9
Boston Yanks 10, 18, 27, 38–39, 42–44, 48–52, 54, 62, 73, 75, 84, 92, 104–05, 128, 148, 166, 170, 177–78, 186, 190
Bowling Green State University 55, 61, 100, 103, 141, 183
Boyle, Leo 139
Breuil, Jim 16, 50–51, 117, 119, 170, 174, 193–95, 199–200, 205, 208–09, 211, 216
Brickels, John 30–31
Briggs, Walter 110, 129
Briggs Stadium 110
Brizzolara, Ralph 37
Brogan, John 85, 124
Brooklyn Dodgers (baseball) 35, 47, 51, 75, 84, 127, 130, 132, 172, 178
Brooklyn Dodgers (football) 35, 47, 53–54, 57–58, 60–62, 65, 67, 69–70, 72, 74–79, 82, 84, 89–91, 100–01, 103–106, 108–109, 111–12, 116, 118–19, 123, 125–27, 129–33, 135, 139–41,

227

144–45, 148, 150–51, 153–54, 156–57, 159, 161–62, 168, 171–72, 174–75, 177–78, 180, 183, 185–86, 188
Brooklyn Dodgers (NFL) 101
Brooklyn-New York football club 178
Brooklyn Tigers 10, 13–14, 27–28, 32, 39, 42, 44, 92
Brown, Paul 3, 21–27, 30–32, 36–38, 40, 45–46, 55, 57, 59, 62, 66, 70, 72, 76–77, 80–81, 86, 91, 93, 98, 100–04, 110–11, 118–19, 121, 124–25, 129, 131, 133–34, 136–41, 143, 147, 149, 156, 158–61, 163–65, 173–74, 179–80, 183, 185, 188, 191–93, 210, 214, 216
Brown, Warren 87
Bryant, J.C. Herbert 84
Buffalo Bills 99–100, 103–104, 106–110, 112–113, 116–117, 120, 122–123, 127, 136, 144, 146, 148, 150–151, 153–155, 157, 159–164, 170–171, 174, 178, 181–184, 186–193, 198–203, 205–208, 210, 211
Buffalo Bisons 47, 50, 58, 61, 63–65, 67, 70–71, 74–76, 78, 82, 98
Buffalo Touchdown Club 199
Buffington, Harry 105
Bumgardner, Rex 157, 211
Burke, Frank 139
Busick, Howard 135–136
Butler, Walter 139
Butts, Wally 88
Byrnes, James F. 19

Canadeo, Tony 138
Canton McKinley high school 55
Card-Pitt 10
Carpenter, Jack 88
Casey, Tom 144
Cason, Jim 158
Castiglia, Jimmy 105
Chappuis, Bob 140, 155, 160, 175
Chicago Bears 5, 8, 11, 13, 36–39, 41, 43, 47, 65, 68–69, 79–80, 85, 90, 95–97, 101, 104–105, 118, 130–31, 133, 137, 151, 153, 159, 166–67, 178, 194, 196, 198
Chicago Cardinals 10, 25, 38, 40, 43, 45, 47, 55, 57, 88, 90, 95, 97, 128, 131, 138, 142, 151, 153, 164, 166, 168–70, 177–78, 186, 190
Chicago Cubs 25, 88
Chicago Hornets 175, 183, 186–187, 189, 191–192, 195, 198–199, 201–202, 205, 208, 219
Chicago Rockets 20, 47, 53–55, 57–59, 61–63, 65–66, 68–69, 70–71, 73–79, 82, 84–85, 93, 95–98, 100–01, 103, 105, 106–09, 11–12, 115, 117–18, 120–24, 126–27, 130–31, 135, 138–40, 142–43, 146–50, 154, 156–57, 160–62, 167–72, 175, 177–78, 183, 217
Chicago White Sox 95
Cincinnati Reds 95
Ciraolo, Frank 87
Civic Stadium (Buffalo) 61, 103, 112, 116, 118–119, 145, 150–151, 184, 187, 191–192, 195, 201, 210–211

Clark, James 208, 213
Clay, Walter 57
Clement, Jimmy 186
Cleveland Browns 2, 9, 22, 24, 30, 39–40, 46, 58–67, 69–72, 74–83, 86, 88–89, 02, 95, 97, 100–103, 106, 107–111, 115, 117–22, 124–29, 133, 135–37, 140–42, 144–64, 166, 169, 170–72, 174, 177–80, 182, 185–87, 189, 191–93, 196, 198, 200–01, 203, 206–14, 216–19
Cleveland Indians 150
Cleveland Indians (football) 8
Cleveland Municipal Stadium 2–3, 23, 25, 27, 44, 48, 50, 59, 64, 67, 70, 75, 104, 109, 117–18, 150–52, 154–55, 158, 162–63, 174, 185, 189–90, 192, 196, 198, 207, 210, 214, 216, 219
Cleveland Panthers 6–7
Cleveland Rams 1, 10, 23–24, 26–27, 29, 35–36, 40–41, 43–45, 48, 52–53, 58, 68, 75, 91, 167
Clowser, Jack 26, 30, 93
Cobbledick, Gordon 18, 66
Colella, Tom 54, 58, 125
Collins, Ted 27, 39, 48–49, 51–52, 62, 73, 84, 166, 170, 190, 199
Collmer, Mickey 105, 118
Columbia Broadcasting System 217
Columbia University 38, 50, 70, 91
Comiskey Park 15, 128
Conerly, Charlie 131–132, 139
Conkright, Bill (Red) 46, 53, 116–117, 190
Cook, Earl 182
Cooke, Bob 171
Corby, Karl 84
Cordovano, Sam 16, 20, 50–51, 68, 70
Cornell University 132
Cox, Bill 34–35, 42, 47–48, 69–70, 79, 89, 106, 112, 120, 127, 129–130, 132, 135
Cravath, Jeff 29
Crepeau, Richard 60
Cross, Hugh 139
Crowe, Clem 193
Crowley, Jim 17, 19, 33, 35, 37, 41, 43, 45–50, 53, 60, 66, 73, 78, 84–86, 92–95, 98, 100, 103, 108, 115, 117–18, 121, 123, 132, 140, 147, 175
Crown, Henry 124

D'Alesandro, Thomas 135–136, 204
Daley, Bill 18, 91–92, 96, 106
Dallas Cowboys 217
Dallas Texans (AFL) 217
Davis, Al 219
Davis, Glenn 79, 90, 92–93, 127–128, 133, 183
Davis, Joe 61
Davis, Lamar 112–113, 146
Davis, Smith 27
Dawson, Lowell (Red) 51, 104, 122, 133, 182, 193–194, 200
Dean, Hal 30–31
DeGroot, Dudley 52, 54, 89, 91, 111, 119, 121, 133

Index

Dellerba, Spiro 141, 147
Detroit Lions 45–46, 49–50, 57, 68, 75, 110, 118, 121, 128–130, 177–178, 210
Detroit Tigers 110, 129
Deutsch, Sam 7
Dietrich, John 22, 55
Dixie League 48, 100
Dobbs, Glenn 18, 60–61, 77, 84, 92, 101, 106, 110–12, 116–17, 137, 143–44, 149, 153, 193, 195
Dobelstein, Bob 185
Donovan, H.L. 37
Dove, Bob 35, 38, 63–4, 66–7, 70
Dowd, Gil 87
Drees, Jack 195
Driskill, Walter 137, 190, 192, 204
Dyson, James 99

Ebbets Field 14, 35, 69, 73–75, 77, 84, 89, 106, 112–13, 116, 120, 144, 153, 155, 161, 172, 186
Edwards, Dan 175
Eisenhower, Dwight D. 128
Elliott, Doc 6
Embry, Robert 138, 162, 171, 204
Eshmont, Len 35, 146, 206
Espey, Jack 79

Fears, Tom 183
Fekete, Gene 33
Fenway Park 148
Filchock, Frank 96
Fitzsimmons, Fred 35, 47–48
Flaherty, Ray 54, 79–81, 83–84, 110, 123, 129, 133, 146–147, 175, 184, 186, 189, 195
Foldberg, Hank 133, 175
Forbes Field 128
Fordham University 17–18
"Four Horsemen" 17, 35
Franck, George 35
Freed, Emerich 58
Freeman, Lee 174
Freitas, Jesse 187
Friedlund, Arthur 207
Fritsch, Ted 55–56, 62, 91
Fyfe, Lyle 129–130

Gafford, Roy 59, 118
Gallagher, Dick 131
Gallery, Tom 28, 32
Gambino, Lu 145–146, 151
Garn, R. Edward 124, 130, 138–139
Gehrig, Eleanor 16, 57, 60, 73
Gehrig, Lou 16
George Wilson's Wildcats 6–7
Georgia Tech 31, 80, 99, 140
Gibron, Abe 211
Gillom, Horace 86, 118, 188
Gilmer, Harry 132, 142
Girard, Earl (Jug) 131
Godfrey, Ernie 29–30

Gompers, Bill 161
Gould, Paul 106
Governali, Paul 18, 38
Graham, Otto 46, 58, 67, 75, 77, 81, 86, 92, 116–118, 120, 125, 128–129, 133, 137, 140, 147, 153, 155, 158–159, 163–164, 180, 188, 193, 202, 209–210, 214
Grange, Red 1–2, 5–7, 11–14, 143
Great Lakes Naval Training Station 22
Green Bay Packers 13, 43, 55–57, 93, 100, 120, 126, 131, 138, 145, 148, 167, 178, 181, 198
Greenwood, Don 54, 58
Gries, Bob 27
Griffin, Don 96
Grimes, Charles 34–35
Grossman, Rex 145
Groves, Leslie 87
Groza, Lou 29, 81, 115, 125, 141, 147, 155, 158–59, 196, 198, 214

Halas, George 5, 13, 39, 60, 65–66, 69, 71, 85, 89, 104, 163, 166–67, 178, 194, 209
Hall, Forrest 155, 158
Hall, Parker 35
Hamilton, Tom 87
Hanley, Dick 25, 38, 55, 63–64, 66, 70–71, 85, 132, 147, 175
Hannegan, Robert 87
Hapes, Merle 96
Harby, Harold 121
Harlow, Dick 79
Hart, Leon 209–210
Harvard University 79
Haynes, Gil 195
Hazelwood, Ted 187
Healey, Bill 99
Heath, Stan 181
Hein, Mel 119, 121
Heisler, Fritz 136
Heisman Trophy 23, 89, 91, 130, 138, 210
Hennie, Sonja 39
Hester, Harvey 18–19, 29, 43, 59–60, 62, 67, 72, 74, 76, 78, 121, 152
Heywood, Ralph 67
Hillenbrand, Billy 96, 105
Hirsch, Ed 162
Hirsch, Elroy (Crazylegs) 35–36, 38, 53, 58, 61, 63, 107, 140, 183
Hoernschmeyer, Bob (Hunchy) 53, 61, 63, 106, 112–113, 123, 150, 175, 186
Hoffberger, Jerry 174, 204
Horvath, Les 23–24, 90
Howard, Bill 87
Hunt, Lamar 217

Indiana University 53, 145
Ingram, Jonas 93–95, 98, 101, 100–111, 113–14, 120–122, 130, 133–136, 139, 143, 146, 154, 156, 162, 168–169, 173, 184
Iowa Pre-Flight 19
Isbell, Cecil 93, 97–98, 116, 133, 145, 182, 190

Jensen, Bob 140
Jersey City Giants 184
Johnson, Gil 180–181
Johnson, Harvey 81, 105, 119, 123, 125, 151, 156, 159, 188–190
Johnson, Nate 128, 141, 146
Jones, Bill (Dub) 123, 140
Jones, Edgar 36–37, 80–81, 125, 155, 163
Judd, Saxon 61

Kane, Michael 52
Kansas City Chiefs 217
Kavanaugh, Ken 39
Keeshin, John 16, 25, 27, 35–36, 38, 40, 42, 45, 47, 50, 53, 61, 63–66, 69–71, 79, 85, 132, 147, 175, 216
Kemp, Ray 60
Kennedy, Bob 146, 193
Kennedy, John F. 60
Kercheval, Ralph 101
Kessing, Oliver 95, 98–99, 116, 133, 162, 173, 175–176, 181–183, 194–196, 205–208
Kezar Stadium 45, 47, 59, 61–62, 71–72, 75–76, 101, 104, 106–107, 123, 144–146, 148, 153–154, 156, 158, 173, 179, 187, 189, 192–193, 202, 207
Kimbrough, John 103, 143–144
Kinard, Frank (Bruiser) 77, 83–84, 86
Kissell, John 211
Klawans, Rufus 48–49, 87
Konetsky, Floyd 104, 113
Kosikowski, Frank 182
Kulbitski, Vic 157

Lahr, Warren 124, 206
Lambeau, Curly 57, 84, 89, 100, 126, 128, 131, 138, 167, 181
Land, Fred 141
Landis, Kenesaw Mountain 35, 95–96
Lane, Frank 86
Lausche, Frank 87
Lavelli, Dante 67, 77, 81, 86, 118, 158
Layden, Elmer 3, 14, 17, 19–21, 27–28, 32–37, 39, 40, 42, 44, 92, 216
Layden, Pete 153
League Park 26, 44
Leahy, Frank 18, 22, 85, 132
Leahy, Marshall 173
Ledvinka, Charles 162
Leicht, Jake 137, 141, 147
Lewis, Cliff 60, 193
Lewis, Franklin 74, 87, 174
Lillard, Joe 60
Lilywhite, Verl 187
Lindheimer, Ben 78, 124, 126, 163, 167–168, 170–172, 174–177, 187, 193, 195, 199, 208
Linehan, Fred 70
Lipscomb, Thomas 58
Little, Lou 50, 87
Livie, R. Bruce 37
Livingston, Bobby 201

Lombardi, Vince 18
Los Angeles Bulldogs 9
Los Angeles Chargers (1960) 217
Los Angeles Dons 41, 45–46, 50–52, 54, 61–62, 64, 66–67, 70–74, 76, 78, 82, 89, 91, 97, 100–101, 103, 105–106, 108–111, 114–116, 120–121, 123–124, 126–127, 134, 137–138, 143–144, 148–149, 151, 154–155, 157–158, 160, 163, 168, 171–172, 174, 176, 178–179, 183–184, 187–188, 190, 192–193, 195–196, 199, 202, 208
Los Angeles Memorial Coliseum 25, 45, 61–62, 67–68, 71, 76, 97, 106, 115, 117, 121, 149–50, 153, 157, 179, 184, 187–88, 193, 195, 202
Los Angeles Rams 46, 51, 54–58, 64, 68, 72, 90, 96, 104, 127–128, 133, 176, 179, 183–184, 196, 208, 214, 218
Luckman, Sid 39, 65–66, 69, 71, 85, 133
Lujack, Johnny 130–131, 133
Luna Park 6–7
Lynch, Jerry 67
Lyne, Daniel 51

MacDonald, Walt 187
Mack, Connie 15, 179
Madigan, Ed 41, 46, 89, 91
Mandel, Fred 46, 49–50, 110, 128–130
Manders, Clarence (Pug) 83–84
Manders, Jack 153
Manhattan College 80
Mara, John 28, 38–40, 49, 122
Mara, Tim 166, 170, 176–177, 180, 200
Mara family 14, 84, 89, 152
Marshall, George Preston 9–10, 19–20, 44, 47, 60, 84, 89, 129, 142, 166, 169, 170–71, 176–77, 180, 185, 194, 200, 208, 213–14
Marshman, Homer 8–9
Martinovich, Phil 118, 120
Massillon Washington high school 21, 55, 86
Mastrangelo, John 185
Mathews, Ned 63–64, 66–67, 70
Mathews, Wid 132
Mayne, Mickey 57, 118, 141, 147
McAfee, George 39
McArthur, Bill 55
McBride, Arthur (Mickey) 16, 18, 22, 24–27, 31, 37, 39, 40–42, 44, 47, 50, 59–60, 69, 80, 85, 87, 89, 111, 125, 132, 134, 136, 139, 167–68, 170–74, 176–77, 185–86, 188–89, 195–96, 200–01, 207, 209, 216–18
McCarthy, Glenn 182, 188, 200, 205, 210
McCarthy, Jim 186, 188
McCormick, Charles 204
McGraw, John 15
McGuire, J. Basil 13
McKeever, Ed 25, 132–33, 139–40, 143–44, 146, 148, 175
Mead, Jim 87
Meagher, Jack 19, 23, 60, 67–68, 70
Meehan, John 11
Mellus, Johnny 161

Memorial Stadium (Baltimore) 37, 78–79, 105, 108, 122–123, 137, 145
Mexican League (baseball) 51
Miami Dolphins 9, 165
Miami Seahawks 23, 47–48, 58–62, 65, 67–69, 71, 73–79, 82, 84, 86, 91–93, 96, 105, 108, 121, 123, 132, 135, 210, 217
Miami University 21
Michalske, Mike 190
Michigan State College 17–18
Miller, Don 86–87
Miller, Edgar (Rip) 37, 44, 79
Miller, Ray T. 18, 27
Mississippi State University 72, 86
Morabito, Tony 16, 20, 97, 127–28, 136, 138, 141, 150, 168, 170–71, 173, 192, 195, 205–07, 217
Morabito, Vic 16, 205–06
Moriarty, Thomas 52
Morris, Max 175
Motley, Marion 2, 55, 60, 72, 75, 77, 81, 86, 113, 125, 128, 146, 163, 184
Municipal Stadium (Philadelphia) 213
Murray, Bill 98
Mutryn, Chet 103, 113, 128, 210

National-American Football League 207–208, 211
National Broadcasting Company 217
National Football League 1, 3–4, 11–13, 17, 21, 24, 28, 32, 34, 37–40, 42–47, 52, 54, 56–58, 69, 72, 74, 80, 84, 87, 90–91, 93, 95–96, 98, 100–102, 105, 108, 120, 126, 128, 138–39, 142–43, 145, 152, 156, 166–169, 171, 173–178, 180–81, 185–86, 194, 199–200, 209, 213–14, 216, 218–19
Neale, Earle (Greasy) 54, 214
Nelson, Bob 77, 86, 128, 187, 202
Nelson, Jimmy 59
Nemeth, Steve 63
Nevers, Ernie 25, 38, 63, 70
New York Bulldogs 180, 186, 190, 194, 198–199, 208, 211–212, 215
New York Giants (baseball) 15, 75, 130
New York Giants (football) 14, 28, 35, 38, 40, 47, 49, 54, 74, 79–80, 90, 96, 120, 128, 131, 139, 152, 159, 166, 173, 178, 185–87, 194, 214, 218–19
New York Titans 217
New York University 34
New York Yankees (baseball) 16, 21, 42, 51, 57
New York Yankees (football) 46, 54, 61–62, 64, 66–67, 70–73, 75–78, 80–84, 88–90, 97–101, 103–107, 109, 112, 115, 118–120, 122–123, 125–126, 131, 134–136, 138, 140–141, 144–145, 149, 151–153, 155–160, 170–172, 174–175, 178–184, 188–189, 192–194, 196, 198, 201–202, 205–207, 212–213
New York Yanks 170, 211–212
Nielsen, Ed 41
Nigro, D.M. 29

Noble, Dave 6
North Carolina Pre-Flight 18
Northwestern University 25

Oakland Raiders 217
O'Brien, Gerry 171
O'Dwyer, Bill 96
Ohio State University 8, 21–22, 24, 26, 29, 30–31, 55, 139, 216
Ohrenberger, Bill 113, 116
Oklahoma City University 181
Oklahoma University 137
Orange Bowl 29, 71, 73, 75, 77, 108
O'Rourke, Charley 110, 137–138
Otis, Sam 6, 18
Owen, Steve 54, 80

Pacific Coast All-Stars 6
Pacific Coast League (baseball) 86
Paffrath, Bob 57
Palmer, Darrell 184
Paris, Alvin 96
Parker, Ace 71, 73, 83–84
Parker, Dan 106
Parsons, Earle 110
Pasquel Brothers 51
Paynes, Roland 11
Pecarovich, Mike 147
Penn State University 72
Perry, Joe 156, 159
Phelan, Jimmy 136, 143–144, 164, 187, 195
Phil-Pitt Steagles 10, 91
Philadelphia Athletics 15, 179, 213
Philadelphia Eagles 10, 44, 54, 64, 84, 89, 92, 128, 152, 164–66, 169, 173, 177, 181, 183, 190, 198, 208, 213–14
Philadelphia Phillies 34–35, 213
Pittsburgh Steelers 10, 44, 60, 91–92, 98, 101, 128, 167, 185, 218
Pollard, Fritz 60
Polo Grounds 5, 14, 38, 74, 79, 120, 177, 186, 190, 194, 198
Pool, Hampton 68–69, 72, 115, 118
Pritchard, Bill 113
Proctor, Dewey 140–141, 145–146
Prokop, Eddie 31, 72–73, 80–81, 140–141, 146
Prokop, Joe 140, 142
Purdue University 54, 93
Pyle, C.C 5–8, 13

Radovich, Bill 77
Ratterman, George 103–104, 107, 109–110, 133, 148, 154–155, 161–162, 182, 187, 193, 199, 202, 206
Reese, Hank 194, 200
Reeves, Dan 23, 27, 43–45, 58, 64, 167, 171, 179, 208, 211
Renfro, Dick 61
Rice, Daniel 124
Rice, Grantland 17
Rice University 19

Index

Rickey, Branch 112, 126, 129–131, 133–134, 140, 156, 171–172, 174, 178–179
Rockne, Knute 136
Rodenberg, Bill 84, 135
Rodenberg, Robert 78–79, 84, 92–93, 97, 112–113, 116, 135, 138
Rooks, Irwin 174
Rooney, Art 44, 60, 167
Roosevelt, Franklin D. 10, 19
Rose Bowl 29
Rosenblum, Max 7
Rubber Bowl 58, 82, 104, 185
Ruby, Martin 77, 86
Ruppert, Jacob 13, 21
Ruppert Stadium 100
Russell, Jack 71
Ruth, Babe 15–16, 145
Ryan, Ray 16
Rykovich, Julie 145
Rymkus, Lou 128, 147

Saban, Lou 125, 155, 163, 207
St. John, Lyn 21–22, 26
St. Louis Cardinals (baseball) 84, 130
St. Mary's of California 136
San Diego Chargers 217
San Francisco Clippers 36, 40, 45, 48, 87
San Francisco 49ers 3, 23, 45, 47, 59, 61–62, 64–67, 70–73, 75–76, 79, 82, 87, 92, 97, 101, 103–110, 112, 117–120, 123–124, 127, 134–138, 141, 144–145, 148, 150–151, 153–161, 168–172, 174, 176–180, 183–187, 191, 193, 196, 199, 203, 205–210, 213–214
Sanders, Orban (Spec) 77, 81, 84, 115, 117, 120, 128, 133, 140, 147, 151, 153, 180
Santa Clara 23
Sauerbrei, Harold 148, 160
Schmidt, Francis 21
Schwartz, Marchy 29
Schwartz, Perry 83–84
Schweiger, Bob 175
Schwenk, Bud 75, 112
Scott, Tom 69–70
Severn Prep 21
Shamrock Bowl 210
Shaughnessy, Clark 79, 201–202
Shaw, Lawrence (Buck) 23, 87, 92, 119, 133, 149, 154–55, 158–59, 180, 206
Sherby, Dan 27, 44, 132, 195–96, 206–09
Shevlin, Agnes 84
Shibe Park 213
Shipkey, Ted 52, 119
Shurnas, Marshall 147
Siebold, H.C. 205
Simonetti, Len 182
Simpson, George 112–113
Sinkwich, Frank 46–47, 50, 109, 138
Smith, Gaylon 54, 56, 58
Smith, Gerald 34–35, 112, 127, 129–130, 132
Smith, Jay 140
Snyder, Bob 41, 121

Soldier Field 15–16, 25, 58, 61, 63, 67, 103, 107–109, 115, 117, 120, 139, 142, 146, 148, 150, 157, 160, 186, 189, 191–92, 195, 198, 201
Sorrell, Allen 16
Southern Conference 145
Southern Methodist University 180
Speedie, Mac 60, 75, 77, 81, 116, 125, 146, 188, 210
Standlee, Norm 106, 187, 206
Stanford University 25, 38, 52
Stevens, Mal 34–35, 53, 60, 69–70
Still, Jim 163, 187
Strader, Norm (Red) 147, 149, 152, 178, 201
Strickler, George 20, 90
Strode, Woody 55, 72
Strohmayer, George 175
Strzykalski, John 110
Stuhldreher, Harry 35–36

Taliaferro, George 202
Taylor, John 105
Tew, Lowell 129
Thayer, Harry 195
Thompson, Alex 84, 89, 122, 152, 156, 165, 169, 173
Thompson, James 174–175, 205
Tittle, Y.A. 129, 137, 141, 145–146, 159, 162, 187
Toohey, Bill 85, 115, 121, 124
Topping, Dan 12–14, 21, 27–28, 32, 38–40, 42, 46, 48, 73, 80, 83–84, 88, 91–92, 97–98, 110, 125, 129, 140, 147, 152, 163, 167–68, 170–71, 178, 181, 194–96, 217
Trafton, George 46
Trans-America Football League 1, 12–14, 34, 216
Trenkamp, Robert 58
Trippi, Charlie 88, 131
Truman, Harry 115
Tryon, Eddie 112–113
Tulane University 51
Tunney, Gene 16, 18
Turner, Clyde 39
Turre, Ernest 16

UCLA 149
United States Football League (1944–1945) 1, 11–14, 34, 216
United States Football League (1983–1986) 216
University of Alabama 59, 129
University of Delaware 98
University of Florida 72
University of Georgia 88
University of Illinois 5, 13, 89
University of Kentucky 37–38
University of Louisville 105
University of Maryland 79, 137, 145–146, 190
University of Michigan 88
University of Minnesota 73
University of Mississippi 132
University of Missouri 54, 136

University of Nevada 55, 72, 86, 181
University of Notre Dame 17, 22–23, 25, 29, 33, 35, 38, 50–51, 53, 85–86, 101, 104, 130, 132, 136, 140, 144, 182, 199, 210
University of Pittsburgh 36
University of San Francisco 132
University of Southern California 29
University of Washington 136
University of Wisconsin 35–36, 131

Vacanti, Sam 107, 146
Valley, Wayne 217
Van Brocklin, Norm 183
Van Buren, Steve 165
Vant Hull, Fred 100
Vardian, Johnny 67
Vincent, Fay T. 113
Voyles, Carl 131, 144, 151, 171, 178

Wagner, Lowell 151
Wallander, Arthur 96
Walsh, Charles (Chile) 26, 36, 46, 54, 56
Walsh, Christy 16, 20, 28
Ward, Arch 1, 3, 15–16, 20, 25, 34, 38, 59, 63, 90, 184, 209, 216, 219
Warrington, Caleb 116
Washington, Kenny 55, 72
Washington Redskins 9, 19, 38, 44, 47, 52, 54, 60, 70, 89, 101, 113, 129, 132–33, 159, 166, 170, 173, 178, 184, 208, 214
Waterfield, Bob 46, 133, 183
Watts, Ray 6

Webb, Del 12–13, 21
Wells, Jim 194
Wendell, Marty 187
West Point 92
Wetzel, Buzz 8–9
Whelan, Tommy 161–162, 182
Whisler, Joe 30–31
Widdoes, Carroll 22, 30
William & Mary 131
Williams, Walt 62
Willis, Bill 2, 55, 60, 72, 86, 128, 184
Willkin, Willie 38, 63–64, 66–67, 70
Wilson, George 6
Wojciehowicz. Alex 18
Wolf, Dick 6
World Football League 216
World Series 95, 150
Woudenberg, John 87
Wright, Red 112
Wrigley, Phil 88
Wrigley Field 25, 36, 65

Yale University 34
Yankee Stadium 8, 12–14, 21, 28, 32, 38–39, 42, 47, 67, 73, 75, 105, 112, 118, 122, 125, 153, 155–57, 159, 170–71, 178, 190, 194, 196, 198, 201–202
Yonkers, Bob 89, 92–93, 127, 184, 200
Young, Buddy 89–90, 97–98, 103, 110, 115, 120, 123, 125, 145, 147, 198
Young, George 163